Divine Beauty Revealed

Divine Beauty Revealed

The Aesthetics of Jonathan Edwards as Seen in His Biblical Theology

Youngrae Kim

PICKWICK *Publications* • Eugene, Oregon

DIVINE BEAUTY REVEALED
The Aesthetics of Jonathan Edwards as Seen in His Biblical Theology

Pickwick Publications
An Imprint of Wipf and Stock Publishers
199 W. 8th Ave., Suite 3
Eugene, OR 97401

www.wipfandstock.com

PAPERBACK ISBN: 979-8-3852-5045-5
HARDCOVER ISBN: 979-8-3852-5046-2
EBOOK ISBN: 979-8-3852-5047-9

Cataloguing-in-Publication data:

Names: Kim, Youngrae [author].

Title: Divine beauty revealed : the aesthetics of Jonathan Edwards as seen in his biblical theology / by Youngrae Kim.

Description: Eugene, OR: Pickwick Publications, 2025 | Includes bibliographical references.

Identifiers: ISBN 979-8-3852-5045-5 (paperback) | ISBN 979-8-3852-5046-2 (hardcover) | ISBN 979-8-3852-5047-9 (ebook)

Subjects: LCSH: Edwards, Jonathan, 1703–1758. | Edwards, Jonathan, 1703–1758—Aesthetics. | Aesthetics—Religious aspects—Christianity. | Aesthetics, Modern—18th century.

Classification: B874.A4 K56 2025 (paperback) | B874.A4 (ebook)

VERSION NUMBER 08/19/25

Contents

Preface

Jonathan Edwards stands as one of the most influential theologians and thinkers in American religious history. His theological insights have been explored through countless lenses—philosophical, historical, pastoral, and ethical—yet among these, his theological aesthetics and biblical hermeneutics hold a distinctive significance. This book, *The Aesthetics of Jonathan Edwards as Seen in His Biblical Theology*, contributes meaningfully to these areas by bridging two essential yet frequently compartmentalized aspects of Edwards's scholarship.

The significance of Edwards's theological aesthetics cannot be overstated. Scholars such as Sang Hyun Lee, Michael McClymond, Gerald McDermott, Oliver Crisp, Kyle Strobel, and Louis J. Mitchell have illuminated Edwards's deep engagement with beauty, excellency, and the divine glory inherent in creation and redemption. His aesthetic vision, deeply embedded in theological convictions, provides profound insights not only into theology proper but also into ethics, spirituality, and practical ministry. Despite this wealth of research, relatively few studies have fully articulated how Edwards's theological aesthetics intersects specifically and systematically with his approach to Scripture.

Similarly, Edwards's biblical hermeneutics, while widely acknowledged as foundational to his thought, remains an area ripe for continued exploration. Although Douglas A. Sweeney and Stephen J. Stein have significantly advanced our understanding of Edwards as a biblical interpreter, there still exists a need for sustained investigation into how Edwards's aesthetic commitments inform his scriptural interpretation and theological formulations. Given that Edwards considered himself foremost a preacher and interpreter of the Bible, comprehending his approach to Scripture is vital for grasping the full scope and intent of his theology.

This book endeavors to address these scholarly gaps by closely examining Edwards's biblical theology through the lens of his theological aesthetics. It argues convincingly that Edwards's vision of divine beauty and excellence not only shapes but is intricately woven into his scriptural interpretations. By doing so, it elucidates how Edwards's aesthetics provides coherence and depth to his theological insights and demonstrates how his biblical hermeneutics reinforce and illuminate his aesthetic vision.

It is my hope that this volume will stimulate further research and dialogue among theologians, historians, and biblical scholars alike, as we continue to appreciate and critically engage with the enduring legacy of Jonathan Edwards.

April 15, 2025
Youngrae Kim

Acknowledgements

I WOULD LIKE TO begin by expressing my sincere gratitude to Wipf and Stock Publishers for their willingness to publish this book. Their support and commitment to theological scholarship have made this project possible, and I am honored to partner with a publisher that has long valued the thoughtful engagement of Christian theology and history.

First and foremost, I render all glory to God, who has redeemed me and granted me the path of life. *Soli Deo Gloria.* This book has come to fruition through the help, encouragement, and wisdom of many people. I express my heartfelt thanks to Dr. Douglas Sweeney, who first opened my eyes to the beauty of Edwards's theology and consistently guided me to read Edwards as a biblical theologian. His warm encouragement and thoughtful advice have left a lasting mark on this work. I am also thankful to Dr. Scott Manetsch, who carefully read my manuscript and offered invaluable suggestions for its improvement. I owe a debt of gratitude to Dr. Kenneth Minkema, who, despite his many responsibilities, generously agreed to serve as an external reader.

I am also grateful to Dr. Peter Lillback, whose mentorship during my time at Westminster Theological Seminary deepened my interest in Jonathan Edwards and encouraged me to pursue this research with faith and rigor.

Finally, I would like to express my deepest thanks to my family. To my father, Rev. Nam Joon Kim, my theological and spiritual mentor, and to my mother, Myung Hee Lee, whose unwavering prayers and faith have sustained me—this work is as much yours as it is mine. To my beloved wife, Eunseon Kim, whose love, patience, and unwavering support have been a constant source of strength and joy—thank you for walking with me through every step of this journey. Without your love, sacrifice, and godly example, none of this would have been possible.

Abbreviations

WJE	*The Works of Jonathan Edwards*. Edited by John E. Smith et al. 26 vols. New Haven, CT: Yale University Press, 1970–2009.
WJEO	*The Works of Jonathan Edwards Online*. New Haven, CT: Jonathan Edwards Center at Yale University, 2008. http://edwards.yale.edu.
KJV	King James Version

Chapter 1

Introduction

The Background of Jonathan Edwards's Thought

There is no doubt that Jonathan Edwards towers as one of the most prominent American theologians of the eighteenth century, having possessed an excellent understanding of science, humanities, languages, literature, philosophy, history, and fine arts, all in addition to theology.[1] He wrote a variety of works utilizing his rich and extensive academic competence and attempted to answer the questions of contemporary philosophers concerning Christianity using their methodology. On the one hand, he maintained the Reformed theology under the Puritan tradition, and on the other hand, he drew from the British Enlightenment, the trend of his contemporary secular studies. These two kinds of backgrounds led later generations to fierce debate. Some scholars like Perry Miller argued that Jonathan Edwards escaped from traditional Puritanism and developed his theology and philosophy using the ideas of the Enlightenment, in particular, John Locke's philosophy.[2] On the other hand, others like

1. Jonathan Edwards started to study Latin at the age six, and he could read Greek and Hebrew. It is very well known that Edwards wrote an essay about spiders at age twelve or nineteen. See Sweeney, *Ministry of the Word*, 35. Moreover, according to Minkema, Edwards "wrote copiously and innovatively on cosmology, being, natural philosophy, light, optics, atoms, and the nature of the mind. He outlined a treatise on a history of the mental world and compiled a stupendous list of subjects on which to write—from the world as 'one vast spheroid' to gravity to comets" (Minkema, "Jonathan Edwards," 3). For more information, see chapter 8 of Nichols, *Jonathan Edwards*, 159–72.

2. According to Peter J. Thuesen, Perry Miller "highlighted his [Edwards's]

Conrad Cherry and Iain Murray opposed the interpretation that Edwards followed the ideas of the Enlightenment and Locke and argued instead that Edwards never departed from a tradition of conservative Christianity.[3] Most scholars recognize that Jonathan Edwards was influenced by both backgrounds—the church tradition and the Enlightenment; thus, it is not easy to evaluate his thought fairly. In this sense, there is need to identify the framework of his thought to gain a better understanding of his intellectual priorities and central concerns.

Jonathan Edwards's Primary Framework of Thought: The Bible

Edwards not only wrote a vast number of books and treatises, but also covered a variety of topics through his writing activities. Despite the various themes of his writings, one thing we can clearly define is that the main purpose of his writings was theological, biblical, and pastoral; that is, the primary foundation of thought for Edwards was the Bible, not secular philosophy. Edwards followed Church traditions, *philosophia ancilla theologiae*, to understand the relationship between philosophy

precocious mastery of Enlightenment philosophy." Moreover, "Miller insisted that Edwards's seeming traditionalism could not always be taken at face value; . . . Consequently, Miller took little interest in Edwards's straightforward engagement with the Bible and regarded his heavily scriptural *History of the Work of Redemption* as scarcely better than a 'story book for fundamentalists.'" In terms of this interpretation, Thuesen evaluates Miller's understanding of Edwards that "Miller's preternaturally modern Edwards, whose appropriation of empirical psychology led him to articulate human self-destructiveness with a force that anticipated Freud or late twentieth-century prophets like Reinhold Niebuhr" (Thuesen, "Edwards's Intellectural Background," 16).

3. One of the most representative theologians who opposed Miller's interpretation of Edwards was Iain Murray. Thuesen introduces a biography of Jonathan Edwards written by Iain Murray and presents Murray's interpretation of Miller's argument regarding Edwards. Thuesen says that Iain Murray "criticized the 'anti-supernatural animus' of Miller and other secular interpreters. Unlike Miller, who repeatedly emphasized Edwards's refashioning of Lockean empiricism, Murray barely mentioned Locke and insisted that philosophy was 'peripheral' to Edwards's thought, which he judged first and foremost as religious" (Thuesen, "Edwards's Intellectural Background," 16). Moreover, Conrad Cherry agreed that "to be sure, Edwards was no slave to his theological heritage," and "it is now patent fact that he turned to his own design the insights of such thinkers as John Locke, Francis Hutcheson and the Cambridge Platonists." However, Cherry refuted the claim that Edwards's thoughts lost connection to traditional Puritanism through his argument that "the interests which occupied Edwards's chief attention were theological interests," and he "broadened and impregnated his Calvinist theology" (Cherry, *Theology*, 4).

and theology. As Avihu Zakai estimates, for Edwards, philosophy was the handmaiden of theology.[4] Therefore, though Edwards developed his ideas using philosophical methodologies, philosophy was not the primary focus of his concerns. As noted above, Edwards developed his ideas based on theology and the Bible. If so, what roles did theology and the Bible play in Edwards's foundation of thought?

Jonathan Edwards has been considered by many as the "greatest theologian"[5] and regarded as "the greatest religious thinker in the history of the Americas."[6] Edwards addressed various kinds of doctrinal and theological topics in his writing, yet his definition of theology was simple and clear. He defined theology, in his words—Christian divinity—as "the doctrine of living to God by Christ."[7] Harry S. Stout, in his preface to volume 22 of the *Works of Jonathan Edwards*, analyzes Edwards's definition of theology and explains how important Edwards considered theology: "Christians should endeavor to grow in this sort of knowledge; they should, as Edwards puts it, 'make a business of it.' God gave humankind the faculty of understanding for this very end. The things of divinity are, in themselves, 'things of superlative excellency' and therefore worthy of being sought."[8]

Edwards's importance in theology is evident in the fact that he wrote articles and books on a variety of theological and doctrinal topics, so much so that even the editing and publishing of his works continued

4. "It is impossible to identify Edwards's natural philosophy with modern scientific thought if only in view of the affinities between his ideas and the medieval Scholastic view which defined theology as the 'Queen of Sciences' and science as 'handmaiden to theology.' . . . In his natural philosophy, Edwards reiterated the medieval view of *philosophia ancilla theologiae*, declaring that 'all arts and sciences, the more they are perfected, the more they issue in divinity, and coincide with it, and appear part of it.' More specifically, he argued, 'after God had shown the vanity of human learning when set up in the room of the gospel,' or 'was pleased to make foolish the wisdom' of classical learning and philosophy after Christ's first coming, 'God was pleased to make it [learning] subservient to the purpose of Christ's kingdom as an handmaid to divine revelation.' In other words, first 'the gospel came to prevail without the help of man's wisdom,' but 'then God was pleased to make use of learning as an handmaid.' Throughout history, Edwards said, 'God has sufficiently shown men the insufficiency of (human reason).' Hence, he repeated over and over that God ordered 'this great increase of learning' of the eighteenth century 'as an handmaid to religion'" (Zakai, *Philosophy of Nature*, 14–15).

5. Schafer, "Jonathan Edwards."

6. McClymond and McDermott, *Theology of Jonathan Edwards*, 23.

7. *WJE* 22:86.

8. Stout, "Preface," in *WJE* 22:81.

after his death. The theological and doctrinal themes he dealt with in his writing are as follows: (1) Antemortem works, including books on the doctrine of Justification—"Justification by Faith Alone" (1738); Pneumatology—"Distinguishing Marks of a Work of the Spirit of God" (1741); the doctrine of the Revival—"Some Thoughts Concerning the Present Revival of Religion" (1742); Eschatology—"Humble Attempt" (1747); the doctrine of the Eucharist—"An Humble Inquiry into the Rules of the Word of God, Concerning the Qualifications Requisite to a Compleat Standing and Full Communion in the Visible Christian Church" (1749); and anthropology—"Freedom of Will" (1754) and "Original Sin (1758)," (2) Books published after his death focused on Ecclesiology—"Ecclesiastical Writings"; the doctrine of God—"Writings on the Trinity, Grace, and Faith"; and the doctrine of Redemption—"A History of the Work of Redemption." In addition to the items listed above, he has written on a wide range of theological topics covered in contemporary systematic theology. His theological writings have helped Edwardian scholars reconstruct and focus on Edwards's theological system.

Edwards's original and traditional theology has had a great impact on countless people and inspired many theologians to study his theology.[9] In particular, modern theological scholars have been influenced by Edwards's God-centered theology, as shown in his definition of theology. These scholars include: H. Richard Niebuhr—a scholar of Christian culture; William C. Spohn in ethics; Edwards Farley in aesthetics; Terrance L. Tiessen in the field of public theology, and many others.[10] Edwards's theological contribution to contemporary scholarship provides further evidence that Edwards's theology played an important role in shaping his ideas.

For Edwards, God's revealed word was of supreme authority, yet he never devalued human reason. He clearly understood the importance of reason; however, he held that reason had significant limitations in the absence of revelation.

Edwards defined reason as "that power or faculty an intelligent being has to judge of the truth of propositions, either immediately, by only looking on the propositions, which is judging by intuition and

9. In the Proquest Dissertation database, I searched for doctoral dissertations and master's theses where the phrase "Jonathan Edwards" is included in the title. As a result, on December 6, 2019, out of a total of 253 dissertations, 108 of them were written on the theme of "theology," and there were 114 papers (69 and 45, respectively) written on the subject of "religion" or "religious history." Only 7 papers were written on the subject of the Bible or biblical study.

10. McClymond and McDermott, *Theology of Jonathan Edwards*, 709–16.

self-evidence; or by putting together several propositions which are already evident by intuition, or at least whose evidence is originally derived from intuition."[11] Rather than devaluing human reason, Edwards argued in terms of the power of reason, that "rational arguments may savingly convince the soul of the truth of the things of religion."[12] Moreover, in his sermon, "The Importance and Advantage of a Thorough Knowledge of Divine Truth," he explained the origin of human reason, which is a faculty to distinguish humanity from "the brutes":

> He [God] hath given to man some things in common with the brutes, as his outward senses, his bodily appetites, a capacity of bodily pleasure and pain, and other animal faculties: and some things he hath given him superior to the brutes, the chief of which is a faculty of understanding and reason. Our business should doubtless much consist in employing those faculties, by which we are distinguished from the beasts, about those things which are the main end of those faculties.[13]

However, he consistently maintained the superiority of revelation to reason.[14] In his sermon, "Light in a Dark World, a Dark Heart," Edwards clarified the limits of reason without revelation:

> Being without revelation, notwithstanding all the light of natural reason, they sunk into brutish ignorance and into such vain, absurd, and ridiculous conceptions of things, that we that have been taught better by divine revelation, can scarce conceive how it was possible for rational creatures to have such thoughts.[15]

Moreover, in his sermon, "The Importance and Advantage of a Thorough Knowledge of Divine Truth," Edwards argued that rational knowledge is a tool for seeking spiritual knowledge: "He [the Apostle] would have the Christian Hebrews seek the one [a spiritual knowledge], in order to the

11. *WJE* 23:359.

12. *WJE* 18:162.

13. *WJE* 22:90.

14. In *The Jonathan Edwards Encyclopedia,* Keith Beuteler argues that Edwards's view on reason is revealed well in his sermon, "Ministers to Preach Not Their Own Wisdom But the Word of God." He quotes that "Ministers are not to preach those things which their own wisdom or reason suggest, but the things already dictated by the superior wisdom and knowledge of God." This quote shows us that "Edwards allowed, ministers do not merely abandon their own reason. Rather they draw the conclusion, reasonable in itself, that God's reasoning is infinitely more penetrating than human reasoning" (Beutler, "Reason," 487–88).

15. *WJE* 19:711.

other [a rational knowledge] . . . it [a spiritual knowledge] is to be sought by the other [a rational knowledge], as its end."[16]

Edwards insisted that the privilege of knowing the "taste" of true revelation—the Bible—was only for believers who had a "new sense of heart" by the Holy Spirit. He argued that a religious experience through the Holy Spirit is an essential prerequisite for the "new sense of heart." He said, "the Spirit convinces men of sin," and "he acts in the mind of a saint as an indwelling vital principle" in contrast with "the mind of a natural man."[17] The Spirit "unites himself with the mind of a saint, takes him for his temple, actuates and influences him as a new, supernatural principle of life and action."[18] Moreover, the Spirit of God "exerts and communicates himself there in his own proper nature."[19] Furthermore, Edwards reveals his understanding of the new "sense of heart" in his sermon.[20] Edwards's new sense of heart was "a true sense of the divine and superlative excellency of the things of religion."[21] Edwards used the parable of honey to explain the taste of the Bible and its relationship with believers.[22] More-

16. *WJE* 22:87.

17. *WJE* 2:410–11.

18. *WJE* 2:411.

19. *WJE* 2:411.

20. In addition to his work, *The Religious Affections,* the new "sense of heart" is clearly described in Edwards's sermon "A Divine and Supernatural Light," which was originally presented in Northampton in 1733 and was subsequently published in Boston the next year. This sense is closely linked to the sense of true beauty. Edwards describes it in a variety of ways, including "a true sense of the divine excellence of the things revealed in the Word of God," "a sense of the loveliness and beauty of that holiness and grace," "the sense of the excellency of Christ," a "sense of true excellence," and a "sense of divine beauty or excellency" (*WJE* 17:406, 413–23).

21. *WJE* 2:413.

22. "Thus there is a difference between having an opinion that God is holy and gracious, and having a sense of the loveliness and beauty of that holiness and grace. There is a difference between having a rational judgment that honey is sweet, and having a sense of its sweetness. A man may have the former, that knows not how honey tastes; but a man can't have the latter, unless he has an idea of the taste of honey in his mind. So there is a difference between believing that a person is beautiful, and having a sense of his beauty. The former may be obtained by hearsay, but the latter only by seeing the countenance. There is a wide difference between mere speculative, rational judging anything to be excellent, and having a sense of its sweetness, and beauty. The former rests only in the head, speculation only is concerned in it; but the heart is concerned in the latter. When the heart is sensible of the beauty and amiableness of a thing, it necessarily feels pleasure in the apprehension. It is implied in a person's being heartily sensible of the loveliness of a thing, that the idea of it is sweet and pleasant to his soul; which is a far different thing from having a rational opinion that it is excellent" (*WJE* 2:413).

over, he confessed that those with a new heart found "the greatest delight in the holy Scriptures, of any book whatsoever. Oftentimes in reading it, every word seemed to touch my heart. I felt a harmony between something in my heart, and those sweet and powerful words."[23]

Briefly, this new sense of heart is like the sense of knowing the taste of honey, which is never known to those who only see the honey with their eyes. Edwards said having a Bible is like having "a large treasure of divine knowledge."[24] He emphasized the importance of studying and interpreting the Bible by saying that:

> These instructions [a book full of divine instructions—the Bible] are accommodated to persons of all capacities and conditions, and proper to be studied, not only by men of learning, but by persons of every character, learned and unlearned, young and old, men and women. Therefore the acquisition of knowledge in these things should be a main business of all those who have the advantage of enjoying the holy Scriptures.[25]

Furthermore, in his "Resolutions," he resolved "to study the Scriptures so steadily, constantly and frequently, as that I may find, and plainly perceive myself to grow in the knowledge of the same."[26] He not only emphasized the divine authority of the Bible, but also gave the Bible the highest authority over all philosophical teachings as well as theology.[27] He argued that "The whole of Christian divinity [theology] depends on divine revelation; for though there are many truths concerning God and our duty to him that are evident by the light of nature, yet no one truth is taught by the light of nature in that manner in which it is necessary for us to know it."[28]

To sum up, for Edwards, the Bible is "a large treasure of divine knowledge" given to believers who have gained a "new sense of heart" by the Holy Spirit, and the Bible has the highest authority over reason or any other intelligent thing when it comes to the knowledge of God.

23. *WJE* 16:797.

24. *WJE* 22:97.

25. *WJE* 22:91.

26. *WJE* 16:755.

27. "Were it not for divine revelation, I am persuaded that there is no one doctrine of that which we call natural religion [but] would, notwithstanding all philosophy and learning, forever be involved in darkness, doubts, endless disputes and dreadful confusion" (*WJE* 13:421).

28. *WJE* 20:52.

Therefore, although Edwards used many rational methodologies to develop his ideas and writings, we can see that God's revealed Word is the basis of his theology.

Here we encounter several important questions regarding the topic of this book: how does knowing that Jonathan Edwards's understanding of beauty centered on biblical interpretation help us understand his foundations of thought? Also, in what ways did Jonathan Edwards's biblical interpretation reflect the insights of beauty found in the Enlightenment and church traditions?

Jonathan Edwards on Beauty

Our knowledge can be divided into two categories: knowledge of God and knowledge of the created world. At this point, Edwards's aesthetics penetrate his entire understanding in that Edwards distinguishes God from the created world based on beauty. Firstly, Edwards located the origin of beauty in the Triune God. He believed that the beauty found in this world is a reflection of the original beauty found in God:

> Because God is not only infinitely greater and more excellent than all other being, but he is the head of the universal system of existence; the foundation and fountain of all being and all beauty; from whom all is perfectly derived, and on whom all is most absolutely and perfectly dependent; of whom, and through whom, and to whom is all being and all perfection; and whose being and beauty is as it were the sum and comprehension of all existence and excellence: much more than the sun is the fountain and summary comprehension of all the light and brightness of the day.[29]

Edwards located the original beauty in God because of God's moral perfection. According to Edwards, all beauty is originated from God's moral perfection so that the soul experiences the true beauty of holiness through His moral perfection.[30] Moreover, Edwards thought that this trinitarian beauty is revealed in His love, regarding the theological

29. *WJE* 8:551.

30. "When the true beauty and amiableness of the holiness or true moral good that is in divine things, is discovered to the soul, it as it were opens a new world to its view. This shows the glory of all the perfections of God, and of everything appertaining to the divine being: for, as was observed before, the beauty of all arises from God's moral perfection" (*WJE* 2:551).

basis for trinitarian persons as the love of the Trinity. In his sermon on Acts 20:28, Edwards noted that "the eternal infinite happiness of the divine being seems to be social, consisting in the infinitely blessed union and felicity of the person[s] of the Trinity so that they are happy in one another; God the Father, God the Son are represented as rejoicing from eternity one in another."[31] He accepted Augustine's understanding of love that love necessarily includes "lover, what is being loved, and love [per se],"[32] and defined the Holy Spirit as "the act of God between the Father and the Son infinitely loving and delighting in each other."[33] He also explained that the Holy Spirit as love is "harmony, excellence and beauty of divinity," claiming the *filioque* in the tradition of Augustine.[34] He further expounded that the Holy Spirit is "DIVINE BEAUTY, love and joy"[35] and "the harmony and excellency and beauty of the Deity."[36]

The reason why the persons of the Trinity can love each other infinitely is self-love on account of the infinite beauty of each person.[37] In terms of God's love, excellence, and beauty, Edwards explained as follows:

> As to God's excellence, it is evident it consists in the love of himself. For he was as excellent before he created the universe as he is now. But if the excellence of spirits consists in their disposition and action, God could be excellent no other way at that time, for all the exertions of himself were towards himself. But he exerts himself towards himself no other way than in infinitely loving and delighting in himself, in the mutual love of the Father and the Son. This makes the third, the personal Holy Spirit or the holiness of God, which is his infinite beauty, and this is God's infinite consent to being in general.[38]

This self-delivering attribute of God's beauty and love is the fundamental beauty and love that is clearly distinguished from the secondary beauty

31. Edwards, "Manuscript Sermons," Beinecke Library, Yale University, quoted in Pauw, *Supreme Harmony*, 76.

32. Augustine, *Trinity* 8.10.14.

33. *WJE* 13:260.

34. "The Father loves because the Holy Ghost is in him. So the Son loves because the Holy Spirit is in him and proceeds from him. So the Holy Ghost, or the divine essence subsisting in divine love, understands because the Son, the divine idea, is in him" (*WJE* 21:133).

35. *WJE* 21:144.

36. *WJE* 13:384.

37. "His infinite beauty is his infinite mutual love of himself" (*WJE* 6:363).

38. *WJE* 6:364.

and love of the created world. Quoting Edwards, McClymond explains that "while all beauty in creatures was a beauty by participation in God's beauty, so all beauty in God derived from God's inmost nature and not from any source outside of God," and "beauty was never something static, but was instead a dynamic and creative principle operating within the Trinity and the created World."[39] Edwards continues: "'Tis peculiar to God that he has beauty within himself, consisting in being's consenting with his own being, or the love of himself in his own Holy Spirit; whereas the excellence of others is in loving others, in loving God, and in the communications of his Spirit."[40]

In contrast, in Edwards's thoughts, the created world is the result of God's emanation of His beauty and excellence. Roland Delattre notes that based on the doctrine of the Trinity, Jonathan Edwards interpreted God's self-sufficiency as "His communicative and creative effulgence."[41] Edwards categorized the explanation of the Trinity into *ad intra* and *ad extra*, the former representing the inner structure of the Father, Son, and Holy Spirit, connected by love and beauty. This inner (*ad intra*) love, beauty, excellence, and glory of God are manifested externally (*ad extra*), which is creation. In other words, since God is infinitely great and good, he made himself his final and ultimate purpose in the creation of the world.[42] In God there is an infinite fullness of goodness, all perfection, all excellence and beauty, and infinite happiness. God created the world "to communicate of his own infinite fullness of good."[43] Therefore, the world is brought close to and united with God through the fullness of God. Since God is the full source of excellence and beauty, and this world was created by this emanation of God's fullness, this world has an image of beauty that resembles God's beauty. According to Edwards:

> THE beauty of the world consists wholly of sweet mutual consents, either within itself, or with the Supreme Being. As to the corporeal world, though there are many other sorts of consents, yet the sweetest and most charming beauty of it is its resemblance of spiritual beauties. The reason is that spiritual beauties are infinitely the greatest, and bodies being but the shadows

39. McClymond and McDermott, *Theology of Jonathan Edwards*, 96–97.

40. *WJE* 6:365.

41. Delattre, *Beauty and Sensibility*, 170.

42. *WJE* 8:421.

43. *WJE* 8:432–35.

> of beings, they must be so much the more charming as they shadow forth spiritual beauties.[44]

Therefore, the beauty of the world is the secondary beauty, and the secondary beauty is the image and shadow of the primary beauty, which is the Triune God.

Jonathan Edwards's aesthetics, in some ways, may seem similar to traditional and contemporary thinkers such as Enlightenment scholars, Augustine, and Neoplatonists. It is true that Edwards developed his aesthetics by borrowing some of their philosophy or methodology; however, his aesthetics, like his other works, were formed centering on his biblical interpretation. Thus, his theological aesthetics has clear differences from the understanding of such thinkers.[45] In this book, I will focus on Edwards's biblical interpretation and his theological aesthetics, but, in order to make a fair analysis of his theological aesthetics, I will partially address his relationship to other scholars and the Western church tradition where it may be needed.

Thesis Statement

Jonathan Edwards's biblical-theological writings, integral to his theological aesthetics, shape a cohesive framework essential for grasping his theological views on beauty.

Review of Literature

Roland André Delattre is a scholar who has contributed a full-fledged study of Jonathan Edwards on Beauty. According to Delattre, "Beauty is, in the first place, fundamental to Edwards's understanding of being."[46] However, while he acknowledges that existing Jonathan Edwards researchers have conducted various studies on the sense of beauty that perceives objective beauty, he insists that the study on beauty itself, the

44. *WJE* 6:305.

45. The Eastern church tradition also has important works on beauty. For instance, in his work *De Imaginibus*, John of Damascus described the beauty of the Trinity. However, this dissertation will focus more on the relationship between the Western Church tradition and Jonathan Edwards, exploring the ways his theological aesthetics is preserved in his biblical interpretation. Furthermore, since Jonathan Edwards clearly engaged with Augustine's ideas on the trinitarian beauty, this paper will focus more on it.

46. Delattre, "Beauty and Sensibility," 3.

object of that sense, has not been sufficiently conducted.[47] For Jonathan Edwards, beauty is the inner and structural principle of being that illuminates the whole system of being. Thus, Delattre argues that, in Edwards's understanding, the existence of God, the moral and religious life of man, and the order of the whole system of existence could best be understood in terms of the reality of beauty.[48] Based on this argument, Delattre estimates that Edwards used beauty as a "platform" for establishing trinitarian doctrine.[49] Another Edwards scholar, Sang Hyun Lee, evaluates dispositional ontology as a key concept in Edwards's theology. He says that, in Edwards's theology, God's disposition is "an excellent disposition" and "the disposition of the true, ultimate beauty."[50] Louis Mitchell regards Edwards as "a preacher and philosopher of beauty."[51] Furthermore, he evaluates how Edwards used the language of beauty to explain many important theological themes about God such as "Trinity, Christ, the Holy Spirit, soteriology, being, community, and ethics."[52] In 1981, Ronald Edwin Strader published his dissertation on Jonathan Edwards's spiritual aesthetics and its relationship to contemporary British philosophy. Like Delattre, Strader also evaluates that Edwards considered beauty to be the fundamental aspect of being.[53] According to him, for Edwards, beauty is both ontological and epistemological so that each aspect of beauty received equal treatment in his philosophical theology, forming a solution to his own tensions due to his various commitments to his own perceived world.[54] By chronologically surveying Edwards's lifetime, Strader analyzes the role of spiritual aesthetics in resolving Edwards's theological and philosophical tensions.[55] Curtis Lee Daugaard wrote his dissertation regarding the topic of God, glory and the good by analyzing Edwards's understanding on aesthetics, excellence and disposition. The most noticeable feature of his argument is that Edwards's idea of glory

47. Delattre, "Beauty and Sensibility," 14.

48. Delattre, "Beauty and Sensibility," 3–5.

49. Delattre, "Beauty and Sensibility," 187. In contrast to Delattre's assessment, William J. Danaher Jr. argues that for Edwards, ontology based on Trinitarian theology was the starting point for his understanding of beauty. See Danaher Jr., *Trinitarian Ethics*, 3.

50. Lee, *Philosophical Theology*, 179.

51. Mitchell, "Theological Aesthetics," 36.

52. Mitchell, "Theological Aesthetics," 36.

53. Strader, "Chronological Development," 131–32.

54. Strader, "Chronological Development," v.

55. Strader, "Chronological Development," v.

is clarified and illustrated by reference to Plato's concepts of the Form of the Good and normative measure. Employing the strong expression "no doubt," Daugaard firmly believes that Edwards's understanding of good comes from Plato's view.[56] Further, his dissertation focuses on developing Edwards's major theoretical components of his philosophical theology.[57]

Including those mentioned above, since 1966, a total of 8 dissertations regarding Edwards's aesthetics have been published in the English-speaking world and submitted to the Proquest/UMI database. However, all of them focus only on the philosophical and theological (i.e., apologetic and systematic theological) aspects of Edwards's aesthetics. According to Douglas A. Sweeney, the key methodology in studying Edwards is to interpret his work under the premise of Edwards as exegete.[58] The Word of God is the pivot that centers Edwards's world of thought, and thus far, no dissertation or monograph has been published regarding Jonathan Edwards's aesthetics by way of his biblical interpretation. As such, current studies have not fully reflected his biblical interpretation of aesthetics. A study on Edwards's theological aesthetics should be researched through a newly integrated understanding of his aesthetics by reinterpreting said aesthetics through the lens of Edwards's interpretation of the Bible. For this research, his *Sermons, Miscellanies, and Blank Bible* should be considered as the main exegetical sources for the study of Edwards's theological aesthetics, and other Yale edition works may frequently be consulted as primary sources to see his understanding on beauty.[59]

Methodology of Research

In order to research overall understanding of Jonathan Edwards's theological aesthetics and his biblical interpretation, the works of Jonathan Edwards in Yale editions will be the main resources as primary sources. In particular, for researching his theological aesthetics, we will consult his *Religious Affections* (*WJE* 2); *Original Sin* (*WJE* 3); *Apocalyptic Writings* (*WJE* 5); *Ethical Writings* (*WJE* 8); *A History of the Work of Redemption* (*WJE* 9); *Typological Writings* (*WJE* 11); *Ecclesiastical Writings* (*WJE*

56. Daugaard, "God, Glory, and the Good," v.

57. Daugaard, "God, Glory, and the Good," vi.

58. Barshinger and Sweeney, *Jonathan Edwards and Scripture*, 249–50.

59. Most of Edwards's sermons are also included in Works of Jonathan Edwards Yale online edition.

12); *Writing on the Trinity, Grace, and Faith* (*WJE* 21); and *Documents on the Trinity, Grace and Faith* (*WJE* 37). For his biblical interpretation, *Sermons and Discourses* (*WJE* 10; 14; 17; 19; 22; 25); *Sermons Series* (*WJE* 42–73); *The Blank Bible* (*WJE* 24); and *The Miscellanies* (*WJE* 13, 18, 20, 23) will be considered. Indeed, there is a clear limit to researching his aesthetics using only the word "beauty," or "beautiful" in his works. But, considering various aspect of beauty, Edwards used synonymous words: excellency, harmony, unity, symmetry, proportion, agreement, consent, union, and love.[60] Thus, this book will address Edwards's understanding of beauty incorporated in his sermons and works using these key terms. Furthermore, published UMI/ProQuest dissertations, articles, and monographs regarding Jonathan Edwards's aesthetics as secondary sources will be addressed to survey existing research.

To understand Jonathan Edwards's intellectual inheritance, both contemporary scholars' and Augustine's works will be considered. On the one hand, British Enlightenment scholars' and Neoplatonists' works will be addressed such as John Locke's *An Essay Concerning Human Understanding* and *Selections from the Writings of Benjamin Whichcote, John Smith and Nathanael Culverwel*, etc. On the other hand, Augustine's *Confessions*, *On Christian Doctrine*, and *The Trinity* will be addressed.[61]

In constructing following chapters of my book (in particular, chapters 4–7) I will adhere to the structure of theological *loci*[62] due to its imperative role in providing a comprehensive and systematic framework essential for rigorous academic inquiry into theological subjects. This methodology will not only facilitate a logically organized exploration of complex doctrinal issues but also ensure doctrinal consistency and integrity throughout the study. By employing the *loci* approach, I will be able to critically engage with each theological theme in its historical, scriptural, and philosophical dimensions, thus fostering a holistic understanding. Moreover, this structure will prove invaluable in contextualizing each doctrinal aspect within the broader narrative of Christian theology, allowing for an interconnected analysis that reflects the depth and breadth of the theological discourse. Consequently, adhering to the framework of theological *loci* is not merely a

60. Jonathan Edwards's vocabulary of beauty can be found in his works such as *Ethical Writings*; *Scientific and Philosophical Writings*; *Apocalyptic Writings*; *Writings on the Trinity, Grace, and Faith*, etc. See Mitchell, "Theological Aesthetics," 37–40.

61. See note 45.

62. The theological *loci* used in this book including the doctrine of God, anthropology, soteriology, Christology, ecclesiology, pneumatology, and eschatology.

structural choice but a scholarly necessity, ensuring that the book upholds academic rigor, maintains doctrinal coherence, and contributes meaningfully to the ongoing theological dialogue.

Expected Contribution

In Christian theology, beauty is not a topic studied as much as truth and goodness. Harold B. Hannum estimates that the latter topics are easy to understand and appreciate because Christians have a general idea of truth and goodness, but beauty is a more difficult subject to grasp.[63] Patrick Sherry points out that although much research has been done on attributes such as God's omniscience and omnipotence, the discussion of God's beauty is missing from these discussions. He goes on to borrow from Hans Urs von Balthasar, pointing out that God's beauty is "His most neglected attribute."[64] In contrast to this theological atmosphere, Jonathan Edwards places beauty at the center of his theology and ethics, having found the essence of beauty in the Trinity and then trying to explain how God's beauty flows into His created world. Moreover, his understanding of beauty permeates the whole of his theology: the doctrine of God, anthropology, soteriology, ecclesiology, Christology, and pneumatology. Therefore, the study of Jonathan Edwards's understanding of beauty in light of his interpretation of the bible will yield a more balanced understanding of what God is like and what the created world is.

In the next two chapters, we will explore the topics of "Jonathan Edwards and the Bible" and "Jonathan Edwards and Beauty," which are essential preliminaries to this project. Subsequent chapters will delve into Edwards's perspectives on divine beauty, human participation in this beauty, and the portrayal of Christ's excellence, highlighting his engagement with biblical texts. Chapter six will be pivotal, focusing on Edwards's defense of Christ's excellence against Deistic critiques, illustrating his theological aesthetics as a counterpoint to the prevalent Deistic thought of his time. Chapter seven will examine Edwards's ecclesiological aesthetics, offering a holistic vision of the church as a community of primary beauty and true virtue, and shedding light on his insights into heavenly aesthetics and the church's evolving beauty and resilience.

63. Hannum, "Truth, Goodness, and Beauty," 34.

64. Sherry, *Spirit and Beauty*, 58, quoted in Balthasar, *Word and Revelation*, 162.

Chapter 2

Jonathan Edwards and the Bible

Introduction

In the 1940s, studies on Jonathan Edwards began in earnest and featured such works as the Pulitzer-winning biography of Edwards by Ola Elizabeth Winslow along with the intellectual study by Perry Miller. *The Works of Jonathan Edwards* series began to be published by Yale University Press in 1957, leading to a renaissance of research into Jonathan Edwards. *The Works of Jonathan Edwards* was completed in 2008 and published in seventy-three volumes (twenty-six *WJE* volumes, forty-seven *WJEO* volumes), and included almost all of Edwards's writings. So far, there are more than 1,300 theses and dissertations about Jonathan Edwards, and books on his life and ideas are still being published.[1] As George Marsden mentioned, the numerous publications that have already appeared may raise skepticism about the need to study more about Jonathan Edwards.[2] However, despite the volume of this prior scholarship, the need for further study yet emerges. Even though much of *The Works of Jonathan Edwards* focuses on his biblical exegetical writings,[3]

1. Based on the WorldCat dissertation database (on May 3, 2022), there are a total of 1,325 volumes of theses and dissertations that include "Jonathan Edwards" in the title.

2. Marsden, *Jonathan Edwards*, xvii.

3. Michael J. McClymond and Gerald R. McDermott classify biblical exegesis in *The Works of Jonathan Edwards* into four categories; furthermore, they assert that his biblical exegetical writings occupy most of his work. "First, there were Edwards's commentaries on scripture, published in fragments within Sereno Dwight's edition of Edwards's

this field remains understudied. In this sense, Stephen Stein notes that "the contemporary renaissance of interest in Edwards has hardly touched this dimension [i.e., his biblical exegeses] of his work."[4] For example, as Douglas A. Sweeney notes, if one consults the index of M. X. Lesser's book *Reading Jonathan Edwards*,[5] headings for "Bible," "Exegesis," "Revelation," and "Scripture" cannot be found.[6] This plainly signals how overlooked the subject of Edwards's biblical interpretation has been. Hence this chapter will examine the relationship between Edwards and the Bible to show why it is necessary to research biblical interpretation in Edwards's studies. Furthermore, it will demonstrate why this book needs to focus on Edwards's biblical interpretation to examine his theological ideas.

Jonathan Edwards and His Puritan Legacy on the Bible

One of the main reasons for insufficient research on Edwards's biblical exegeses lies with the decision of some scholars to interpret Edwards as a theologian, philosopher, theorist, or revivalist, rather than as an exegete. It is true that he performed all of these roles admirably, but the more essential and the main concern for him was the Bible. The debate on Edwards's theological identity was broached early on, when Perry Miller defined Edwards's thought as "the simplest, and most precise, definition of Edwards's thought is that it was Puritanism recast in the idiom of empirical psychology."[7]

writings in 1829–1830, and full form in Stephen Stein's transcriptions of the 'Notes on the Apocalypse' (1977), 'Notes on Scripture' (1998), and 'Blank Bible' (2006), as well as the jointly edited 'Typological Writings' (1993). Taken collectively, these exclusively exegetical works fill five volumes in the Yale edition and include almost 2,500 pages of printed text. Yet there is more: Edwards's more than 1,200 extant sermon manuscripts contain a great deal of biblical exegesis. Furthermore, biblical exegesis is an integral part of such published works as 'Religious Affections,' 'Original Sin,' 'End of Creation,' 'Miscellanies,' and other writings. Finally, a number of exegetical texts were in preparation for future publication at the time of Edwards's death, notably the notebook for a 'Harmony of the Old and New Testaments,' running to some five hundred manuscript pages. Were one to extract the strictly exegetical elements of the sermons, and add them to the works already noted, the sum might come to 5,000 printed pages of material—a large fraction of the total word count of Yale University Press' Edwards" (McClymond and McDermott, *Theology of Jonathan Edwards*, 167).

4. Stein, "Spirit and the Word," 123.

5. An annotated bibliography of Jonathan Edwards studies from 1729 to 2005. See Lesser, *Reading Jonathan Edwards*, 613–73.

6. Sweeney, *Edwards the Exegete*, 8.

7. Miller, *Jonathan Edwards*, 62.

Miller and other scholars who agreed with his thought argued that Jonathan Edwards escaped from traditional Puritanism and developed his theology and philosophy using the ideas of the Enlightenment, in particular, Locke's philosophy.[8] Brad Walton explained that Miller's reasoning was as follows: "In order to make Edwards an effective voice against contemporary liberalism, Miller needed, on the one hand, to dissociate Edwards from the puritan tradition and, on the other, to identify him with Enlightenment currents of thought."[9] Many scholars agreed with Miller's interpretation of Edwards. Partrica J. Tracy and Ralph J. Coffman described Miller as "the most challenging of all" or "a master of Puritan thought,"[10] while Everett H. Emerson and John E. Smith, like Miller, argued that Edwards's thoughts were "so original . . . it is misleading to call him a puritan,"[11] and that "Locke's thought had a commanding influence upon him."[12]

On the other hand, many scholars opposed the interpretation that Edwards followed the ideas of the Enlightenment and Locke's thoughts, and claimed, instead, that Edwards did not depart from a tradition of conservative Christianity.[13] Conrad Cherry agreed that "to be sure,

8. According to Peter J. Thuesen, Perry Miller "highlighted his [Edwards's] precocious mastery of Enlightenment philosophy." Moreover, "Miller insisted that Edwards's seeming traditionalism could not always be taken at face value . . . Consequently, Miller took little interest in Edwards's straightforward engagement with the Bible and regarded his heavily scriptural *History of the Work of Redemption* as scarcely better than a 'story book for fundamentalists.'" In terms of this interpretation, Thuesen evaluates Miller's understanding of Edwards that "Miller's preternaturally modern Edwards, whose appropriation of empirical psychology led him to articulate human self-destructiveness with a force that anticipated Freud or late twentieth-century prophets like Reinhold Niebuhr" (Thuesen, "Edwards's Intellectual Background," 16).

9. Walton, "Formerly Approved and Applauded," 5–6. In addition, he says, "Miller's reading of Edwards's religious psychology as essentially a product of Enlightenment and empiricist thought has by no means gone unchallenged, it has proven remarkably influential and enduring, and has been frequently repeated" (6).

10. Murray, *Jonathan Edwards*, xxix.

11. Emerson, *Puritanism in America*, 150.

12. Smith, *Jonathan Edwards*, 25.

13. One of the most representative theologians to oppose Miller's interpretation of Edwards was Iain Murray. Thuesen reveals Murray's interpretation about Miller and Edwards by introducing a biography of Edwards, which is written by Iain Murray. Thuesen says that Iain Murray "criticized the 'anti-supernatural animus' of Miller and other secular interpreters. Unlike Miller, who repeatedly emphasized Edwards's refashioning of Lockean empiricism, Murray barely mentioned Locke and insisted that philosophy was 'peripheral' to Edwards's thought, which he judged first and foremost as religious" (Thuesen, "Edwards's Intellectual Background," 16).

Edwards was no slave to his theological heritage," and "it is now patent fact that he turned to his own design the insights of such thinkers as John Locke, Francis Hutcheson and the Cambridge Platonists." However, Cherry refuted the claim that Edwards's theological concerns lost connection to traditional Puritanism, arguing that "the interests which occupied Edwards's chief attention were theological interests," and he "broadened and impregnated his Calvinist theology."[14] Moreover, contrary to Miller's claim, Cherry argued that "Perry Miller, to whom every contemporary student of Edwards and the Puritans is profoundly indebted, leads one to conclude that Edwards is to be appreciated primarily at points other than where traditional Calvinist tenets receive extensive treatment."[15] Arguing that "the sense of the heart was fundamental in Calvinism,"[16] Terrence Erdt defined Edwards's thought as "the Calvinist psychology of the heart."[17] Paul Helm agreed that, "There is no doubt that Locke's *Essay* [*Concerning Human Understanding*] was a major factor in the philosophical development of Jonathan Edwards."[18] However, he stressed that "the use of Lockean terminology does not commit Edwards to the position Miller claims for him."[19] Moreover, he argued that "Edwards was not an empiricist, and it is too much to say that his philosophy was Locke-inspired; he draws on arguments from 'the new way of ideas' only when these serve his wider aims."[20] Finally, Norman Fiering also opposed the proposition that Locke's thoughts had a dominant intellectual influence on Edwards's ideas. He argued that "on hardly any single point in moral philosophy does he follow Locke, and in logic and metaphysics his differences from Locke are fundamental."[21]

The reason why this discussion is important is that if Edwards is understood as a Calvinist in Puritan[22] tradition, his theology would also

14. Cherry, *Theology*, 4–5. He assumes that "Edwards's Puritan ancestors would themselves have delighted in Edwards's efforts to feed new life into theology with the broadest possible learning."

15. Cherry, *Theology*, 3.

16. Erdt, "Calvinist Psychology," 178.

17. Erdt, "Calvinist Psychology," 166.

18. Helm, "Locke and Edwards:," 51.

19. Helm, "Locke and Edwards," 54.

20. Helm, "Locke and Edwards," 51.

21. Fiering, *Moral Thought*, 37.

22. In this chapter, I am going to demonstrate that Jonathan Edwards shared the Puritan conviction of the authority and usefulness of the Bible in the Christian life. Therefore, it is revealed in advance that even though some characteristics of Puritans

have developed within that tradition. One of the most obvious characteristics of Puritans is to consider the Bible important. In *The Writings of a Puritan's Mind,* C. Matthew McMahon defines a two-fold ideology of the Puritans. "(1) They knew their Bible well and consequently wrote deeply and passionately about it, and (2) They put their knowledge about Christ into action."[23] Joel R. Beeke and Randall J. Pederson assert five major concerns which are embraced by Puritans, and two of them are related to the Bible: (1) "The Puritans sought to search the Scriptures, collate their findings, and apply them to all areas of life"; (2) "The Puritans were passionately committed to focusing on the Trinitarian character of theology"; (3) "In common with the Reformers, the Puritans believed in the significance of the church in the purposes of Christ"; (4) "In the great questions of national life presented by the crises of their day, the Puritans looked to Scripture for light on the duties, power, and rights of king, Parliament, and citizen-subjects"; (5) "In regard to the individual, the Puritans focused on personal, comprehensive conversion."[24] Sweeney argues that one of three main types of reform, which Puritans grasped, is that "pastors should root their preaching in God's word—not perfunctorily but profoundly. . . . [I]t should 'open' in simple terms the spiritual contents of the Bible."[25]

The biblical-centered characteristics of the Puritans are also evident in the Westminster Confession, "the doctrinal standard for Puritan theology."[26] Many confessions, which contain the doctrinal lessons of the Protestant faith, address the doctrine of God as the first chapter. For instance, The Scots Confession of Faith, written at Edinburgh in 1560, begins with the confession and acknowledgment of the Trinity and His attributes. This confession was written by six Johns (John Winram, John Spottiswoode, John Willock, John Douglas, John Row, and John Knox), all reformed in their theology, and was used as the standard confession of the Presbyterian Church of Scotland until 1648 when the Westminster Confession was selected as the standard. In addition, many other

revealed in the following statements may be also shared with other Christian denominations such as Lutherans or Pietists, the following statements are aimed at focusing on and examining the relationship between Edwards and the Puritan tradition, rather than proving where Edwards's Christian denomination belonged.

23. McMahon et al., *Writings*, 9.

24. Beeke and Pederson, *Meet the Puritans*, xvii.

25. Sweeney, *American Evangelical Story*, 31.

26. Gleason and Kapic, "Who Were the Puritans?," 22.

confessions, such as the Belgic Confession (1561), Augsburg Confession (1530), and Gallican Confession (1559), address the doctrine of God as the first chapter. However, the Puritan document, the Westminster Confession of Faith begins with the statement of the Holy Scripture, suggesting how closely Puritan theology is connected to the Bible.

There may be many interpretations of Jonathan Edwards, but incontestably he takes a clear Puritan stance in his attitude to the Bible and its message. In his book *Jonathan Edwards' Exegesis of Genesis: a Puritan Hermeneutic?,* comparing Puritans's and Edwards's hermeneutics, Doug Landrum says that "Edwards maintained an adherence to Puritan exegesis within the natural sense."[27] In regard that "Puritanism derived from Reformed theology and denied Arminianism,"[28] Hyun-Jin Cho argues that "Edwards played a leading role to defend a Calvinist view" and "enthusiastically responded to the Arminian challenge with his sermon on justification."[29] In particular, Edwards clearly criticized Arminianism and defended Calvinist view on justification in his sermon "Justification by Faith Alone." Furthermore, suggesting that "Edwards was more of a Puritan than [Perry] Miller or his revisionists concede," Harry S. Stout evaluates Edwards as one of the "defenders of the Puritan legacy."[30] Notably, Stout also uses a lot of Edwards's sermons to analyze these Puritan tendencies, showing how these sermons[31] demonstrate Edwards's commitment to federal theology in the Puritan tradition.[32]

27. Landrum, *Exegesis of Genesis*, 7.

28. Cho, *On Justification*, 35.

29. Cho, *On Justification*, 57–58.

30. Stout, "Puritans and Edwards," 275–88.

31. The passages of the sermons are Jonah 3:10 (1727); Acts 19:19 (1736); 2 Chr 23:16/Exod 19:6 (1737); Josh 7:12 (1744/1755); Lev 26:3–13 (1745); 1 Kgs 8:44–45 (1745/1755); 2 Chr 20:27–29 (1745); Ps 111:5 (1745); Jer 51:5 (1745/1757), Neh 4:14 (1746); Exod 33:19 (1746/1754); Ps 60:9–11 (1755); and Isa 33:19–24 (1746/1756). For more information, see Stout, "Puritans and Edwards," 277–87.

32. According to Stephen J. Stein, "Cherry's study sets to rest another mistaken notion fostered by Perry Miller's biography, namely, that Edwards avoided using the language and concepts of Puritan covenant theology . . . as Cherry shows, Edwards relied heavily upon the covenant, writing at many places." Furthermore, Stein defines Edwards as "a covenant theologian properly associated with the earlier Puritan tradition," evaluating that Perry Miller distorted some parts of Edwards's traditional theology due to his antagonism toward Orthodox Christianity. Even though Miller described Edwards as "a modern intellectual hero, fighting against the entrenched forces of wealth and traditionalism in the Connecticut River valley," and he "succeeded in that objective," Stein argues that the "Edwards disclosed in Cherry's volume is a figure far more consistent with eighteenth-century realities, one deeply indebted to the theological traditions of

According to Stein, before the publication of Cherry's *The Theology of Jonathan Edwards*, there was no serious attempt to address the biblical elements of Edwards's theology outside the conservative evangelical camp, and Perry Miller's premise that Edwards deviated from the Puritan tradition was widely accepted, resulting in disregard of Edwards's biblical interpretation.[33] As this section has demonstrated, however, scholars now recognize that Jonathan Edwards affirmed many important features of the Puritan tradition, including its commitment to the central place of the Bible in the Christian life.[34]

Human Reason and Revelation

Undoubtedly, the Bible is very important for Jonathan Edwards, but there may be still some doubt about the relationship and priority between human reason and special revelation for him. In practice, he was a theological and philosophical warrior who had to survive in the battlefield of the eighteenth-century Enlightenment. The contact with Enlightenment philosophies was an inevitable reality for Edwards the scholar, and he had a good grasp of Enlightenment philosophies. Thus, as we have seen above, there are many debates about Edwards's stance between human reason and God's revelation.[35] The fact that Edwards was immersed in

the sixteenth and seventeenth centuries." The reason why this fact is important is that Miller's distorted evaluation of Edwards causes one to miss "the primary commitments the latter had made to Reformed dogmatics, scriptural interpretation, and the collective experience of the faithful." Therefore, the fact that Edwards was "a covenant theologian properly associated with the earlier Puritan tradition" is an important premise for understanding his theology and aesthetics based on his biblical interpretation. (Stein "Preface," in Cherry, *Theology*, x–xi).

33. Cherry, *Theology*, x–xi.

34. For further discussions about Edwards's relationship with the Puritans, see Sanborn, "Puritanic Philosophy," 401–21; Smith, *Jonathan Edwards*; Lovelace, "Afterword," 298–309; Lee, *Princeton Companion to Jonathan*, xxvii, 331; McClymond, *Encounters with God*, 194; Landrum, *Exegesis of Genesis*; Smith, "Puritanism and Enlightenment," 195–226.

35. No one can deny the fact that Edwards valued both God's revelation and human reason. With no doubt, Jonathan Edwards was a sincere Christian leader who led the Great Awakening and was a faithful believer. However, the assessment of Edwards's scholarly commitments (i.e., his philosophy and theology), not his religious faith, is variously divided. On the one hand, he is regarded as one of the many Christian Enlightenment figures of his time, and on the other as a faithful Christian who fought to defend the authority of the Bible against rationalism. This debate became more complicated in the eighteenth century with the emergence of a new understanding of the

the thought of the Enlightenment (in particular, Locke's empiricism) has been supported by testimony from Samuel Hopkins, who studied theology with Jonathan Edwards at Northampton:

> In his second year at college, and the thirteenth of his age, he read Locke on human understanding, with great delight and profit. His uncommon genius, by which he was, as it were by nature, formed for closeness of thought and deep penetration, now began to exercise and discover itself. Taking that book into his hand, upon some occasion, not long before his death, he said to some of his select friends, who were then with him, that he was beyond expression entertained and pleased with it, when he read it in his youth at college; that he was as much engaged and had more satisfaction and pleasure in studying it, than the most greedy miser in gathering up handsful of silver and gold from some new discovered treasure.[36]

Moreover, William Smith, who was Edwards's fellow professor, "recalled, 'he [Edwards] seemed to be of a logician and a metaphysician by nature; but greatly improved by art and study. He had imbibed the sentiments of the great Mr. Locke; these grew in him as in native soil.'"[37] As they testified, Edwards's philosophical interest in exploring Enlightenment thinkers like John Locke raises the question of whether the Bible was really at the center of Edwards's thought. The fact that the Bible was very important to him cannot be denied in itself, but the question of whether it had an absolute position in comparison to other philosophical studies still remains.

It is an undeniable fact that Edwards was influenced by contemporary Enlightenment thinkers and used their methodologies. In the editor's introduction of *The Works of Jonathan Edwards vol 26, Catalogues of Books,* Peter J. Thuesen notes hundreds of secular philosophers that

relationship between Enlightenment and religion. Traditional scholars such as Edwin S. Gaustad interpreted the relationship between Enlightenment-reason and piety-faith as a confrontational relationship. However, in recent years, scholars such as Michael J. McClymond and Gerald R. McDermott reject this interpretation based on the fact that most Enlightenment scholars were religious. This more integrated understanding of the eighteenth-century perspective on revelation and reason allows for a more suitable assessment of Edwards. For more information on conflicting assessments of Enlightenment, see Gaustad, *Great Awakening in New England*; McClymond and McDermott, *Theology*.

36. Hopkins, *Life and Character*, 3.

37. Edwards's obituary, *New York Mercury*, April 10, 1758, 1, quoted in Marsden, *Jonathan Edwards*, 62.

Edwards was interested in: for instance, English Enlightenment philosophers—John Locke, Isaac Newton, and Ephraim Chambers; Scottish philosophers—David Fordyce, Francis Hutcheson, Henry Home (Lord Kames), and David Hume; Cambridge Platonists—John Norris and Ralph Cudworth; Newtonian Metaphysician—Andrew Baxter; French Philosophers—Nicolas Malebranche and René Descartes, and many more.[38] However, Sweeney argues that Edwards had much more interest in biblical scholars:

> Three hundred years after his birth, half a century into what some have called the Edwards renaissance, few have bothered to study Edwards' massive exegetical corpus. While preoccupied with his place in America's public life and letters—and failing to see the public significance of his biblical exegesis—we have ignored the scholarly work he took most seriously. . . . We know a great deal now about his ethics, metaphysics, Calvinism, and aesthetics—not to mention his pastoral labors and his role in the Great Awakening—few know much at all about his exegetical work. Although we know quite a lot about his engagement with the leading philosophical men of his day, we know little of his work with Matthew Poole, Philip Doddridge, Matthew Henry, Arthur Bedford, John Owen, or Humphrey Prideaux—biblical scholars all. Yet they were steady, staple sources of his study day to day—more than Locke, Berkeley, and Newton. They rarely played as great a role in shaping his scholarly agenda, but they played a greater role in its execution. He spent decades, quite literally, poring over their biblical writings, doing his most important work with them at hand.[39]

Edwards was aware of the importance of human reason while clearly aware of its limitation. On the other hand, many Enlightenment scholars argued for the superiority of human reason over divine revelation. This fact can be clearly confirmed by comparing Edwards and Locke's perceptions of human reason and revelation.

Many people believe that Locke was a representative philosopher of Enlightenment who focused on the power of reason,[40] but Locke regarded

38. For more information, see Thuesen, "Editor's Introduction," in *WJE* 26:1–113.

39. Sweeney, *Edwards the Exegete*, 7.

40. One of the main reasons why Locke received this evaluation is that the scholars who succeeded Locke's thought, have emphasized the power of reason. For instance, John Toland, who "claimed to base his general position upon a philosophy similar to that of John Locke," argues that "there is nothing in the Gospel contrary to reason, nor above it; and that no Christian doctrine can be properly called a mystery" (Toland,

himself as a Christian.[41] Moreover, in contrast with many scholars of the Enlightenment, Locke agreed that the Bible is the revealed Word of God:

> Let him study the Holy Scripture, especially the New Testament. Therein are contain'd the Words of Eternal Life. It has God for its author; Salvation for its End; and Truth, without any mixture of Error for its Matter. . . . And my reason is, because the Christian religion is a revelation from God Almighty, which is contained in the Bible; and so all the knowledge we can have of it must be derived from thence.[42]

Furthermore, in the editor's introduction of *Original Sin*, Holbrook argues that Edwards "counted Locke as a significant commentator upon the Scriptures."[43] By accepting this core doctrine of Christianity, Locke seems to have an orthodox understanding of Christianity, but the problem is that he accepted not only the authority of God's revelation but also the authority of reason. Moreover, he places revelation under the regulation of reason. This fact is revealed well in his *Essay on Human Understanding*:

> Reason and faith not opposite, for faith must be regulated by reason. There is another use of the word reason, wherein it is opposed to faith: which, though it be in itself a very improper way of speaking, yet common use has so authorized it, that it would be folly either to oppose or hope to remedy it. Only I think it may not be amiss to take notice that, however, faith be opposed to reason, faith is nothing but a firm assent of the mind: which, if it be regulated, as is our duty, cannot be afforded to anything but upon good reason; and so cannot be opposite to it. He that believes without having any reason for believing, may be in love with his own fancies; but neither seeks truth as he ought, nor pays the obedience due to his Maker, who would have him use those discerning faculties he has given him, to keep him out of mistake and error.[44]

"Christianity Not Mysterious," 4). Although Locke argued that there was a disagreement between Tolland and himself, Toland's argument shows that people perceived Locke as the scholar who considered reason to have priority over revelation. Jackson and Lake, *Beginnings of Christianity*, 410.

41. The fact that he regarded himself as a Christian appears in his books such as *A Letter Concerning Toleration*; *A Paraphrase and Notes on the Epistles of St Paul*; and *The Reasonableness of Christianity*.

42. Locke, *Correspondence*, 56.

43. As a basis for his assertion, he points to the fact that Edwards partially quoted Locke's interpretation in his *Interleaved Bible*. See *WJE* 3:78.

44. Locke, *Essay*, IV, XVII, 24. According to Nicholas Wolterstroff, Locke's intention

Thus, we can affirm that even though Locke accepted God's revelation, he broke away from the absolute authority of the Bible; ultimately, he set forth the proof of reason as the rational basis of all faiths:

> In all things, therefore, where we have clear evidence from our ideas, and those principles of knowledge I have above mentioned, reason is the proper judge; and revelation, though it may, in consenting with it, confirm its dictates, yet cannot in such cases invalidate its decrees: nor can we be obliged, where we have the clear and evident sentience of reason, to quit for the contrary opinion, under a pretence that it is matter of faith: which can have no authority against the plain and clear dictates of reason.[45]

The definition of Locke's reason, faith, and revelation clearly illuminates Locke's thought. In Locke's definition, "*Reason*, therefore here, as contradistinguished to *Faith*, I take to be the discovery of the Certainty or Probability of such Propositions or Truths, which the Mind arrives at by Deductions made from such *Ideas,* which it has got by the use of its natural Faculties, *viz,* by Sensation or Reflection."[46] On the other hand, he defines faith and revelation as follows: faith "is the Assent to any Proposition, not thus made out by the Deductions of Reason; but upon the Credit of the Proposer, as coming from GOD, in some extraordinary way of Communication . . . This way of discovering Truths to Men we call Revelation."[47] He agrees with the existence of faith and revelation. However, he argues that revelation must be regulated by reason before the revelation is accepted and believed. He clearly recognizes that there is a realm of propositions "above reason," and he acknowledges that God's revelation is in that realm.[48] According to Locke, the propositions are "purely the proper Matter of Faith."[49] Moreover, he argues that "Revelation, where God has been pleased to give it, must carry it against the probable conjectures of Reason."[50] In this vein, he seems to agree with the

to write his *Essay on Human Understanding* was to address the difficulties encountered in discussing matters of morality, revelation, and religion. See Wolterstorff, "Locke's Philosophy of Religion."

45. Locke, *Essay,* IV, VIII, 6.
46. Locke, *Essay*, IV, XVII, 2.
47. Locke, *Essay*, IV, XVII, 2.
48. Locke, *Essay,* IV, XVII, 23.
49. Locke, *Essay,* IV, XVIII, 7.
50. Locke, *Essay,* IV, XVIII, 8. See also Jolly, "Locke on Faith and Reason," 441–46.

higher authority of revelation than reason. But his argument presupposes an important premise: in order to confirm whether the revelation is true, judgment of reason must be preceded.[51] Therefore, he cleverly says that revelation has higher authority than reason, but if we analyze all his arguments, we can confirm that reason, which has the role of verifying the truth of revelation, ultimately has a higher authority.

On the other hand, Jonathan Edwards believed that human reason has a significant limitation without God's revelation. In his sermon, "Like in a Dark World, a Dark Heart," Edwards defines God's revelation as follows:

> It reveals God to the soul, and enables it to apprehend him as he is, and to have a right apprehension of the perfections and glory of that being who is the being of beings, the first and the last. And proportionably, as it discovers him, it gives a right understanding of all other things.[52]

Moreover, in *The Miscellanies*, Edwards clearly states that it is God who reveals Himself. He argues that "God is a communicative being . . . this communication is really only to intelligent beings."[53] Moreover, God created spirits "to have communion" with him and, the aim of God's creation is "communication of himself, which he intended throughout all eternity."[54] Thus, in Edwards's understanding, God's revelation is not the simple knowledge that is simply imparted by Him. Rather, revelation is God's "communication of himself" toward spirits.[55]

Edwards clarifies the necessity of revelation. In his sermon, "True Nobleness of Mind," Edwards emphasizes the necessity of God's revelation that God "created us to serve him and to enjoy him." So, Edwards argues that God "should some way reveal himself to mankind; that he should give them some revelation wherein he should teach them concerning his nature and will, and reveal things of another world to them, and tell them the way how they obtain peace with him and enjoy his favor."[56]

Edwards defines reason as "that power or faculty an intelligent being has to judge of the truth of propositions, either immediately, by

51. "It still belongs to reason to judge of the truth of its being a revelation" (Locke, *Essay*, IV, XVIII, 8).

52. *WJE* 19:725.

53. *WJE* 13:410.

54. *WJE* 13:339; 8:443.

55. *WJE* 13:273.

56. *WJE* 14:232.

only looking on the propositions, which is judging by intuition and self-evidence; or by putting together several propositions which are already evident by intuition, or at least whose evidence is originally derived from intuition."[57] Edwards never devalued human reason. Rather, in terms of the power of reason, he argues that "rational arguments may savingly convince the soul of the truth of the things of religion."[58] Moreover, in his sermon, "The Importance and Advantage of a Thorough Knowledge of Divine Truth," he explains the origin of human reason which is a faculty to distinguish from the brutes:

> He [God] hath given to man some things in common with the brutes, as his outward senses, his bodily appetites, a capacity of bodily pleasure and pain, and other animal faculties: and some things he hath given him superior to the brutes, the chief of which is a faculty of understanding and reason. Our business should doubtless much consist in employing those faculties, by which we are distinguished from the beasts, about those things which are the main end of those faculties.[59]

However, Edwards, unlike Locke, clearly reveals the superiority of revelation over reason.[60] In his sermon, "Like in a Dark World, a Dark Heart," Edwards clarifies the limits of reason without revelation. He argues that "being without revelation, notwithstanding all the light of natural reason, they sunk into brutish ignorance and into such vain, absurd, and ridiculous conceptions of things, that we that have been taught better by divine revelation, can scarce conceive how it was possible for rational creatures to have such thoughts."[61] Moreover, in his sermon, "The Importance and Advantage of a Thorough Knowledge of Divine Truth," Edwards argues that rational knowledge is a tool for seeking spiritual knowledge. He says, "He [the Apostle] would have the Christian

57. *WJE* 23:359.

58. *WJE* 18:162.

59. *WJE* 22:90.

60. In *The Jonathan Edwards Encyclopedia*, Keith Beuteler argues that Edwards's view on reason is revealed well in his sermon, "Ministers to Preach Not Their Own Wisdom But the Word of God." He quotes this sermon that "Ministers are not to preach those things which their own wisdom or reason suggest, but the things already dictated by the superior wisdom and knowledge of God." "This quote shows us that, for Jonathan Edwards, ministers do not merely abandon their own reason. Rather they draw the conclusion, reasonable in itself, that God's reasoning is infinitely more penetrating than human reasoning" (Beutler, "Reason," 486–88).

61. *WJE* 19:711.

Hebrews seek the one [a spiritual knowledge], in order to the other [a rational knowledge] . . . it [a spiritual knowledge] is to be sought by the other [a rational knowledge], as its end."[62] Thus, we can clearly affirm that Edwards takes the opposite position from Locke's claim that revelation should be judged by reason.

Jonathan Edwards argues that the Scripture is "a miraculous gift" and "a prefect rule" which has no need "to be added to."[63] Moreover, he notes:

> Were it not for divine revelation, I am persuaded that there is no one doctrine of that which we call natural religion [but] would, notwithstanding all philosophy and learning, forever be involved in darkness, doubts, endless disputes and dreadful confusion. There are many things, now they are revealed, seem very plain, and as if we could easily arrive at a certainty of them if we never had had a revelation of them. It is one thing to see that a truth is exceeding agreeable to reason, after we have been told it and have had it explained to us, and have been told the reasons of it; and another to find it out, and clearly and certainly to explain it, by mere reason.[64]

This different understanding of the relationship between human reason and revelation brings critical distinction of the relationship in his biblical interpretation. Locke regarded himself as a Christian, but his biblical interpretation was reason-centric and sometimes had deistical characteristics. For instance, his biblical interpretation on some fundamental articles such as original sin, God's eternal punishment, Christology, and soteriology could not have been accepted by Puritan theologians like Jonathan Edwards.[65]

For example, Locke's understanding of original sin depended on his empirical epistemology, in particular, the theory of *tabula rasa*. According to Locke, human beings can only acquire ideas through their senses and experiences. On the one hand, all human beings in the Bible have religious sense; on the other hand, they also have antagonism toward God because they have turned away from God since the Fall so that every human being is born with a sinful tendency. In this vein, what is Locke's understanding of original sin? Locke acknowledges the existence

62. *WJE* 22:87.

63. *WJE* 8:363.

64. *WJE* 13:421.

65. For more on John Locke's comparison of Christian doctrine with Latitudinarianism, see Polinska, "John Locke," 173–94.

of original sin. However, he does not accept that everyone should be eternally punished because of Adam's sin because, in his thought, this kind of punishment is not suitable for God's goodness and justice.[66]

Locke agrees that Adam's sin is the fact; furthermore, he accepts that Adam's disobedience brought serious consequences. However, Locke's understanding of the consequences of Adam's sin and imputation of original sin is very different from how Christian theologians have traditionally interpreted Scripture. He argues that "death came on all men by Adam's sin."[67] His claim is evident in his interpretation of Romans 5:12.[68] As he interprets this passage, Locke argues that since Adam broke the law of God, as a result, man began to die. In other words, the result of Adam's sin was the loss of man's immortality, and man became mortal.[69] Moreover, Locke stubbornly rejects that men are eternally punished because of original sin. He argues that, despite God's goodness and justice, if humans should go to hell because of Adam's sin, it is "a strange way of understanding a Law."[70] This understanding of original sin also affects his understanding of the universality of sin. In his interpretation of Romans 3:23, which is another representative verse of original sin, he interprets the word "all" as Jewish and Gentile, not all mankind.[71] This shows that Locke denies the imputation of sin from Adam and the eternal punishment of God for that sin.

Locke's understanding of Christ and redemption begins with a similar understanding as that of traditional Christianity. In his book, *the Reasonableness of Christianity*, he refutes those who claim that redemption

66. Locke, *Reasonableness of Christianity*, 5.

67. Locke, *Reasonableness of Christianity*, 6.

68. "Therefore, just as sin came into the world through one man, and death through sin, and so death spread to all men because all sinned" (Rom 5:12).

69. Locke, *Paraphrase*, 522–23; *Reasonableness of Christianity*, 6–7.

70. "This is so clear in these cited places, and so much the current of the New Testament, that nobody can deny, but that the Doctrine of the Gospel is, that Death came on all Men by Adam's sin; only they differ about the signification of the word Death. For some will have it to be a state of Guilt, wherein not only he, but all his Posterity was so involved, that everyone descended of him deserved endless torment in Hell-fire. I shall say nothing more here how far, in the apprehensions of Men, this consists with the Justice and Goodness of God, having mentioned it above: But it seems a strange way of understanding a Law, which requires the plainest and directest words, that by Death should be meant Eternal Life in Misery. Could anyone be supposed by a Law, that says, For Felony you shall die, not that he should lose his Life, but be kept alive in perpetual exquisite Torments? And would anyone think himself fairly dealt with, that was so used?" (Locke, *Reasonableness of Christianity*, 7).

71. Locke, *Paraphrase*, 508.

is unnecessary, and he argues that their claim makes Christ "nothing but the restorer and preacher of pure natural religion; thereby doing violence to the whole tenor of the New Testament."[72] But, like his understanding of revelation and original sin, his understanding of Christ and redemption also has a crucial difference from the traditional Christian understanding. He acknowledges that Christ's redemption is "deliverance from that, to which a man in subjection or bondage,"[73] but he refutes substitution of Christ for his work of redemption in his biblical interpretation.[74] However, at the same time, he argues that the Church was "purchased with his [Christ's] own Blood" in his interpretation of Ephesians 1:14.[75]

Locke's view of Christ and salvation seems to derive from his doctrines of original sin and Christ's nature. John C. Higgins-Biddle, who is the editor of Locke's book *The Reasonableness of Christianity*, claims that "Locke . . . continued to argue that the phrase 'Son of God' did not originally imply Christ's divinity."[76] His understanding of God's wrath[77] on all sinners from original sin and his presentation of Christ's nature seems to have led Locke to fail to integrate Christ's two-fold roles as messiah and redeemer of the sins of mankind; as a result, he did not understand that

72. Locke, *Reasonableness of Christianity*, 5.

73. Locke, *Paraphrase*, 508.

74. Locke's rejection of the doctrine of substitution is evident through his theological position as a Latitudinarian. According to Wioleta Polinska, Locke's major concern is to confirm that "the redemption in Christ is gratis, which makes any notion of the ransom paid to God unacceptable to him." In his biblical interpretation of Romans 5:15, Locke claims that the restoration through Jesus Christ's suffering, crucifixion was from the exuberant bounty and good-will of Christ towards men, who at the cost of his own painful death, purchased life for them, not making a payment to God. In this sense, Polinska argues that "what Locke rejects is . . . the doctrine of substitution. . . . he rejects the idea implied in the doctrine of substitution that our guilt was imputed to Christ while Christ's righteousness was imputed to all humanity" (Polinska, "John Locke," 180–86).

75. Locke, *Paraphrase*, 619.

76. Higgins-Biddle, "Introduction," lxx.

77. In terms of God's wrath, interpreting Deuteronomy 32:35 in his 1741 sermon, "Sinners in the Hands of an Angry God," Jonathan Edwards reveals that divine justice, mercy, and wrath all belong to God. "The sword of divine justice is every moment brandished over their heads, and 'tis nothing but the hand of arbitrary mercy, and God's mere will, that holds it back. . . . The bow of God's wrath is bent, and the arrow made ready on the string, and justice bends the arrow at your heart, and strains the bow, and it is nothing but the mere pleasure of God, and that of an angry God, without any promise or obligation at all, that keeps the arrow one moment from being made drunk with your blood" (Edwards, *The Sermons*, 51, 57).

the doctrine of satisfaction and the doctrine of substitution are organically connected doctrines.

In short, Locke's understanding of the doctrine of Original Sin clearly suggests his attitude toward the relationship between reason and revelation. Locke seems to advocate both revelation and reason. However, as analyzed by W. M. Spellman, Locke's theory of *tabula rasa* conflicts with the traditional biblical interpretation of the corruption of mankind by Adam's original sin.[78] In other words, Locke's understanding of Original Sin eventually becomes conclusive evidence that Locke placed the judgment of human reason above revelation. As David Hume evaluates, for Locke, "faith was nothing but a species of reason, that religion was only a branch of philosophy."[79] This attitude of Locke is clearly different from Edwards's understanding of the relationship between human reason and revelation.

Unlike Locke, Edwards's understanding on the fundamental articles followed carefully the traditional orthodox view of Scripture. In his book, *Original Sin,* Edwards defines original sin as "the innate sinful depravity of the heart."[80] Moreover, he argues that original sin means not only a corruption of human nature but also the imputation of Adam's sin and "to partake of the punishment of that [Adam's first] sin."[81] Edwards obviously held to a Reformed understanding of original sin; but at the same time, he did not hesitate to have conversation with Enlightenment scholars and to use their writings and arguments to develop his theology. For instance, according to C. A. Holbrook, an editor of *Original Sin* in the Yale edition, Jonathan Edwards "had seemed inclined to accept" Locke's interpretation of "personal identity." He did not accept Locke's argument because Edwards discovered an error in his argument, but he was "ever ready to count Locke on his side." Moreover, Holbrook notes that "Turnbull's citation from Newton was also quarried to buttress Edwards' principal theses." He did not ignore human reason and secular academic methodology, but he clearly understood the limitation of human reason: "the proofs that have been extant in the world, *from trial and fact*, of the depravity of men's nature, are inexpressible, and as it were infinite, beyond the representation of all comparison and similitude."[82]

78. Spellman, "Christian Estimate," 476.

79. Hume, *Dialogues*, 14.

80. *WJE* 3:107.

81. *WJE* 3:107.

82. *WJE* 3:187 (italics added).

Edwards's understanding of original sin and the punishment for it becomes more apparent in his sermons. In those, Edwards explicitly asserts the fact that everyone is a sinner, and affirms the Fall and its consequences, God's punishment, along with the reality of hell. Unlike Locke, Edwards argues that everyone is a sinner since Adam's fall. In his sermon, "the Reality of Conversion," Edwards argues that conversion is a "mighty work of God on their [men's] hearts, changing their natures and infusing principles that strengthened them and carried 'em far beyond the strength of nature."[83] Here Edwards argues that human nature must be changed. In interpreting Amos 3:3, he asserts that man must be united with God, and that a person with a nature opposite to God cannot associate with God: "No men have union with God without conformity to God . . . 'Tis unreasonable to suppose that God would ever admit any person into union with him, to dwell with him and enjoy him, whose nature is contrary to his."[84] And, he calls those who have the opposite nature to God "those that remain in a natural condition."[85] Thus, we can see that Edwards in this sermon, unlike Locke, argues that all humans have one of two natures, of which those, who have the unconverted natures, remain in a natural condition.[86] Moreover, he argues that regardless of "old, young, bond and free, poor, wicked," everyone needs conversion.[87] This means that everyone under the influence of original sin is a sinner.

In his sermon, "He that Believeth Shall Be Saved," Edwards clarifies Adam's representation on the basis of a Reformed understanding of the fall of Adam and original sin: "If Adam had never fallen, then he would have had eternal life on his own account, and for his own goodness. But now, we have fallen and lost our goodness, we are saved only for Christ's sake."[88] Through his interpretation of Adam's representation of all human beings, we can also know that Edwards clearly argues that all the descendants of Adam are sinners.

Edwards's understanding of original sin leads to an understanding of God's punishment as a result of the sin. He says, "all men have sinned

83. Edwards, *Sermons*, 89.

84. Edwards, *Sermons*, 85.

85. Edwards, *Sermons*, 92.

86. Edwards suggests Paul as a representative figure who was converted from a sinful nature. Edwards, *Sermons*, 86.

87. Edwards, *Sermons*, 103.

88. Edwards, *Sermons*, 114.

and deserve to be damned. All men are naturally full of sin."[89] Moreover, he argues that the judgment of God against a sinner will surely take place, the souls of sinners will go to hell, and the judgment will never end.[90]

In his best-known sermon, "Sinners in the Hands of an Angry God," Edwards also explicates original sin and its results. As I stated above, Locke argues that because God is righteous, eternal punishment by original sin does not fit God's attributes. On the other hand, Edwards argues that sinners "deserve to be cast into hell; so that divine justice never stands in the way, it makes no objection against God's using his power at any moment to destroy them."[91] Without stopping here, Edwards interpreted John 3:18 that sinners "already under a sentence of condemnation to hell . . . every unconverted man properly belongs to hell."[92] Moreover, according to Edwards, John 8:23 tells us that sinners "are from beneath [hell]."[93] Finally, by arguing that in the "nature of sinners" "corrupt principles . . . [is] reigning power in them," unlike Locke's "*tabla rasa*," Edwards clarifies the existence of sinful nature and corrupt principles which originated from original sin.[94]

Furthermore, unlike Locke, who cannot affirm that Christ is the Son of God, in his sermon "I Know My Redeemer Lives," Edwards states that Jesus Christ is the redeemer and that Christ is risen from the dead, as God-man, and Christ is "the Son of the living God."[95] Furthermore, in contrast to Locke, Edwards clearly reveals his understanding of the doctrine of substitution. In his sermon, "He That Believeth Shall Be Saved," Edwards explains the reason why believing in Christ is the only way to be saved by Christ, that "Christ has suffered for us, and has satisfied for our sin, and has paid down a sufficient price for our salvation. He has done all. There is nothing for us to do now but only believe in Christ, and with all our hearts to come to him for salvation."[96]

Therefore, we can confirm that Edwards's understanding of original sin and the relationship between Christ and redemption, which are revealed in his sermons, has a clear difference from Locke's understanding

89. Edwards, *Sermons*, 117.

90. Edwards, *Sermons*, 116–17.

91. *WJE* 22:405.

92. *WJE* 22:406.

93. *WJE* 22:406.

94. *WJE* 22:407.

95. Edwards, *Sermons*, 143, 148.

96. Edwards, *Sermons*, 114.

of human nature and Christology; furthermore, this obvious difference reveals a clear distinction between those who look at the Bible as subservient to human reason and those who look at the Bible as God's revelation.

Jonathan Edwards's Primary Role: Pastor

Patricia J. Tracy has argued that "Jonathan Edwards, the most famous revivalist of the eighteenth century, has been extensively studied as a philosopher-theologian; but, strangely, his career as a pastor . . . has received only minimal attention."[97] However, Edwards devoted himself to his role as a pastor and preacher, wherein "his chief professional concern was the saving of souls, and most of his intellectual activity revolved around an attempt to restate the Calvinist dogma he had inherited so that its meaning would be clear and emotionally affecting when preached in the meetinghouse."[98] After a brief tenure as pastor of a Presbyterian church in New York city in 1722–1723 and a Congregational church in Bolton in 1723–1724, Edwards succeeded his maternal grandfather Solomon Stoddard as pastor of Northampton Church on February 11, 1729.[99] In this role, his primary concern was to preach and minister to his congregation until his dismissal from the Northampton church on June 22, 1750. After his dismissal, he began to devote himself to the work of the Stockbridge Indian Mission, and from August 8, 1751, he was once again dedicated to the Church of Stockbridge as a pastor. At the end of his life he served as the president of the College of New Jersey in Princeton at the last moment of his life; but, most of his life was filled with his duties as a pastor.

In order to understand the relationship between Edwards as a pastor and his devotion to biblical interpretation, an understanding of the characteristics of pastors in eighteenth-century New England should precede. A pastor has diverse duties and priorities depending on the times, culture, countries, or denominations, but, the primary obligation of pastors in most Protestant churches is studying and preaching the Bible for their congregation. This was certainly the case in Puritan New England:

97. Tracy, *Jonathan Edwards, Pastor*, 4.

98. Tracy, *Jonathan Edwards, Pastor*, 4.

99. Before he served the church as a senior pastor, "from late in 1726 till late in 1728 (when Stoddard's health declined), Edwards preached once every Lord's Day and 'lectured' once a week, adding a third sermon per week to his already busy schedule as he turned twenty-five" (Sweeney, *Ministry of the Word*, 57).

> The center of attention in the Puritan meeting house was the pulpit, or "the desk," as New Englanders commonly dubbed it for its importance as the locus of biblical scholarship in their midst. . . . Their clergy shed their vestment (ornate liturgical clothes), preaching instead in academic gowns that symbolized their calling to learned, biblical ministry (rather than sacramental priesthood). . . . Edwards' world was strikingly different from ours. Its pastors worked as theologians. Its theologians worked as pastors. People expected ordained clergy to spend the bulk of their time in study, preparing to minister the Word to them in depth and rich detail. . . . They paid attention to words, biblical words most of all. Many knew their Bibles well, believing their lives depended upon it.[100]

In this sense, Edwards spent most of his time as a pastor, studying, teaching, and preaching the Bible. If his primary and major role was not as a pastor but as a scholar or philosopher, he would have spent more time and effort for his academic achievement. However, Edwards devoted himself to his pastoral role so he could confess that he did his best in his ministry. In his farewell sermon preached at the First Precinct in Northampton (June 22, 1750), his devotion and efforts as a pastor can be seen:

> I have spent the prime of my life and strength in labors for your eternal welfare. You are my witnesses, that what strength I have had, I have not neglected in idleness, nor laid out in prosecuting worldly schemes, and managing temporal affairs, for the advancement of my outward estate, and aggrandizing myself and family; but have given myself to the work of the ministry, laboring in it night and day, rising early and applying myself to this great business to which Christ appointed me.[101]

Furthermore, the fact that his primary concern should be interpreting the Bible for preaching as a pastor can be revealed by the proportion of his biblical interpretations in his works. Among the total of seventy-three volumes of *The Works of Jonathan Edwards* Yale edition, there are six volumes of *Sermons and Discourses*,[102] two volumes on Scripture,[103] one volume of *Sermon Notebooks*,[104] thirty volumes of sermon series,[105]

100. Sweeney, *Ministry of the Word*, 25, 30.
101. Edwards, *Sermons*, 217.
102. *WJE* 10; 14; 17; 19; 22; 25.
103. *WJE* 24; 15.
104. *WJE* 36.
105. *WJE* 42–73.

and other volumes which have his biblical interpretation.[106] His rich and abundant studies and sermons involving biblical interpretation illustrate how important he considered the Bible as a pastor.

Conclusion

For Jonathan Edwards, a Christian's "duty towards God" is "knowing what that religion is"; furthermore, he asserts that "we must know not only that [God] exists, and what manner of being he is, but also must know the mutual concern he has with us, etc."[107] In this sense, Edwards believes in the fundamental necessity of revelation, in particular, the Bible.[108] He confesses that "when I have read the Scripture most, I have evermore been most lively, and in the best frames."[109] As a successor to the Puritan theological legacy, Edwards centered his ideas and thoughts on the Bible, just as his ancestors did. It is also true that he selectively embraced Enlightenment ideas, a philosophical approach of his time, but unlike many Enlightenment philosophers, he placed God's revelation over human reason. Finally, Edwards established his identity as a pastor above all other roles, and as a pastor, he spent "the prime of his life" studying and preaching the Bible.[110] Therefore, in order to properly address Edwards's theology and aesthetics through his writings, an understanding of his biblical interpretation must be laid out.

106. Most of his writings contain his interpretation of the Bible, but the following books especially illustrate his biblical interpretation: *Original Sin* (*WJE* 3); *Apocalyptic Writings* (*WJE* 5); *A History of the Work of Redemption* (*WJE* 9); *Typological Writings* (*WJE* 11); *Ecclesiastical Writings* (*WJE* 12); *Writings on the Trinity, Grace, and Faith* (*WJE* 21); *Original Sin Notebook* (*WJE* 34); *Charity and Its Fruits* (*WJE* 35); and his *Miscellanies* (*WJE* 13; 18; 20; 23). For additional analysis of Jonathan Edwards's exegetical works by Michael J. McClymond and Gerald R. McDermott, see note 67.

107. *WJE* 23:254. For further understanding of his argument on the relationship between the revelation and Christian religion (or faith), see "Necessity of Revelation. Christian Religion" (*WJE* 23:253–64).

108. He accepted the benefit of general or natural revelation, but in terms of the knowledge of our salvation, he clearly delimited the light of nature. "The light of nature teaches that religion that is necessary to continue in the favor of God that made us. But it cannot teach us that religion that is necessary to our being restored to the favor of God after we have forfeited it" (*WJE* 23:264).

109. *WJE* 16:786.

110. Edwards, *Sermons*, 217.

Chapter 3

Jonathan Edwards on Beauty

Introduction

The term "aesthetic" first appeared in Alexander Gottlieb Baumgarten's 1735 master's thesis, *Philosophical Meditations on Some Matters Pertaining to Poetry*.[1] Baumgarten derives this term from Greek philosophers and Church fathers.

> The Greek philosophers and the Church fathers have already carefully distinguished between *things perceived* [αἰσθητά] and *things known* [νοητά]. It is entirely evident that they did not equate *things known* with things of sense, since they honored with this name things also removed from sense (therefore, images). Therefore, *things known* are to be known by the superior faculty as the object of logic; *things perceived* [are to be known by the inferior faculty, as the object] of the science of perception, or *aesthetic*.[2]

Although the term "aesthetics" itself was first introduced in the eighteenth century, the theme of "beauty" as "theological aesthetics" has been addressed as an important theological subject from the early church era to the present day. In particular, the theme of beauty is one of the most important subjects that ran through Edwards's theological world. Ironically, however, the expressions "beautiful" and "beauty" are not often used in his work to encompass his entire theology. How, then, can the

1. Guyer, "Monism and Pluralism," 133.
2. Baumgarten, *Reflections on Poetry*, 78 (italics added).

theme of beauty be at the core of Edwards's theology and thinking? What terms did Edwards use to express the beauty of God and the beauty of the created world? Was Edwards's understanding of beauty original with him, was it a product of the philosophy of the Enlightenment; was it in continuity with the Western church tradition? Answering these questions, this chapter will address Edwards's core understanding of beauty.

Theological Aesthetics in the Western Church Tradition

St. Augustine on Beauty

Scholars who have studied Augustine, agree that his philosophy and theology have had a profound effect on Western intellectual history, beyond Western church history. Furthermore, Augustine's academic influence is not limited to the domain of philosophy and theology but also extends to the aesthetics of Western church traditions. In this sense, renowned Polish aesthetician and art historian Władysław Tatarkiewicz's evaluation of Augustine as "the founder of the Christian aesthetics of the West" is remarkable.[3]

The reason understanding of beauty is important to Augustine is that this is the point at which the two major pillars of his thought, Hellenism and Hebraism, are in harmony.[4] Augustine was educated extensively in Latin culture and Hellenism, where he encountered the aesthetics of Cicero, Plato, and the aesthetics of the Stoic school. Under the influence of Hellenism, he maintained his understanding of *Symmetria* as the essence of beauty and *Asymmetria* as the essence of ugliness,[5] beginning with Pythagoras and continuing to the Stoics.[6] Around 385, he encountered Plotinus's treatise "On Beauty," and he was greatly assisted by Plotinus's

3. Tatarkiewicz, *History of Aesthetics*, 2:47.

4. According to Floyd Anderson, "Saint Augustine lived in an age when the divisions between the Hellenic and the Hebraic ideals were great, arguably, greater than at any other time in the history of the West. His great achievement is that he effected a convergence of these two rival traditions—a convergence that represents probably the most successful synthesis of Hebraism and Hellenism in Western history" (Anderson, "De Doctrina Christiana," 102).

5. Augustine, *De vera religione* 30.55; 31.57; 32.60; 95.77; *De Musica* 6.10.28; 6.12.38.

6. This Pythagorean point of view was maintained by Plato, Aristotle, the Stoics, and Cicero. See Tatarkiewicz, *History of Six Ideas*, 222–23. For those scholars, *symmetria* was a synonym for beautiful arrangement (227), and Augustine maintained this concept of *symmetria*.

aesthetics, which focused on discovering the ultimate good and the cause and source of all beautiful things. Unlike Hellenistic aesthetics, which used *symmetria* as the source of beauty, Plotinus's aesthetics viewed the role of beauty as the action of returning to the One. Augustine found harmony between Hellenism and Hebraism after encountering Plotinus. Through Plotinus's methodology, he realized that there was inferior beauty and lofty beauty, and so he reached the pinnacles of his aesthetics: Prime beauty—*Simplicitas Dei* (divine simplicity) and *Pankalia* (beauty of the created world).[7] This understanding of Augustine on beauty was later inherited by Jonathan Edwards to help form the core of his aesthetics.

Augustine's passion and qualifications for the study of aesthetics were confirmed in his first article, "On the Beautiful and the Fitting" (*De pulchro et apto*), which he wrote in his youth.[8] His reference to this work appears in his *Confessions*, where he defines what makes love or what we love beautiful by quoting from his writings in *De pulchro et apto*: "Do we love anything but the beautiful? What, then, is the beautiful? And what is beauty? What is it that attracts us and draws us to things which we love? For, unless grace and beauty of form were in them, they certainly would not draw us to themselves."[9] After his Christian conversion, however, he reflects on his phase as a Manichean, correcting this beauty as "the lower kind of beauties."[10] For Augustine, who experienced the beauty of God, the true beauty is the unchangeable truth which leads him into the One, God.[11]

In his *Against Academicians*, through the "two sisters" metaphor (the love of beauty, *philocalia*, and the love of wisdom, *philosophia*), Augustine reveals that we must escape sensuous and physical beauty and instead seek the noble beauty of wisdom and truth.[12] In addition, Augustine does not treat philosophy as a cool and refined abstraction but compares it to the bright appearance of a bride. By glimpsing the beauty of that appearance, a man can stoke an incredible fire in the soul, and he is also surprised and blazing with excitement as he becomes a holy admirer, seeking the beauty of wisdom and truth and leaving behind all

7. Augustine, *Confessions* 10.34.51; *De vera religione* 27.43; *De natura boni* 3.

8. This early work of Augustine, written when he was a professor of rhetoric in Carthage, was lost.

9. Augustine, *Confessions* 4.13.20.

10. Augustine, *Confessions* 4.13.20; 10.28.38.

11. Augustine, *De vera religione* 34.63; 36.66.

12. Augustine, *Against the Academicians* 2.6–7.

other fascinations.[13] As such, since Augustine's true beauty is related to truth, he seeks to find the way to reach true beauty in the perception of order in the world.[14] Furthermore, he emphasizes that it is reason, not sense, that perceives and judges the beauty found in the order.[15]

According to Augustine, God is the best beauty that human beings should seek and desire.[16] So he confessed that the further he was from God, the more that beauty "wasted away."[17] For him, the source of "beauty" and "goodness" is God, and God's "beauty" and "goodness" are the *principia essendi* of all beings.

> THE highest good, than which there is no higher, is God, and consequently He is unchangeable good, hence truly eternal and truly immortal. All other good things are only from Him, not of Him. For what is of Him, is Himself. And consequently if He alone is unchangeable, all things that He has made, because He has made them out of nothing, are changeable.[18]

His statements about the relationship between "goodness" and "beauty" are also found in his *Confessions*.

> Thou who art beautiful, for they are beautiful; Thou who art good, for they are good; Thou who doth exist, for they exist, too. Yet, they are not beautiful, they are not good, they do not exist, in the same way as Thou, their Creator; in comparison with Thee, they are neither beautiful, nor good, nor do they even exist.[19]

13. Augustine, *Against the Academicians* 2.3–6.

14. Augustine's arguments sometimes sound Platonic, in particular in his writings regarding "love." As we have seen above, this is associated with Augustine's balance between Hebraism and Hellenism. Anders Nygren's explanation is helpful to understand it: "The question of influence of the Eros and the Agape motifs on Augustine's life and religious outlook seems to be very closely connected with the much-disputed question of the influence of Neoplatonism and Christianity on his inner development. He took over the Eros idea substantially from Neoplatonism, and what he possesses of the idea of Agape he has obviously got from the New Testament, especially from the Pauline writings. . . . He thinks he can find a remarkably large measure of agreement between them. . . . He has done more than any other, by combining things Neoplatonism and Christian, to import the Eros motif into Christianity" (Nygren, *Agape and Eros*, 458–59).

15. Augustine, *On Order* 2.6; 32; 34; 39; Chadwick, *Augustine*, 47–48.

16. Augustine, *Confessions* 10.34.53.

17. Augustine, *Confessions* 2.1.1.

18. Augustine, "Concerning the Nature of Good," 351.

19. Augustine, *Confessions* 11.4.6.

To Augustine, the Trinity is perfect beauty, and his personal perfection is confirmed by the love flowing in the Trinity: "In that supreme triad is the source of all things, and the most perfect beauty, and wholly blissful delight."[20] Furthermore, he confesses that the trace of the Trinity, the source of beauty, is found in the created world he created. It is impossible to understand the mystery of the Trinity with human reason, but the grandeur and beauty of the created world can give us a knowledge of God the Creator.[21]

In summary, for Augustine, true beauty comes from God, the highest beauty, and it is a very low level of beauty that humans are attracted to (without God) and think of as beautiful. Goodness and beauty are inseparable from each other as *principia essendi*, and all beings can confirm the beauty of their being in God, the *summum bonum*. In addition, the Trinity is bound by love, due to the complete beauty of each hypostasis, and this trinitarian beauty can be traced in the created world.[22]

Edwards does not directly cite Augustine's aesthetics in his writings. Looking at the structure of Edwards's aesthetic logic, however, confirms the significant influence of Augustine. For example, Edwards describes the beauty of the Trinity using Augustine's structure of the trinitarian relationship of love. Augustine repeatedly describes the Father as "Lover," the Son as "Beloved," and the Holy Spirit as "Love Itself."[23] In this sense, he argues that since God is love (John 4:8), God should be triune. Likewise, Edwards states that the excellence and beauty of the Trinity is the reason for the three Persons' mutual love.[24]

Thomas Aquinas on Beauty

As Umberto Eco points out, "most of the aesthetic issues that were discussed in the Middle Ages were inherited from Classical Antiquity," including not only from ancient philosophy but also "from the Bible and from the Fathers"; but "these were absorbed into a new and systematic

20. Augustine, *Trinity* 6.10.12. In this sense, he explains the Trinitarian hypostases as the Lover, the Beloved, and the Love (8.10.14).

21. Augustine, *Trinity* 15.2.3.

22. For further information of Augustine's aesthetics, see Bychkov, "What Does Beauty," 197–212; Chapman, *Saint Augustine*; "Some Aspects," 46–51; Tatarkiewicz, *History of Aesthetics*; Eco, *Art and Beauty*.

23. Augustine, *Trinity* 8.10.14; 9.2.2. See also 9.5.8.

24. *WJE* 6:363–65.

philosophical world."[25] In other words, aesthetics in the Middle Ages had both continuity and originality. However, considering that the theme that appeared constantly and repeatedly in the Middle Ages was "the beauty of being in general," and that the concepts of beauty and goodness were used cosmologically, medieval aesthetics were not very original, deviating only slightly from Augustinian tradition but as a kind of an extension and development of that tradition.[26]

The theology of Thomas Aquinas, the Dominican priest who lived in the golden age of medieval culture in the thirteenth century, was one important example of the medieval Scholasticism. Aquinas is an indispensable figure, not only in theology and philosophy but also in the history of aesthetics.[27] By saying, "Beauty and goodness in a thing are identical fundamentally; for they are based upon the same thing, namely, the form; and consequently goodness is praised as beauty," he reveals his understanding of the classical view of truth, goodness, and beauty, wherein beauty and goodness are the same subject.[28] However, he logically divides good and beautiful as follows:

> But they differ logically, for goodness properly relates to the appetite (goodness being what all things desire); and therefore it has the aspect of an end (the appetite being a kind of movement towards a thing). On the other hand, beauty relates to the cognitive faculty; for beautiful things are those which please when seen. Hence beauty consists in due proportion.[29]

According to Aquinas, beauty is based on the concept of goodness but is distinguished by an additional relationship with cognitive ability towards this concept. More precisely, goodness is fulfilled when it attains what it desires, whereas beauty is fulfilled when it is recognized. In this sense, he argued that beauty is related to the rational senses of sight and hearing, and through these senses the desire for beauty is fulfilled.

> The beautiful is the same as the good, and they differ in aspect only. For since good is what all seek, the notion of good is that which calms the desire; while the notion of the beautiful is that

25. Eco, *Art and Beauty*, 4.

26. Eco, *Art and Beauty*, 17.

27. Tatarkiewicz considers Aquinas's aesthetic achievements as comparable to Kant's. Tatarkiewicz, *History of Aesthetics*, 2:246.

28. Aquinas, *Summa Theologica* I, q.5, a.4, ad.1.

29. Aquinas, *Summa Theologica* I, q.5, a.4, ad.1.

> which calms the desire, by being seen or known. Consequently those senses chiefly regard the beautiful, which are the most cognitive, viz. sight and hearing, as ministering to reason; for we speak of beautiful sights and beautiful sounds. But in reference to the other objects of the other senses, we do not use the expression "beautiful," for we do not speak of beautiful tastes, and beautiful odors. Thus it is evident that beauty adds to goodness a relation to the cognitive faculty: so that "good" means that which simply pleases the appetite; while the "beautiful" is something pleasant to apprehend.[30]

In his understanding, beauty and goodness are "identical fundamentally"[31] In particular, he regards "moral beauty" as same as "*honestum*—moral goodness."[32] Nevertheless, beauty and goodness are different in meaning because "goodness relates to appetite while beauty relates to cognition."[33]

Aquinas argues that in order for beauty to be established, three conditions—perfection, proportion, and clarity[34]—must be met, because defective beings (imperfection) are ugly and beauty dwells in clarity and proportion.[35] He also describes these three appropriate conditions of

30. Aquinas, *Summa Theologica* II-I, q.27, a.1, ad.3.

31. Sevier, *Aquinas on Beauty*, 14.

32. Sevier, *Aquinas on Beauty*, 6–7.

33. Sevier, *Aquinas on Beauty*, 14.

34. Christopher Sevier's explanation on Aquinas's beauty is helpful to understand this issue. "Aquinas gives us three formal conditions of beauty: proportion (or harmony), integrity (or perfection), and splendor (or color). One may also think of these three as constituting a kind of order, which is itself identifiable with beauty." Aquinas "enumerates the three conditions of beauty: integrity or perfection (*integritas sive perfectio*), due proportion or harmony (*debita proportio sive consonantia*), and brightness or clarity (*claritas*). . . . *proportio* represents the oldest known, and most widespread, philosophical theory of beauty." An object "has certain sensory qualities expressing certain underlying formal features, namely, proportion, clarity, and integrity" (Sevier, *Aquinas on Beauty*, 4, 105, 122). See also, Aquinas, *The Summa Theologica*, I, q.39, a.8. An understanding of the relationship between proportion and beauty is also found in Augustine. According to Henry Chadwick, "Augustine was struck by the pervasiveness of mathematical order in the cosmos, and this had been a prominent theme in the Cassiciacum dialogues. There his vindication of providence is in substance aesthetic and Plotinian: i.e., the chiaroscuro of light and dark contribute to the beauty of the whole. But this beauty is not merely a subjective feeling; it is grounded in numbers. There is precision not only in the inanimate environment, but also in the processes of human life, as is obvious from the study of embryology which shows how the embryo reaches each successive stage of development at constant and exact intervals of time. Moreover, Augustine added, the beauty of a building depends on its mathematical proportions" (Chadwick, *Augustine*, 48).

35. Aquinas, *Summa Theologica* I, q.39, a.8; II-a II-ae, q.180, a.2.

beauty, referring to the Son's appropriateness, "Species or beauty," while talking about the inherent appropriateness of the Trinity:

> According to which "eternity" is appropriated to the Father, "species" to the Son, "use" "to the Holy Ghost." . . . Species or beauty has a likeness to the property of the Son. For beauty includes three conditions, "integrity" or "perfection," since those things which are impaired are by the very fact ugly; due "proportion" or "harmony"; and lastly, "brightness" or "clarity," whence things are called beautiful which have a bright color.[36]

These vocabularies of beauty, especially as they are based on the trinitarian relationship, connect with Augustine[37] in the past and Edwards in the future.

Beauty in the Pre-Enlightenment Church Tradition

The Reformation era saw sharp debates between the Reformers and Roman Catholic theologians on the issue of icons and religious art, so the Reformers were not readily advocating Christian aesthetics. However, the Reformers, including John Calvin (1509–1564), also maintained a traditional position on the beauty of God and the beauty of creation. John T. McNeill, in *The History and Character of Calvinism*, reveals John Calvin's expressions on the beauty of God and His created world:

> He likes to praise an apt expression, using words such as "beautiful," "elegant," "splendid." . . . There are in Calvin's work numerous passages of striking beauty in appreciation of the forms of nature. . . . When he describes the exhilaration of beauty, he

36. Aquinas, *Summa Theologica* I, q.39, a.8, c.

37. See Sevier's explanation as follows: "What Augustine makes clear, in the passage to which Aquinas defers, is that the equality of the Son to the Father consists in part due to the absolute approximation of the Son to the Father, of the image to the exemplar. . . . It is in this sense of image, as exact likeness, that both Augustine and Aquinas may be said to hold the view that 'beautiful' is an appellation properly applied only to God, since this exact representation of the Father can be found in no created thing, but in the Son alone. It is in this sense that beauty in things is merely relative to, and dependent upon, the beauty of God by way of participation. . . . God is Beauty itself, and everything else is merely called 'beautiful' by participation in God (or Beauty itself). God alone is what Dionysius calls the 'Supersubstantial Beautiful' (*Supersubstantiale vero pulchrum pulchritudo*), the Cause of the harmony and splendor in all other things (*causa consonantiae et claritatis in omnibus*)" (Sevier, *Aquinas on Beauty*, 110–11).

habitually speaks of it as an intimation of the bounty, and of the presence, of God.[38]

Furthermore, citing Old Testament and New Testament verses, he explains that God is the origin of beauty, and that the world he created is a reflection of God's beauty—"mirror" according to his expression—which consists of elaborate harmony and balance.

> wherever you turn your eyes, there is no portion of the world, however minute, that does not exhibit at least some sparks of beauty; while it is impossible to contemplate the vast and beautiful fabric as it extends around, without being overwhelmed by the immense weight of glory. Hence, the author of the Epistle to the Hebrews elegantly describes the visible worlds as images of the invisible (Heb 11:3), the elegant structure of the world serving us as a kind of mirror, in which we may behold God, though otherwise invisible. For the same reason, the Psalmist attributes language to celestial objects, a language which all nations understand (Ps 19:1), the manifestation of the Godhead being too clear to escape the notice of any people, however obtuse. The apostle Paul, stating this still more clearly, says, "That which may be known of God is manifest in them, for God has showed it unto them. For the invisible things of him from the creation of the world are clearly seen, being understood by the things that are made, even his eternal power and Godhead" (Rom 1:20).[39]

As William A. Dyrness explains, "consistent with the reformers," all of Calvin's theology and thought are closely related to the "transcendence of God."[40] This means that Calvin and other reformers' understanding on beauty is also related to the beauty of transcendence of God. This kind of beauty is brilliantly revealed in two points: the glory of creation and Christ's salvation. In terms of the glory of creation, Calvin said that humans can look at God through the glory of His created world, and in this respect, the glory of creation is like a "mirror" and a "theatre" that

38. McNeill, *History*, 232.

39. Calvin, *Institutes* 1.5.1.

40. "In another sense one might argue that all of Calvin's thought is related in one way or another to the active direction and transcendence of God. Consistent with the reformers generally Calvin begins with the insistence on the 'otherness' of God and opposes any thought of mixing God with anything created—an impulse that, in part, respond to all the spiritual practices that had grown up in the Middle Ages" (Dyrness, *Visual Culture*, 64).

makes us see the beautiful glory of God invisible.[41] Furthermore, Calvin regarded Christ's redemptive works for the salvation of the world as the "highest expression of God's splendor."[42] Jonathan Edwards inherited this understanding of God's beauty and the beauty of the created world as a reflection of God's beauty from his reformed predecessors. In particular, he embraced the idea of a "mirror" and a "theatre" in terms of relationship between God's creation and His glory.[43] Edwards understood God's beauty as primary beauty and the beauty of the created world as secondary beauty; the beauty of the created world is a reflection of the creator's original beauty.[44]

John Owen (1616–1683), one of the most important Puritan writers, described the "fresh taste" on "spiritual things," that is given to converted believers.[45] In his book, *Of the Mortification of Sin in Believers; the Necessity, Nature, and Means of It: With a Resolution of Sundry Cases of Conscience Thereunto Belonging* (1656), he explained the new joy of tasting the grace of Christ based on John 6:67–68. Furthermore, using a parable of the person who came out from a dungeon, he described the appreciation of the beauty felt by the converted believer:

> As a man that hath been long kept in a dungeon, if brought forth on a sudden into the light of the sun, finds so much pleasure and contentment in it, in the beauties of the old creation, that he thinks he can never be weary of it, nor shall ever be contented on any account to be under darkness again; so is it with souls when first translated into the marvellous light of Christ, to behold the beauties of the new creation. They see a new glory in him, that hath quite sullied the desirableness of all earthly diversions. And they see a new guilt and filth in sin, that gives them an utter abhorrency of its old delights and pleasures; and so of other things.[46]

Interpreting Galatians 6:14, he argues, "If the heart be filled with the cross of Christ, it casts death and undesirableness upon them all; it leaves no

41. Dyrness, *Visual Culture*, 72–75.

42. Dyrness, *Visual Culture*, 73.

43. Dyrness, *Visual Culture*, 75.

44. For more studies on the aesthetics of the Protestant reformers, see Zachman, *Image and Word*; Koerner, *Reformation of the Image*.

45. Owen, *Works*, 6:290.

46. Owen, *Works*, 6:291.

seeming beauty, no appearing pleasure or comeliness, in them."[47] In other words, Owen argues for a beauty that cannot be found without experiencing the cross of Christ, and the person who experiences the cross has a new sense of discernment of true beauty. He believes that the believer's obedience under the grace of the cross of Jesus Christ gives the believer a beauty "that is an overbalance for the evil of the remainders of sin."[48]

This kind of new sense of beauty among converted believers can be seen in Jonathan Edwards's understanding on a new sense of heart. In his *Personal Narrative,* he describes "a new sense" that he experienced while reading 1 Timothy 1:17.[49] After experiencing this new sense, he learned anew about Christ's atonement and the grace of salvation; and furthermore, this sense led him to perceive and meditate on the "beauty and excellence of his person."[50] This sense made him aware of the beauty of God in the created world that he had never felt before.

> And scarce anything, among all the works of nature, was so sweet to me as thunder and lightning. Formerly, nothing had been so terrible to me. I used to be a person uncommonly terrified with thunder: and it used to strike me with terror, when I saw a thunderstorm rising. But now, on the contrary, it rejoiced me. I felt God at the first appearance of a thunderstorm. And used to take the opportunity at such times, to fix myself to view the clouds, and see the lightnings play, and hear the majestic and awful voice of God's thunder: which often times was exceeding entertaining, leading me to sweet contemplations of my great and glorious God. And while I viewed, used to spend my time, as it always seemed natural to me, to sing or chant forth my meditations; to speak my thoughts in soliloquies, and speak with a singing voice.[51]

The new sense made him feel the true beauty of the created world, and further meditate on God's glory and excellence through it. His personal experience of this new sense is thus consistent with the new sense of the believer described by John Owen.

In short, the concept of beauty understood by many theologians in the patristic and medieval periods in Western Christianity is not a

47. Owen, *Works*, 6:250.

48. Owen, *Works*, 7:556.

49. *WJE* 16:792.

50. *WJE* 16:793.

51. *WJE* 16:794.

reliance on a subjective sense, but rather, it is an objective idea as an absolute conceptual criterion. Most theologians, including Augustine and Aquinas, do not treat beauty as an independent subject but within the unity of truth, goodness, and beauty, especially in the context of explaining the perfection of hypostases of the Trinity. This understanding does not change significantly, even after the Reformation. Moreover, John Owen describes a new sense that enables converted believers to discern true beauty, a fresh taste of the spiritual things of believers. His understanding anticipates to Jonathan Edwards's understanding of *a new sense of heart*.

The British Enlightenment and Aesthetics

The study of the influence of Locke's philosophy on eighteenth-century British aesthetics began in earnest after 1963, when Jerome Stolnitz published his essay "Locke and the Categories of Value in Eighteenth-century British Aesthetic Theory."[52] When we consider Locke's influence on British philosophy and the humanities, we might be surprised that studies of his aesthetics did not begin until the mid-twentieth century. It is difficult clearly to analyze the impact of Locke's philosophy on aesthetics, since Locke rarely mentions beauty or art directly in his work. But Locke is very important in providing a new approach to analyzing beauty through his empiricist epistemology. This is evidenced by Locke's influence and the empirical approach among thinkers such as the Third Earl of Shaftesbury, Joseph Addison, Francis Hutcheson, David Hume, Edmund Burke, Alexander Gerard, and so forth.

Stolnitz asserts, however, that it is hard to find a philosophical work more important in the history of aesthetics than Locke's *An Essay Concerning Human Understanding* (1689). Stolnitz argues that "Locke's attitude toward the arts and beauty may . . . be said to fall between calculated indifference and hostility."[53]

> The eighteenth century, the "classic" age in the history of aesthetic thought, was the first to develop aesthetics as an autonomous discipline. . . . The British nowhere use the words "aesthetic" or "aesthetics"; yet it is simply frivolous to allow this to decide who "created" aesthetic theory, as we know it. Still, the

52. Stolnitz, "Locke," 40–51.

53. Stolnitz, "Locke," 41.

> British "critics," as they called themselves, were, like everybody else, nurtured on Locke.[54]

In his *Essay Concerning Human Understanding*, Locke describes beauty as complex ideas or mixed modes that result from the synthesis of color and shape and arouse pleasure to the viewer.[55]

To better understand this, we need to look at Locke's definition of "idea" and its classification. William Uzgalis explains Locke's definition of "idea": "The term 'idea,' Locke tells us . . . 'stands for whatsoever is the Object of the Understanding, when a man thinks.'"[56] He describes ideas as simple ideas, complex ideas, and an infinitive idea.

In *Essay*, the term "simple ideas" refers to a kind of idea that is not complex in itself and contains only a single phenomenon or concept; that one idea does not change or divide into other ideas.[57] These simple ideas are supplied to the mind by sensation and reflection, and it is impossible to find or construct them in the mind, no matter how high the mind. In other words, for simple ideas, the mind has to passively accept them. The simple idea has four characteristics: passive, unchangeable, irreplaceable, and indestructible. The simple idea is sensation or reflection of the sensation; so, since the simple idea cannot come into existence in the mind without accepting the sensation of reflection, the simple idea is passive.

Once the mind has these simple ideas, it cannot change or destroy them, nor can they be replaced with new ones at will:

> The mind can neither make nor destroy them. . . . [I]t is not in the power of the most exalted wit, or enlarged understanding, by any quickness or variety of thought, to invent or frame one new simple idea in the mind, not taken in by the ways before mentioned: nor can any force of the understanding destroy those that are there.[58]

Furthermore, Locke divides simple ideas into four categories in accordance with the different ways they approach the mind:

> First, then, There are some which come into our minds by one sense only. Secondly, There are others that convey themselves into the mind by more senses than one. Thirdly, Others that are had

54. Stolnitz, "Locke," 40.
55. Locke, *Essay* 2.12.5.
56. Uzgalis, "John Locke."
57. Locke, *Essay* 2.2.1–2.
58. Locke, *Essay* 2.2.2.

> from reflection only. Fourthly, there are some that . . . are suggested to the mind by all the ways of sensation and reflection.[59]

Light, colors, noises, sounds, tones, tastes, smells, hot, cold, and solidity belong to the first category of simple ideas. The simple notions of the second category are primarily related to seeing and touching, which include "space or extension, figure, rest, and motion."[60] "The idea of perception, and idea of willing, we have from reflection," and this includes "Perception, or Thinking; and Volition, or Willing."[61] Lastly, the category of simple ideas of both sensation and reflection includes "pleasure or delight, and its opposite, pain, or uneasiness; power; existence; unity."[62]

In contrast, complex ideas refer to a certain combination of simple ideas created by the mind.[63] As mentioned above, the mind is entirely passive in relation to the acceptance of simple ideas, but using the simple ideas as the basis or source material, the mind can actively create ideas through combination and synthesis, which are called complex ideas:

> The acts of the mind, wherein it exerts its power over its simple ideas, are chiefly these three: (1) Combining several simple ideas into one compound one; and thus all complex ideas are made. (2) The second is bringing two ideas, whether simple or complex, together, and setting them by one another, so as to take a view of them at once, without uniting them into one; by which way it gets all its ideas of relations. (3) The third is separating them from all other ideas that accompany them in their real existence: this is called abstraction: and thus all its general ideas are made. This shows man's power, and its ways of operation, to be much the same in the material and intellectual world. For the materials in both being such as he has no power over, either to make or destroy, all that man can do is either to unite them together, or to set them by one another, or wholly separate them.[64]

Locke argues that complex ideas can be created as infinitely complex and varied, but in the end everything can be reduced to three items

59. Locke, *Essay* 2.3.1. Examples of each category are as follows: (1) color, sound, smell, and taste; (2) size, shape, extension, and motion; (3) remembrance, discerning, reasoning, judging, knowledge, and faith; and (4) unity, existence, pleasure, pain, and substance.

60. Thilly, *History of Philosophy*, 335; Locke, *Essay* II.5.

61. Locke, *Essay* 2.6.1–2.

62. Locke, *Essay* 2.7.1.

63. Thilly, *History of Philosophy*, 336.

64. Locke, *Essay* 2.12.1.

of mind: modes, substances, and relations.[65] Among these three items, we should pay particular attention to the complex of ideas of modes. He calls the ideas of modes "complex ideas which, however compounded, contain not in them the supposition of subsisting by themselves, but are considered as dependences on, or affections of substances."[66] The reason we should focus on this kind of idea is that Locke mentions "beauty" as an example of a complex idea of mode: "There are others compounded of simple ideas of several kinds, put together to make one complex one;—e.g., beauty, consisting of a certain composition of colour and figure, causing delight to the beholder . . . a combination of several ideas of several kinds: and these I call mixed modes."[67]

The important thing we can take from this is that, for Locke, "beauty" is not something that comes to the mind. Simple ideas are passively given to the mind, while complex ideas are those that the mind actively combines with other ideas. However, if "beauty" is one of the mixed modes—that is, complex ideas—then beauty is not passively given to the mind, but the mind combines with other ideas. Furthermore, since beauty is evaluated differently according to the judgment of each person's mind as such a complex idea, then we can conclude that, for Locke, beauty cannot exist as an absolute idea in the world.

In this sense, Locke's view of beauty differs greatly from other pre-Enlightenment scholars and theologians—in particular Augustine who emphasized the simplicity of God as an original beauty. Edwards also later emphasized the simplicity of the divine beauty of the Trinity, in a manner similar to that of Augustine.

One of the most important Enlightenment figures who influenced Edwards's study of beauty was Francis Hutcheson (1694–1746). Hutcheson accepted Locke's terms and methodology for his study on beauty, but he did not follow Locke's understanding of beauty as a complex idea. In his book *An Inquiry into the Original of Our Ideas of Beauty and Virtue* (1725), Hutcheson introduces important concepts for beauty: original (absolute) beauty and comparative (relative) beauty, sense of beauty.

> Beauty is either Original or Comparative; or, if any like the Terms better, Absolute, or Relative: Only let it be observ'd, that by Absolute or Original Beauty, is not understood any Quality suppos'd to

65. Dicker, *Locke on Knowledge* 63. See also Stuart, *Locke's Metaphysics*, 16.

66. Locke, *Essay* 2.12.4.

67. Locke, *Essay* 2.12.5.

> be in the Object, which should of itself be beautiful, without relation to any Mind which perceives it: For Beauty, like other Names of sensible Ideas, properly denotes the Perception of some Mind; so Cold, Hot, Sweet, Bitter, denote the Sensations in our Minds, to which perhaps there is no resemblance in the Objects, which excite these Ideas in us, however we generally imagine that there is something in the Object just like our Perception.[68]

Hutcheson recognizes the special internal senses involved in the judgment of beauty. By that, he means an inner sense which accepts beauty, just as the eyes are the sense organ which accepts colors and ears are the sense organ which accepts accept sounds. In other words, when the object that causes the sense of beauty is given to the sense, we have no choice but to think of the sense of beauty, regardless of our will, just as with the action of the external senses.

> Let it be ovbserv'd, that in the following Papers, the Word Beauty if taken for the Idea rais'd in us, and a Sense of Beauty for our Power of receiving this Idea. (I.IX). . . It is of no consequence whether we call these Ideas of Beauty and Harmony, Perceptions of the External Senses of Seeing and Hearing, or not. I should rather chuse to call our Power of perceiving these Ideas, an INTERNAL SENSE, were it only for the Convenience of distinguishing them from other sensations of Seeing and Hearing, which men may have without Perception of Beauty and Harmony.[69]

Among the seventeenth- and eighteenth-century British Enlightenment scholars, the Cambridge Platonists are an indispensable group when referring to Edwards's academic background.[70] Wilson H. Kimnach states that John Smith (1618–1652), who was one of the representative Cambridge Platonists, was Jonathan Edwards's "favorite rhetorician"[71]; furthermore, Kimnach argues that "the source of Edwards' terminology

68. Hutcheson, *Inquiry* I.XVII.

69. Hutcheson, *Inquiry* I.IX–X.

70. According to McClymond and McDermott, Edwards's teaching on divinization has a background in the seventeenth-century Cambridge Platonists' writings. Moreover, Edwards cited John Smith's *Select Discourses* (1660) and Ralph Cudworth's *True Intellectual System of the Universe* (1678) in his writings, and he added these works in his *Catalogue* of reading. In his early period, Edwards read Henry More's works and he "shared with him and other Cambridge Platonists a deep aversion to materialistic philosophy" (McClymond and McDermott, *Theology of Jonathan Edwards*, 413–16).

71. See *WJE* 10.

was probably the Cambridge Platonist John Smith."[72] Although some Cambridge Platonists like Nathaniel Culverwell (1619–1651) mentioned beauty in their works,[73] compared to the influence of Cambridge Platonists on Edwards's academic methodology, there are little notable features about their aesthetics themselves.[74] However, the aesthetics of Anthony Ashley Cooper (1671–1713, the third Earl of Shaftesbury, in short Shaftesbury), who was closely linked to the Cambridge Platonists, are treated as important in British aesthetics in the seventeenth and eighteenth centuries, along with Hutcheson.

Shaftesbury was influenced by Cambridge Platonists such as Henry More (1614–1687) and Benjamin Whichcote (1609–1683). Like the Cambridge Platonists, Shaftesbury's "conception—expounded in the *Inquiry*—of the universe" is a harmonious system with good order.[75] As Richard Glauser and Anthony Savile evaluate, "Shaftesbury's notion of beauty is classical" since he "equates beauty with a formal quality which he calls variously 'harmony,' order,' 'symmetry,' 'design,' 'proportion' or 'numbers.' It is thus a complex property, for harmony and proportion imply relations of different parts or elements to each other."[76] Shaftesbury classifies beauty into three degrees: (1) *the dead forms* "which bear a fashion and are formed, whether by man or nature, but have no forming power, no action or intelligence"; (2) "*the forms which form* . . . have intelligence, action and operation" (i.e., human being); and (3) beauty, "*which forms not only such as we call mere forms but even the forms which form*"

72. Mitchell, "Experience of Beauty," 55n1.

73. "The Candle of the Lord do's not shine so clearly as it was wont, must it therefore be extinguisht presently? is it not better to enjoy the faint and languishing light of this Candle of the Lord, rather then to be in palpable and disconsolate darknesse? There are indeed but a few seminal sparks left in the ashes, and must there be whole floods of water cast on them to quench them? 'Tis but an old imperfect Manuscript, with some broken periods, some letters worn out, must they therefore with an unmerciful indignation rend it and tear it asunder? 'Tis granted that the picture has lost its glosse and beauty, the oriency of its colours, the elegancy of its lineaments, the comelinesse of its proportion; must it therefore be totally defac'd? must it be made one great blot? and must the very frame of it be broken in pieces? Would you perswade the Lutanist to cut all his strings in sunder, because they are out of tune? and will you break the Bowe upon no other account, but because it's unbended? because men have not so much of Reason as they should, will they therefore resolve to have none at all?" (Culverwell, *Elegant*, 3–4, quoted in Lamprecht, "Innate Ideas," 561).

74. For more information on Cambridge Platonists' aesthetics, see Hedley, "Reason and Beauty in Cambridge Platonism."

75. Glauser and Savile, "Aesthetic Experience in Shaftesbury," 32.

76. Glauser and Savile, "Aesthetic Experience in Shaftesbury," 26–27.

(i.e., God).[77] He considered the higher grade more beautiful because the beautifying is the really beautiful, not the beautified.[78] In other words, God is the most beautiful. The human mind is more beautiful than art or natural objects, and the divine mind is more beautiful than the human mind. Human beings, formed by God, but with formative power, are able to distinguish beauty or ugliness through the ability given by God and make beautiful things based on it. Furthermore, in Shaftesbury's mind, "beauty is one of the evidences of the goodness of God."[79]

In this sense, Shaftesbury's aesthetics looks similar to Edwards's aesthetics. Like Shaftesbury, Edwards regarded God's beauty as the primary beauty, and the secondary beauty was formed by the primary beauty. However, there is an irreconcilable difference between Edwards's aesthetics and Shaftesbury's aesthetics, which are influenced by Neoplatonism. Shaftesbury regarded the nature of religion as the "disinterested love" to God.[80] He emphasized the harmony between faith and human reason; in particular, he "develops his aesthetics as a defense of the essential goodness of human nature and the power of reason in leading to goodness."[81] As Joseph Addison, who described the Puritans as having "a morbid obsession with death," Shaftesbury regarded the human reason, leading to the existence of a reasonable God, as the essence of true religion, not "enthusiasm, or blind devotion to obscure doctrines."[82]

Jonathan Edwards embraced the methodology and terminology of the theory of taste from British Enlightenment aesthetics. Edwards applied Hutcheson's understanding of the sense of beauty:

77. Shaftesbury, *Characteristics,* 323. Glauser and Savile further subdivide the beauty of the three classes of Shaftesbury into seven classes: "(1) unbeautified dead forms (zero degree of beauty); (2) beautiful dead forms that are relatively simple qualities; (3) beautified dead forms that are works of art; (4) beautified dead forms that are natural beings; (5) art itself, which is a beautifying principle, hence not a dead form, but not a forming form either, since it is not a mind, but a product of finite mind; (6) forming forms which are finite minds (these are at least triply beautifying in that they animate bodies, produce works of art, and are capable of self-improvement towards moral goodness and virtue); and finally God, the infinite forming form of finite forming forms, from whom, as we shall see, all beauty flows directly or indirectly. The higher one moves in the hierarchy, the greater the reality of beauty" (Glauser and Savile, "Aesthetic Experience in Shaftesbury," 31).

78. Shaftesbury, *Characteristics*, 322.

79. Louie, "Theological Aesthetics," 35.

80. Shaftesbury, *Characteristics*, 268.

81. Louie, "Theological Aesthetics," 35.

82. Louie, "Theological Aesthetics," 35.

> There is such a kind of taste of the mind as this, which philosophers speak of, whereby persons are guided in their judgment of the natural beauty, gracefulness, propriety, nobleness and sublimity of speeches and actions, whereby they judge as it were by the glance of the eye, or by inward sensation, and the first impression of the object.[83]

Even more, Edwards directly mentioned that the characteristic of secondary beauty (the beauty of the created world, which reflects God's primary beauty) is the same as Hutcheson's understanding of beauty. He agreed with Hutcheson's expression of beauty, "uniformity in the midst of variety" and "the consent or agreement of different things, in form, quantity, etc."[84]

Edwards went a step further, however, developing it into "a divine taste" given to believers: "There is likewise such a thing as a divine taste, given and maintained by the Spirit of God, in the hearts of the saints, whereby they are in like manner led and guided in discerning and distinguishing the true spiritual and holy beauty of actions."[85] He refers to this "divine taste" as "a new sense of heart":

> From hence it follows, that in those gracious exercises and affections which are wrought in the minds of the saints, through the saving influences of the Spirit of God, there is a new inward perception or sensation of their minds, entirely different in its nature and kind, from anything that ever their minds were the subjects of before they were sanctified. For doubtless if God by his mighty power produces something that is new, not only in degree and circumstances, but in its whole nature, and that which could be produced by no exalting, varying or compounding of what was there before, or by adding anything of the like kind; I say, if God produces something thus new in a mind, that is a perceiving, thinking, conscious thing; then doubtless something entirely new is felt, or perceived, or thought; or, which is the same thing, there is some new sensation or perception of the mind, which is entirely of a new sort, and which could be produced by no exalting, varying or compounding of that kind of perceptions or sensations which the mind had before; or there is what some metaphysicians call a new simple idea.[86]

83. *WJE* 2:283.

84. *WJE* 8:562–63.

85. *WJE* 2:283.

86. *WJE* 2:205. For further explanation, see Erdt, "Calvinist Psychology"; "Sense

In other words, Edwards focused on the passive character of Locke's "simple ideas." He believed that the human mind cannot make or control simple ideas; the ideas can be only passively received. As such, Edwards thought that a new sense of heart can also be received by the Holy Spirit. Edwards's epistemology was evident in his sermon "A Divine and Supernatural Light." He argued that a religious experience through the Holy Spirit is an essential prerequisite for the "new sense of heart."

He said, "the Spirit convinces men of sin," and "he acts in the mind of a saint as an indwelling vital principle" in contrast with "the mind of a natural man."[87] The Spirit "unites himself with the mind of a saint, takes him for his temple, actuates and influences him as a new, supernatural principle of life and action."[88] Moreover, the Spirit of God "exerts and communicates himself there in his own proper nature."[89] In this sense, we can confirm that Edwards focuses on the inner senses acquired passively by the Holy Spirit. Furthermore, Edwards reveals his understanding of the "new sense of heart" in his sermon. Edwards's new sense of heart was "a true sense of the divine and superlative excellency of the things of religion."[90] In this sermon, the honey metaphor Edwards uses helps us to understand his "new sense of heart":

> Thus there is a difference between having an opinion that God is holy and gracious, and having a sense of the loveliness and beauty of that holiness and grace. There is a difference between having a rational judgment that honey is sweet, and having a sense of its sweetness. A man may have the former, that knows not how honey tastes; but a man can't have the latter, unless he has an idea of the taste of honey in his mind. So there is a difference between believing that a person is beautiful, and having a sense of his beauty. The former may be obtained by hearsay, but the latter only by seeing the countenance. There is a wide difference between mere speculative, rational judging anything to be excellent, and having a sense of its sweetness, and beauty. The former rests only in the head, speculation only is concerned in it; but the heart is concerned in the latter. When the heart is sensible of the beauty and amiableness of a thing, it necessarily

of the Heart"; LaShell, "Jonathan Edwards and the New Sense"; Minkema, "Dordtian Philosophe."

87. *WJE* 2:410–11.

88. *WJE* 2:411.

89. *WJE* 2:411.

90. *WJE* 2:413.

> feels pleasure in the apprehension. It is implied in a person's being heartily sensible of the loveliness of a thing, that the idea of it is sweet and pleasant to his soul; which is a far different thing from having a rational opinion that it is excellent.[91]

Briefly, this new sense of heart is a sense of the divine taste among believers, given by God, such as the sense of knowing the taste of honey, which is never known to those who only see honey with their eyes.

We have briefly examined the background of Edwards's theological aesthetics. We have seen that, beginning with Augustine, Christian thinkers thought that God's simplicity, excellence, and perfection, were other expressions or implications of his beauty; so, too, we have noted Edwards's connections to and distinctions from British Enlightenment aesthetics. In the remainder of this chapter we'll explore characteristics of Edwards's aesthetics, gaining some of the basic background knowledge needed for the following chapters.

Important Characteristics of Jonathan Edwards on Beauty

In order to discuss Edwards's theological aesthetics in the next chapters, we need to look at the important characteristics of his aesthetics.[92] For Edwards, beauty was more fundamental than just a sensual and philosophical subject. In his thought, the beauty is "consent, agreement, or union of being to being,"[93] and virtue is "the beauty of those qualities and acts of the mind that are of a moral nature."[94] Furthermore, "charity or love is the sum of all saving virtue,"[95] and true virtue "most essentially consists in benevolence to Being in general."[96] In this sense, he believed that the origin of beauty stems from the Holy Trinity, especially from the perfection of hypostases of the Trinity, the union among the Trinitarian hypostases, the holiness of God, and the simplicity of God. Douglas Sweeney and Owen Strachan reveal Edwards's understanding of seven attributes of God's beauty: eternality and self-existence, greatness,

91. *WJE* 2:413.

92. There are many important features in Edwards's theological aesthetics, and more details will be covered in the next chapter, where we will look only at the prerequisite conditions essential for understanding Edwards's aesthetics.

93. *WJE* 8:561.

94. *WJE* 8:539.

95. *WJE* 8:104.

96. *WJE* 8:540.

loveliness, power, wisdom, holiness, and goodness. These attributes of God's beauty relate to his understanding of God's primary beauty and reflected the secondary beauty of the created world.

Primary Beauty and Secondary Beauty

Jonathan Edwards found his understanding of beauty from the relationship with being.[97] According to Edwards, beauty is divided into a "general" and "particular" beauty: the former is a comprehensive, universal, perfect beauty, while the latter is a beauty that appears only in limited conditions or relationships.[98] Thus, he explains that a "general beauty" is true virtue.

> By a "particular" beauty I mean that by which a thing appears beautiful when considered only with regard to its connection with, and tendency to some particular things within a limited and, as it were, a private sphere. And a "general" beauty is that by which a thing appears beautiful when viewed most perfectly, comprehensively and universally, with regard to all its tendencies, and its connections with everything it stands related to. The former may be without and against the latter. . . . That only, therefore, is what I mean by true virtue, which is that, belonging to the heart of an intelligent being, that is beautiful by a general beauty, or beautiful in a comprehensive view as it is in itself, and as related to everything that it stands in connection with.[99]

How then can a being's true beauty be defined? Edwards found the answer to this question in "consent, agreement, or union of being to being."[100]

> If it has its seat in the heart, and is the general goodness and beauty of the disposition and exercise of that, in the most

97. "The category of being is fundamental to Edwards's aesthetic theory, namely, his conception of beauty" (Stout, "Being," 66).

98. Edwards also called these two kinds of beauty "primary" and "secondary" beauty, or "essential" and "secondary" beauty. Delattre argues that Edwards preferred to use "essential" and "secondary" beauty rather than "primary" and "secondary" beauty (Delattre, *Beauty and Sensibility*, 17). Moreover, Edwards also referred to primary beauty as true spiritual beauty, spiritual original beauty, and true moral beauty, and secondary beauty as inferior beauty and natural beauty (*WJE* 8:564–65, 573). Even when Edwards needed to emphasize the difference, he referred to the former as a true beauty and the later as a false and confined beauty (*WJE* 6:344).

99. *WJE* 8:540.

100. *WJE* 8:561.

> comprehensive view, considered with regard to its universal tendency, and as related to everything that it stands in connection with; what can it consist in, but a consent and good will to Being in general? Beauty does not consist in discord and dissent, but in consent and agreement. And if every intelligent being is some way related to Being in general, and is a part of the universal system of existence; and so stands in connection with the whole; what can its general and true beauty be, but its union and consent with the great whole?[101]

For Edwards, the beauty of a being is the beauty in the relationship with others who should be related with the being—in particular, in the relationship with God, who is the ultimate cause and goal of other beings. This is because "God is not only infinitely greater and more excellent than all other being, but he is the head of the universal system of existence; the fountain of all being and all beauty,"[102] and "all beauty consists in similarness" to God.[103] In other words, a general beauty (or a primary beauty) is the beauty that exists in the agreement and consent of being in general, God. This agreement is not related to God's natural quality but to God's moral quality (revealing God's holiness, such as love, mercy, and justice). Thus, general beauty exists in a relationship in which the human being as a spiritual being is in agreement and consent with God, being in general.

On the other hand, a particular beauty (or a secondary beauty) is an "image" and shadow of a general beauty. Edwards gives several examples to explain secondary beauty. Secondary beauty is not unique to the spiritual being but is called by various names, such as regularity, order, unity, symmetry, proportion, harmony. Specific examples are as follows: the correspondence of the sides of an equilateral triangle, such as the equilateral triangle/square, the harmony of the colors and shapes of the spaces on the chessboard, the balance between the parts of the human face, and the various melodies of music matching and coordination, etc. In addition, unity and harmony among immaterial things are secondary beauties: social order, wisdom, justice, duty, and virtue belong to secondary beauties.[104]

> Yet there is another, inferior, secondary beauty, which is some image of this, and which is not peculiar to spiritual beings, but is

101. *WJE* 8:540–41.
102. *WJE* 8:551.
103. *WJE* 6:334.
104. *WJE* 8:561, 568–72.

> found even in inanimate things: which consists in a mutual consent and agreement of different things in form, manner, quantity, and visible end or design; called by the various names of regularity, order, uniformity, symmetry, proportion, harmony, etc.[105]

Elsewhere, Edwards also explains secondary beauty as follows:

> As bodies, the objects of our external senses, are but the shadows of beings, that harmony wherein consists sensible excellency and beauty is but the shadow of excellency; that is, it is pleasant to the mind because it is a shadow of love. When one thing sweetly harmonizes with another, as the notes in music, the notes are so conformed and have such proportion one to another that they seem to have respect one to another, as if they loved one another.[106]

Edwards argued that in the common grace of God, people can feel joy in the harmony, balance, and proportion of a secondary beauty, even if they do not know God, the archetype of a secondary beauty.[107] However, he emphasized that beauty, or partial beauty, which is not connected with God—being in general—is false beauty, and that only a primary beauty is the true beauty.[108]

Eighteenth-Century Deism and Jonathan Edwards's Understanding of God as a Communicative Being

Edwards's understanding of Primary-Secondary beauty is derived from his understanding of God: God has a disposition to communicate himself to creatures.[109] In order to understand it, we need to appreciate the context of his contemporary theological setting. Edwards's theological object of controversy was deism. This can be seen in Edwards's efforts to refute deists in his works. According to Sweeney, "more than 25 percent

105. *WJE* 8:561–62.

106. *WJE* 6:380.

107. *WJE* 8:565.

108. *WJE* 6:344.

109. "For God having from eternity from his infinite goodness designed to communicate himself to creatures, the way in which he designed to communicate himself to elect beloved creatures, all of them, was to unite himself to a created nature, and to become one of the creatures, and to gather together in one all elect creatures in that creature that he assumed into a personal union with himself, and to manifest to them and maintain intercourse with them through him" (*WJE* 18:389).

of Edwards's 'Miscellanies,' the most famous of his private theological and philosophical notebooks, treated either deism itself or the issues raised by deists."[110] Deists tried to remove all supernatural and irrational content from the Bible and to ignore doctrines such as God's absolute sovereignty and transcendental revelation.

As Hans Frei explains, "the credibility of special divine communication and (later on) of divine self-presentation" was at the heart of the deistic controversy.[111] In other words, deists argued that God created the world but does not present himself to or interfere with the created world; furthermore, they denied the immanence and personality of a God who communicates with his created world.[112]

In opposition to the deistic argument, Edwards argues that God is a person who communicates with his creature in his love, and that the end of God's creation is related to "an emanation of his own infinite fullness."[113] Edwards argues that "the thing which God aimed at in the creation of the world, as the end which he had ultimately in view, was that communication of himself, which he intended throughout all eternity."[114] This argument led to the following statements: God is the infinite and eternal Being, so it takes an infinite amount of time for a creature to learn about God and his beauty. If the purpose of God's creation is to reveal his excellence, beauty, and glory to the created world, it takes eternal time for creature to know and rejoice in God's infinite beauty. Therefore, God must continue to communicate with his creatures forever and to reveal his beauty to them. In this sense, against the deistic view of God, Edwards's understanding of theological aesthetics should be established on the prerequisite that God is a communicative Being who constantly reveals his beauty to his created world.

Jonathan Edwards's Vocabulary of Beauty

The use of the synonyms of "beauty" was a tradition that existed from the pre-Edwards period. The ancient Greeks expressed "beauty" with the

110. Sweeney, "Edwards, Jonathan," 309.

111. Frei, *Eclipse of Biblical Narrative*, 54.

112. "Deism negates God's immanence in favor of his transcendence. Deists have included François-Marie Voltaire, Thomas Jefferson, and Thomas Paine" (Geisler, *Big Book*, 16).

113. *WJE* 8:435.

114. *WJE* 8:443.

word καλόν, which includes not only the objects of the senses but also the meaning of the characteristics of the soul. Furthermore, the word τέχνη, which means "art," is also a word that can be applied to all kinds of general skills or techniques. In a broad sense, all beautiful things are good (ἀγαθόν) and all good things have an order of harmony (ἁρμονία) and symmetry (συμμετρία).[115] Aristotle, for instance, in his *De Caelo*, considered that all the regular movements of the world in the cosmological order produced harmonious music.[116]

Given this traditional understanding of the terms of beauty, it is not surprising that Jonathan Edwards used a variety of terms for "beauty" in his writings: excellency (or excellence), symmetry, proportion, harmony, agreement, consent, union, and love.[117] Furthermore, in terms of glory as synonym of beauty, in his interpretation of Isaiah 33:17,[118] Edwards explains that "beauty is often put for glory and prosperity, as Isaiah 28:1, and Ezekiel 27:3–4, Ezekiel 27:11, and Ezekiel 28:12, Ezekiel 28:17, as Ezekiel 28:20 of this context."[119] This fact shows that in his theology, "beauty" is not just a sensory concept but a comprehensive and fluid term. He expressed beauty through these various words because in most cases the beauty he spoke about is used to express God or the created world, which is manifested in the relationship with God.

Edwards used the term "excellence" to describe "beauty."[120] He defined "excellency" as follows: "The consent of being to being, or being's consent to entity. The more the consent is, and the more extensive, the greater is the excellency."[121] In order to better understand this expression, we must look at his other explanation of being and relationship. Edwards further argued that excellence exists in equality, accepting the ideas of contemporary thinkers that excellence is referred to as harmony, symmetry, and proportion, as beauty expressed in different terms.[122] According to Edwards,

115. Tatarkiewicz, *History of Aesthetics*, 1:25–26, 34.

116. Aristotle, *Aristotelis De Caelo* 2.9.290b.12–23.

117. Mitchell, "Theological Aesthetics," 37.

118. "Thine eyes shall see the king in his beauty; they shall behold the land that is very far off" (Isa 33:17 KJV).

119. *WJE* 15:145.

120. *WJE* 6:344.

121. *WJE* 6:336.

122. *WJE* 6:332.

> For being, if we examine narrowly, is nothing else but proportion. When one being is inconsistent with another being, then being is contradicted. . . . One alone, without any reference to any more, cannot be excellent; for in such case there can be no manner of relation no way, and therefore, no such thing as consent. Indeed, what we call "one" may be excellent, because of a consent of parts, or some consent of those in that being that are distinguished into a plurality some way or other. But in a being that is absolutely without any plurality there cannot be excellency, for there can be no such thing as consent or agreement.[123]
> [O]ne alone cannot be excellent, inasmuch as, in such case, there can be no consent. Therefore, if God is excellent, there must be a plurality in God; otherwise, there can be no consent in him.[124]

In summary, excellence is in harmony with proportion, and in order for harmony and proportion to exist, there must be a relationship between two or more beings, so excellence must be pluralistic. His understanding of excellence, harmony, and plurality constitutes an important basis for Edwards's theology of the Trinity and trinitarian beauty. As will be discussed in more detail in the following chapters, the full excellence and beauty of each hypostasis of the Trinity arouses perfect and eternal love for each other.

Conclusion

The term "aesthetics" itself was established in the modern era, but in the history of philosophy and the church, theologians and philosophers have continued to seek answers to the question of what beauty is. The Western church's tradition of beauty was inherited by Jonathan Edwards through St. Augustine, Thomas Aquinas, reformers such as John Calvin, and Puritans such as John Owen. In particular, Augustine's understanding of the excellence and beauty of each hypostasis of the Trinity and the trinitarian union of love among hypostases greatly influenced Edwards in establishing his theological aesthetics.[125] Post-Augustine theologians, mentioned

123. *WJE* 6:336–37.

124. *WJE* 13:284.

125. In terms of the relationship between Jonathan Edwards and Augustine traditions, the explanation of McClymond and McDermott is helpful. "Thomas Schafer commented on 'how often Edwards came down on the side of Augustine' on a whole variety of theological issues. Edwards's biographer, George Marsden, referred to Edwards as 'the American Augustine' and invoked a number of parallels between Edwards

earlier in this chapter, also interpreted beauty around the themes of harmony among hypostases of the Trinity or God's excellence, and this influenced Edwards to employ synonyms of beauty and to understand how God's beauty relates to the created world.

Edwards embraced the Western church tradition as well as the methodologies of the Enlightenment philosophers of his time. He developed his discussion of beauty by using the language of his time to enable the reader of his time to understand and argue with adversaries. However, he did not follow the philosophy of the seventeenth- and eighteenth-century British Enlightenment but developed his own understanding by using their methodology. For instance, he tried to explain the concept of "a divine taste" by using the terms of British aesthetics—theory of taste—and to account for converted believers' "new sense of heart" by using the vocabulary of Hutcheson's aesthetics—"sense."

Edwards emphasized the obvious difference between God's primary beauty, which is the archetype of beauty, and the secondary beauty of the created world: God, the primary beauty, has revealed his beauty to the world through creation, and the created world reveals its secondary beauty as a reflection of God's primary beauty. In his time, his major theological adversaries were the Deists, who argued that God created the world but does not present himself to or interfere with the created world. Against the arguments of Deists(or those who are more moderate yet still possess misguided understandings), Edwards's understanding of beauty helped explain the characteristics of God, who revealed his beauty to the created world and communicated with the world. Edwards referred to God's beauty with various synonyms, such as excellence, symmetry, proportion, harmony, agreement, consent, union, and love,[126] which are linked to his understanding to the Trinity, the archetype of beauty.

---

and the early Christian thinker. Edwards's major writings may be compared with those of Augustine. *Freedom of the Will* and *Original Sin* correspond to Augustine's anti-Pelagian writings. Personal Narrative is something like the *Confessions. The History of Redemption* might be compared with *City of God*. Edwards's *Discourse on the Trinity* mirrored Augustine's *On the Trinity* both in theme and argument. Edwards's sixteen-lecture volume on divine and human love, *Charity and Its Fruits*, expounded a major theme of Augustine's writings. Both the content of their theologies and the genre of their works show analogies" (McClymond and McDermott, *Theology of Jonathan Edwards*, 696–70). For further information, see also Smith, "Jonathan Edwards."

126. Mitchell, "Theological Aesthetics," 37.

With this understanding of Edwards's aesthetics, the following chapters will examine how Edwards's aesthetics connects to theology, and evaluate his theological aesthetics based on his biblical interpretation.

Chapter 4

Jonathan Edwards's Biblical Aesthetics on the Being of God

Introduction

JONATHAN EDWARDS BELIEVED THAT God is the foundation of true beauty, the archetype of all beauty, and primary beauty.[1] This idea of the relationship between God and beauty was not Edwards's unique perception,[2] but undoubtedly, Edwards's understanding of God's beauty permeated his theology and philosophy as a whole. That the center of Edwards's theology is the beauty of God is supported by many Edwardsean scholars. In *Jonathan Edwards on Beauty*, Douglas A. Sweeney and Owen

1. "God is God, and distinguished from all other beings, and exalted above 'em chiefly by his divine beauty, which is infinitely diverse from all other beauty" (*WJE* 2:298).

2. As Louis J. Mitchell points out, "terms such as 'beauty' and 'excellency' were not uncommon in seventeenth- and eighteenth-century" (Mitchell, "Theological Aesthetics," 36). Moreover, the understanding of God as beauty can be found in Augustine in the Western Christian tradition and in Plato in the ancient Greek philosophical tradition. See Tatarkiewicz, *History of Aesthetics*, 2:47. According to Plato, "'the divine beauty' is 'pure and clear and unalloyed, not clogged with the pollutions of mortality and all the colours and vanities of human life,' and that it is 'the true beauty, simple and divine'" (Wooddell, "Aesthetic Christian Apologetics," 117). However, Edwards's and the Platonists' understanding of who God is, the subject of beauty, has a clear distinction. Edwards's understanding of God's existence is much closer to Augustine than Plato. Augustine regarded God as "infinitely beautiful" and "identical with . . . greatness and beauty" (Augustine, *Confessions* 1.4.4; 4.16.29). For more discussion on this issue, see chapter 3 of this book.

Strachan argue that "the center of Edwards's theology" is "the Lord God, who formed the first link in a cycle of beauty that begins with creation and runs its course to heaven."[3] Likewise, according to Louis J. Mitchell, "Edwards' vision of beauty . . . begins and ends with God."[4] Furthermore, Belden C. Lane notes that "Edwards argued that God's ravishing beauty is the first and most important thing to be said of God."[5] As demonstrated by these evaluations by scholars, the beauty of God should be considered first in examining Edwards's aesthetics.

In the chapters that follow (4–7), each chapter will address important themes in Jonathan Edwards's theological aesthetics. Edwards's philosophical works and existing studies related to each topic are first addressed, after which Edwards's biblical interpretation of the topic is considered.

Edwards's Philosophical Examinations on the Beauty of God's Being and of the Trinitarian Unity

According to Jonathan Edwards, for "the nothingness" or "not being of nothing" to exist somewhere is absolutely impossible, inconceivable, and meaningless because "the words 'absolute nothing' and 'where' contradict each other."[6] The concept of *nothing* is entirely subordinate to the concept of *existence* because the point at which *existence* ends is to become *nothing existence*. Based on this logic, Edwards argues that the "eternal being must be infinite and omnipresent."[7] Moreover, for Edwards, "God is a necessary being."[8] Kin Yip Louie describes Edwards's argument for God's

3. Strachan and Sweeney, *Jonathan Edwards on Beauty*, 24–25.

4. Mitchell, "Theological Aesthetics," 36.

5. Lane, *Ravished by Beauty*, 173.

6. *WJE* 6:202. "A state of absolute nothing is a state of absolute contradiction. Absolute nothing is the aggregate of all the absurd contradictions in the world, a state wherein there is neither body, nor spirit, nor space: neither empty space nor full space, neither little nor great, narrow nor broad, neither infinitely great space nor finite space, nor a mathematical point; neither up nor down, neither north nor south (I don't mean as it is with respect to the body of the earth or some other great body, but no contrary points nor positions nor directions); no such thing as either here or there, this way and that way, or only one way. When we go about to form an idea of perfect nothing we must shut out all these things" (206).

7. "It gives as great a shock to the mind to think of pure nothing in any one place, as it does to think of it in all; and it is self-evident that there can be nothing in one place as well as in another, and so if there can be in one, there can be in all. So that we see this necessary, eternal being must be infinite and omnipresent" (*WJE* 6:202).

8. "God is a necessary being, as it is impossible but that God should exist, because there is no other way" (*WJE* 18:122).

being as combining Edwards's understanding of existence and of God's being[9] as a necessary being: God, who is a necessary being, "guarantees that nothingness is an impossibility" and "encompasses all possibilities of existence."[10] In his article "Of Being" (1721), Edwards reveals that through the inference about existence and absolute nothingness, "we see this necessary, eternal being must be infinite and omnipresent."[11] Since God is a "necessary, eternal, infinite and omnipresent being,"[12] God entails the existence of all being.[13]

For Edwards, the Divine being cannot be separated from His beauty. The nature of virtue is "beauty or excellency," and "true virtue" is "truly beautiful."[14] The nature of true virtue consists in "true and general beauty of the heart," and true virtue "must chiefly consist in love to God; the Being of beings."[15] In other words, God is "the *first* objective ground of that love, wherein true virtue [i.e., true beauty] consists."[16] In this sense, according to Roland André Delattre, Edwards understood that beauty is fundamental to being, and in Edwards's understanding, even beauty is fundamental to God's being.[17] Considering both facts, namely that the Divine being con-

9. Edwards's further considerations on the being of God are well illustrated in his *Miscellanies* (e.g., 27a, 91, 124, 125a, 134, 199, 200, 267, 268, 269, 274, 312, 333, 365, 383, 587, 650, 749, 976). The lists of the Edwards's *Miscellanies* on the being of God are found in APM, "Being of God."

10. Louie, "Theological Aesthetics," 91–92. Kin Yip Louie adds the following explanation to avoid misunderstanding that the expression "a necessary being" may cause: "Edwards' concept of necessary being is different from the contemporary of necessary being as expressed in, for example, Alvin Plantinga, *The Nature of Necessity*, chapter 10. For Edwards, God is necessary not only in the sense of existing in every possible worlds, but God is necessary in the sense of being the ground for the possibility of having any worlds at all. Edwards' argument is closer to the Third Way of Aquinas' Five Ways (*Summa Theologica* 1.2.3) than modern modal arguments of God. Aquinas argues from the contingency of all beings in the world to the existence of a necessary being undergirding the existence of our world" (Louie, "Theological Aesthetics," 92n6).

11. *WJE* 6:202.

12. *WJE* 6:203.

13. Edwards describes this statement as follows: "all the space there is not proper to body, all the space there is without the bounds of the creation, all the space there was before the creation, is God himself" (*WJE* 6:203).

14. *WJE* 8:539. Louis Joseph Mitchell notes that "for Jonathan Edwards true virtue was that which was founded on *the primary beauty* of benevolence to being in general" (Mitchell, "Experience of Beauty," 23 [italics added]).

15. *WJE* 8:540–50.

16. *WJE* 8:550.

17. "Beauty, in the first place, [is] fundamental to JE's understanding of being. Beauty is the first principle of being, the inner, structural principle of Being-itself,

tains the existence of all being and that the fundamental of God's being is beauty, it is concluded that God's being contains all beauty.[18]

In Edwards's understanding, since God is "infinitely the greatest being," He is "infinitely the most beautiful and excellent."[19] In this sense, Louie notes that in terms of God's being and Divine beauty, Edwards connects God, who is "the universal being," to God's infinity—one of God's essential attributes. Since God is infinite, God's being includes the existence of all beings, and His beauty is "the prototype of all other beauty."[20] God reveals Himself in His Divine "being, infinite greatness, and excellency."[21] Furthermore, "God is not only infinitely greater and more excellent than all other being, but he is the head of the universal system of existence."[22] Therefore, He must be "the foundation and fountain of all being and all beauty" because everything comes from Him perfectly, and everything depends on Him perfectly and absolutely.[23] Thus, Edwards describes God's being and beauty by saying that God's "being and beauty is as it were the sum and comprehension of all existence and excellence: much more than the sun is the fountain and summary comprehension of all the light and brightness of the day."[24]

To consider the beauty of God's being in Edwards's theological aesthetics, what cannot be overlooked is the divine beauty in the trinitarian unity. For this consideration, two factors should be addressed: (1) that

---

according to which the universal system of being is articulated. Beauty is also the measure and objective foundation of the perfection of being—of excellence, goodness, and value—and is, therefore, the basis for JE's way of affirming and construing the ultimate unity of being and good in God. . . . Beauty is, in the second place, fundamental to JE's understanding of divine being: . . . it is first among the perfections of God; it constitutes in itself the perfection of all the other divine attributes; it provides a major clue to his doctrine of Trinity; and it defines his understanding of the nature of the divine transcendence and immanence, and of the relation between with respect to God's creation, governance, and redemption of the world" (Delattre, "Beauty and Sensibility," 2–3).

18. "Only beings can be beautiful; non-beings have no capacity for beauty. Since God is the ground of all existence, God is also the ground of beauty. All beauty is a participation in divine beauty firstly because a being can be beautiful only when God calls it into existence" (Louie, "Theological Aesthetics," 93).

19. *WJE* 8:550.

20. Louie, "Theological Aesthetics," 93–94.

21. *WJE* 8:551.

22. *WJE* 8:551.

23. *WJE* 8:551.

24. *WJE* 8:551.

the being of God is an ontologically relational being and (2) that beauty must be expressed only in the plural.

Through his understanding of Edwards's ontology—dispositional ontology, Sang Hyun Lee argues that Edwards regards being as proportion or beauty, and this aesthetic-ontological category "refers to the content or character of disposition and habits."[25]

> Disposition and beauty are two ways of looking at the same reality. "Disposition" refers to the dynamic aspect of beauty, while "beauty" refers to the manner or direction of disposition. The nature of things, in other words, is disposed to be actively related in a beautiful way. True beauty is God's beauty. For anything to exist, it must be both disposed to and actually react in a fitting way to the true beauty of God.[26]

According to Lee, Jonathan Edwards believes that "God's disposition to operate as God, in other words, is the essence of the divine being."[27] Lee continues:

> "It is God's essence to incline to communicate Himself," writes Edwards. And this "disposition to communicate Himself" is what "we must conceive of as being originally in God as a perfection of his nature." Edwards goes on to resolve the communicative disposition of God into "a disposition effectually to exert Himself, or to exert Himself in order to an effect."[28]

Furthermore, in Edwards's understanding, "God . . . is also true beauty and a knowing and loving being, God's being is essentially the sovereign disposition to know and love the true beauty and to continue to know and love it."[29] In this sense, for Edwards, God is "*essentially relational*" because beauty is a relation of "consent," which is a relation of "proportion and harmony."[30]

25. *WJE* 21:7. See also *WJE* 6:335–36.

26. *WJE* 21:7.

27. Lee, *Philosophical Theology*, 175.

28. Lee, *Philosophical Theology*, 175. Quotes are from "Miscellanies" (*WJE* 2:207, 152).

29. *WJE* 21:8.

30. *WJE* 21:8 (italics added).

In Edwards's understanding, without plurality, there can be no beauty or excellency of being, since beauty is proportion,[31] "being's uniting, consent, or propensity to Being."[32]

> One alone, without any reference to any more, cannot be excellent; for in such case there can be no manner of relation no way, and therefore, no such thing as consent. Indeed, what we call "one" may be excellent, because of a consent of parts, or some consent of those in that being that are distinguished into a plurality some way or other. But in a being that is absolutely without any plurality there cannot be excellency, for there can be no such thing as consent or agreement.[33]

In this regard, Edwards argues that "one alone cannot be excellent, inasmuch as, in such case, there can be no consent. Therefore, if God is excellent, there must be a plurality in God; otherwise there can be no consent in him."[34] Thus, considering that God is essentially a relational being, God is true beauty, and God's beauty is revealed in His plurality, it can be concluded that the beauty of God's being should be understood within his trinitarian unity.

In terms of the beauty of trinitarian unity, Edwards argues that "as to God's excellence, it is evident it consists in the love of himself," and God's "infinite beauty is his infinite mutual love of himself."[35] Moreover, Edwards notes the hypostatic mutual love in the Trinity: "But, he [God] exerts himself towards himself no other way than in infinitely loving and delighting in himself, in the mutual love of the Father and the Son."[36] Edwards's understanding of trinitarian unity based on mutual love appears to be an Augustinian understanding of the Trinity.[37] However,

31. *WJE* 6:332–35.

32. *WJE* 8:29.

33. *WJE* 6:337.

34. *WJE* 13:284.

35. *WJE* 6:363–64.

36. *WJE* 6:364.

37. Sang Hyun Lee argues that Edwards proposed a new concept of divine unity based on "*perichoresis*," breaking away from Augustine's and the Western church's understanding of the doctrine of Trinity which focuses on divine simplicity. To support his argument, Lee quoted Edwards's statement as follows: "In order to clear up this matter, let it be considered, that the whole divine essence is supposed truly and properly to subsist in each of these three—viz. God, and his understanding, and love—and that there is such a wonderful union between them that they are after an ineffable and inconceivable manner one in another; so that one hath another, and they have

Edwards more actively emphasizes the role of the Holy Spirit in the trinitarian unity of the three persons. In particular, with regard to the Holy Spirit, Edwards argues that the mutual love between the Father and the Son "makes the third, the personal Holy Spirit or the holiness of God, which is his infinite beauty, and this is God's infinite consent to being in general."[38] Furthermore, Edwards claims that the Holy Spirit "is the act of God between the Father and the Son infinitely loving and delighting in each other. Sure I am, that if the Father and the Son do infinitely delight in each other, there must be an infinitely pure and perfect act between them, an infinitely sweet energy which we call delight."[39]

Edwards's Biblical Interpretations on the Beauty of God's Being and of the Trinitarian Unity

The following explanation by Amy Plantinga Pauw reveals the legitimacy of this book's purpose, reconsidering Edwards's theological aesthetics based on his biblical interpretation:

> Even in his youthful brashness about the powers of unaided reason, Edward's explicit reliance on Scripture for his exposition of the Trinity reflected the conviction that divine revelation was "exceeding needful" for correct theological understanding.

communion in one another, and are as it were predicable one of another. As Christ said of himself and the Father, 'I am in the Father, and the Father in me' [John 10:14], so may it be said concerning all the persons of the Trinity: the Father is in the Son, and the Son in the Father; the Holy Ghost is in the Father, and the Father in the Holy Ghost; the Holy Ghost is in the Son, and the Son in the Holy Ghost" (*WJE* 21:133). Lee claims that Edwards followed the Augustine-Western tradition of the doctrine of the Trinity in the spring of 1728, however, his understanding was transferred to a stronger *perichoretic* formula in his "Discourse on the Trinity" a few years later. See Lee, *Trinity*, 61–63. For more information, see the editor's introduction in *WJE* 21:2–27. However, many other Edwardsean scholars such as Douglas A. Sweeney, Stephen R. Holmes, and Oliver Crisp hesitate to agree with Lee's understanding of this issue. In their view, although Jonathan Edwards focused more on the trinitarian personalities, he also certainly affirmed divine simplicity. For instance, Crisp argues that there is "no evidence that Edwards rejected divine simplicity." He continues, in Edwards's passages in his "Discourse on the Trinity," Edwards "clearly endorses the pure act account, of which divine simplicity is a corollary" (Crisp, *Jonathan Edwards on God and Creation*, 101–7). See Holmes, "Response," 108–9; Crisp, "Ontology," 1–20; McClymond and McDermott, *Theology of Jonathan Edwards*, 661.

38. *WJE* 6:364.

39. *WJE* 13:260.

> Without God's declaration to humanity concerning "what manner of being he is," human reason is helpless.[40]

Furthermore, in terms of knowing the divine perfections, Edwards stresses the limitation of human understanding and the importance of God's Word for knowing the perfection and excellencies of God as follows:

> Indeed the perfections of God are such a theme as the strongest, best instructed, and most knowing Christians know but infinitely little of; no, nor the bright intelligences of the higher world. *The most understanding* there may spend all their lives' time, yea, an eternity, in learning and discovering more and more, and yet *never arrive to a perfect knowledge*; it is a bottomless ocean of wonders that we can never comprehend, but yet may with great pleasure and profit dive further into it. It would be greatly to the advantage of our souls, if we understood more of the excellency and gloriousness of God. . . . Wherefore, I shall not presume to speak of *the excellencies of God* any further than he has taught and instructed us in *his Word*.[41]

In his sermon "God's Excellencies," based on Psalms 89:6,[42] Edwards notes God as the infinitely glorious and excellent being.[43] Referring to Psalms 90:2, 4,[44] Edwards argues that God received "his power, his wisdom, his excellency, his glory, his honor, and [his] authority . . . from none other" because God's being "never had a beginning" and "never was made."[45] God's excellency is the greatest and original excellency because "all other excellencies proceed from him as the fountain, for he has made them all," and he must have "all that excellency in himself."[46] To summarize, Edwards defines God's being by saying, "God's is an infinite excellency,

40. Pauw, "Trinity," 51.

41. *WJE* 10:417–18 (italics added).

42. "For who in the heaven can be compared unto the LORD? Who among the sons of the mighty can be likened unto the LORD?" (Ps 89:6 KJV).

43. As we have seen above, for Edwards, God's excellency is a synonym of God's beauty. "[This] text is another instance, wherein the *infinite gloriousness* and *excellency of God* is held forth to us, by *its being* so transcendent above the greatest and highest creature" (*WJE* 10:416 [italics added]).

44. "Before the mountains were brought forth, Or ever thou hadst formed the earth and the world, Even from everlasting to everlasting, thou art God. . . . For a thousand years in thy sight Are but as yesterday when it is past, And as a watch in the night" (Ps 90:2, 4 KJV).

45. *WJE* 10:418–19.

46. *WJE* 10:420.

infinite glory, and beauty itself; he is an infinite, eternal, and immutable excellency; he is not only an infinitely excellent being, but a being that is infinite excellency, beauty, and loveliness."[47]

Edwards extends the beauty of God's being to the beauty of the Trinity in various ways. By exegeting the Hebrew word אֱלֹהִים in Genesis 3:1 and 3:22, he argues that the word אֱלֹהִים significantly reveals "the three persons of the Trinity" and "a plurality of persons in the Godhead."[48] Based on Peter van Mastricht's (1630–1706) exegesis,[49] he parses אֱלֹהִים in Genesis 3:1 as follows:

> The word is *Elohim* from the radix אָלָה, "adjurare," signifying the three persons of the Trinity confederated together as to the grand scheme and design of the creation, as they are in the eternal covenant of redemption. . . . And also from אֵל, *deus*, from the radix איל, *fortitudo*, signifying the power of the Creator. *Elohim* is the plural number of *El*, with the insertion of the letter ה out of the name *Jehovah*, as was in the change of the names of Abraham and Sarah.[50]

Furthermore, in his exegesis on Genesis 3:22, Edwards repeatedly argues that the word אֱלֹהִים reveals a plurality.[51] He states that the reason the word אֱלֹהִים has respect to a plurality is that "when God refers to his words, he speaks of a plurality, saying, 'Behold, the man is become as one of us.' And so that the word *Elohim*, as 'tis a word in the plural number, so does properly carry a plurality of persons in its signification, for the word

47. *WJE* 10:421.

48. *WJE* 24:123, 139–40.

49. *WJE* 24:123n6.

50. *WJE* 24:123.

51. In order to support his exegesis, Edwards quoted James Knight's (1672–1735) sermons: "It may be worthwhile to reflect on the words which the serpent spake to deceive our first parents. 'God doth know (saith he) that in the day you eat thereof, then your eyes shall be opened, and ye shall be as gods (or rather as God, the one God), knowing good and evil.' For the word *Elohim* is so used from the beginning of Genesis to this very place for the one God, and the design of the tempter was to make them believe that by tasting of the fruit, which God had forbidden, they might come to the knowledge and wisdom of God, even of the same God who gave them the precept. When therefore God saith, 'The man is become as one of us,' the meaning is this: he is become as God, for he hints at the promise that the serpent had made, which was a likeness to God [Gen 3:5] and not to angels. But 'one of us' is an indefinite term, and equally applicable to each of the persons meant and comprehended in the name God, and consequently one with the true God" (*WJE* 24:139). James Knight's original work is *Eight Sermons Preached at the Cathedral Church of St. Paul, in Defence of the Divinity of our Lord Jesus Christ, and of the Holy Spirit* (London, 1721), quoted in *WJE* 24:139n8.

'us' denotes a plurality of persons."[52] Edwards stresses that "nothing can be more evident than that expression, 'one of us,' has respect to more than one." Moreover, Edwards opposes those who argue that the plural meaning of אֱלֹהִים refers to angels or other superior creatures, not to God, and emphasizes that both usages of אֱלֹהִים in Genesis 3:22 (God himself mentions) and 3:5 (the serpent mentions) "refer to confining the plurality to the deity."[53] In addition, by interpreting connected words with the word אֱלֹהִים, he enhances his interpretation of the plurality of the word אֱלֹהִים. For instance, by interpreting the verb הִתְעוּ in Genesis 20:13, he says:

> Not only is the word *Elohim* in the plural number, but it is joined to a verb of the plural number in Genesis 20:13, "When God caused me to wander from my Father's house." The word hithgnu, הִתְעוּ, "caused to wander," is in the plural number. This is agreeable to the use of plural verbs, adjectives and pronouns in Genesis 1:26, Genesis 3:22, Genesis 11:7.[54]

Moreover, he interprets the adjective קָדוֹשׁ in Joshua 24:19 that it is used as a plural with אֱלֹהִים קְדֹשִׁים—אֱלֹהִים, as Edwards translated, "he is the holy Gods."[55] Therefore, he identifies the grammatical explanation that "a plural substantive and adjective are used here concerning the true God," and this grammatical usage can be found in 1 Samuel 4:8; Daniel 4:8, 9, 18; 5:11; Isaiah 6; and Revelation 4.[56]

Before proceeding to a more detailed discussion of Edwards's understanding of the Trinity and God's beauty, I wish to address a brief explanation to prevent any misunderstanding of Edwards on the doctrine of the Trinity. Edwards emphasizes God's plurality in his various works, but he likewise emphasizes God's one Essence. For instance, in his *Miscellanies,* by interpreting the words אֱלֹהִים and יהוה, he argues:

> The very frequent joining of the word *Elohim*, a word in the plural number, with the word *Jehovah*, a word in the singular number . . . seems to be a significant indication of the union of several divine persons in one Essence. The word *Jehovah* signifies as much as the word Essence, and is the proper name of

52. *WJE* 24:140.
53. *WJE* 24:140.
54. *WJE* 20:486.
55. *WJE* 23:175.
56. *WJE* 23:176.

> God, with regard to his self-existent, eternal, all sufficient, perfect and immutable Essence.[57]

As an example of his interpretation, he exegetes Deuteronomy 6:4: "Moses seems to have regard to something remarkable in thus calling *Elohim*, the plural, so often by the singular name Jehovah, [especially] in that remark which he makes for the special observation of God's people Israel."[58] Furthermore, Edwards suggests a more proper translation of this passage. In particular, he recommends translating "יְהוָה אֱלֹהֵינוּ יְהוָה | אֶחָד" into "Jehovah, our divine persons, is one Jehovah."[59] This reveals that Jonathan Edwards follows the traditional Nicene formula by stressing both the plural divine personalities and also one divine essence.

Here, one question becomes pertinent: how does the fact that God is the Trinity relate to the beauty of God's being? As described above, Jonathan Edwards stresses there is no excellency and beauty without a plurality.[60] This can be found in his biblical interpretation as well. In his interpretation of 1 John 1:3,[61] Edwards mentions the excellency of the trinitarian fellowship in the unity of the Trinity: "This is the common excellency and joy and happiness in which they all are united; 'tis the bond of perfectness by which they are one in the Father and the Son, as the Father is in the Son, and [he in him]."[62] Furthermore, Edwards argues that God's "infinite beauty is his infinite mutual love of himself. . . . God is the prime and original being. . . . But he exerts himself towards himself no other way than in infinitely loving and delighting in himself, in the mutual love of the Father and the Son."[63] In other words, Edwards believes the hypostatic mutual love of the Trinity is the beauty of the infinite God's being. This fact likewise can be found in his biblical interpretation. Concerning the central theme of Trinitarian beauty, Edwards focuses on *Αγαπε* in 1 John 4:8 and 4:16: "ὁ μὴ ἀγαπῶν οὐκ ἔγνω τὸν θεόν, ὅτι ὁ θεὸς

57. *WJE* 20:487. In terms of these words in plural and singular numbers, he noted that "as may be seen in places referred to in the English Concordance, under the words Lord God, Lord his God, Lord my God, Lord our God, Lord their God, Lord thy God, Lord your God."

58. *WJE* 20:487–88.

59. *WJE* 20:488.

60. *WJE* 6:337. For the explanation of the editor of this work, see also 84–85.

61. "That which we have seen and heard declare we unto you, that ye also may have fellowship with us: and truly our fellowship is with the Father, and with his Son Jesus Christ" (1 John 1:3 KJV).

62. *WJE* 21:130.

63. *WJE* 6:363–34.

ἀγάπη ἐστίν (1 John 4:8)"; "*Ὁ θεὸς ἀγάπη ἐστίν, καὶ ὁ μένων ἐν τῇ ἀγάπῃ ἐν τῷ θεῷ μένει, καὶ ὁ θεὸς ἐν αὐτῷ μένει* (1 John 4:16)."[64] He interprets that we "find no other attributes of which it is said that they are God in Scripture, or that God is they, but Λογος and *Αγαπε*, the reason and *the love of God*."[65] Moreover, in his sermon "Heaven is a world of love," Edwards illustrates God, who is the fountain of love, by using a metaphor of the sun, which is the fountain of light:

> For God is the fountain of love, as the sun is the fountain of light. And therefore the glorious presence of God in heaven fills heaven with love, as the sun placed in the midst of the hemisphere in a clear day fills the world with light. The Apostle tells us that God is love, 1 John 4:8. And therefore seeing he is an infinite Being, it follows that he is an infinite fountain of love. Seeing he is an all-sufficient Being, it follows that he is a full and overflowing and an inexhaustible fountain of love. Seeing he is an unchangeable and eternal Being, he is an unchangeable and eternal source of love.[66]

In Edwards's understanding, God loves His Idea,[67] and Christ is "the Eternal, necessary, Perfect, substantial & Personal Idea which G[od] hath of himself."[68] He notes that the Bible accounts for who the Son of God is—His "being in the form of" God and His "express & Perfect Image & Representation,"[69] and as supporting passages, he quotes 2 Corinthians 4:4; Philippians 2:6; Galatians 1:15; and Hebrews 1:3.[70] Furthermore, by interpreting Exodus 33:14, Edwards argues the relationship between God

64. The original Greek passages are quoted in NA28.

65. *WJE* 21:132 (italics added).

66. *WJE* 8:369.

67. Edwards, *Unpublished Essay*, 93.

68. Edwards, *Unpublished Essay*, 85. In this essay, Edwards used the following abbreviations: Chh. = church, or churches; F. = Father; G. = God; G.H. = Ghost; Gosp. = Gospel; H.G. = Holy Ghost; L = Lord; L. J. X. = Lord Jesus Christ; So. = Son; Sp. = Spirit, or Spirits; SS. Scriptures (or Scripture); X. = Christ; Xtians. = Christians.

69. Edwards, *Unpublished Essay*, 85.

70. "In whom the god of this world hath blinded the minds of them which believe not, *lest the light of the glorious gospel of Christ, who is the image of God, should shine unto them*" (2 Cor 4:4); "*Who, being in the form of God,* thought it not robbery to be equal with God" (Phil 2:6); "*Who is the image of the invisible God*, the firstborn of every creature" (Col 1:15); "*Who being the brightness of his glory, and the express image of his person*, and upholding all things by the word of his power, when he had by himself purged our sins, sat down on the right hand of the Majesty on high" (Heb 1:3 KJV). The phrases Edwards quoted are italicized.

and the Son, who is a perfect and infinite Idea of God. Exodus 33:14 provides the account that Christ "is called the face of" God, and the word "presence" in the original (i.e., פָּנֶה) "signifies face, looks, form or appearance," and the root of this word (פָּנָה) "signifies to look upon or behold."[71] Through this interpretation, he argues that Christ—the Son of God—is the perfect and eternal idea of God himself as His "own face in a looking glass."[72]

> What can be so Properly & fitly called so with Respect to G[od] as God[']s own Perfect Idea of himself whereby He has every moment a view of His own essence: this Idea is that face of God which G[od] sees as a man sees his own face in a looking glass. [']Tis of such form or appearance whereby G[od] eternally appears to himself. The root that the original word comes from signifies to look upon or behold: now what is that which G[od] looks upon or beholds in so Eminent a manner as he doth on his own Idea or that perfect Image of himself which he has in view. This is what is eminently in God[']s Presence & is therefore called the angel of God[']s presence or face. Isai. 63,9. . . . [T]hat the Son of G[od] is God[']s own eternal and Perfect Idea is a thing we have yet much more expressly Revealed in God[']s Word.[73]

To summarize, God loves the idea of Himself, and Christ is the face of God and His perfect and eternal idea. Therefore, the Father loves His perfect idea, the Son. Since God's "infinite beauty is his infinite mutual love of himself,"[74] this divine relationship of love signifies God's mutual beauty.

Next, Edwards interprets how the relationship of love between the Father and the Son connects with the Holy Spirit. Through his interpretation of Proverbs 8:30, "I was daily his delight, Rejoicing always before him," Edwards argues that the Holy Spirit, who is the third person of the Trinity, is the "eternal & most Perfect & essential act of the divine nature," the "Godhead being . . . begotten by God[']s loving an Idea of himself," and "an Infinitely holy & sacred energy arises between the F[ather] & Son in mutually Loving & delighting in each other."[75] He explains that the

71. Edwards, *Unpublished Essay*, 88.

72. Edwards, *Unpublished Essay*, 88.

73. Edwards, *Unpublished Essay*, 88–89.

74. *WJE* 6:363–64.

75. Edwards, *Unpublished Essay*, 93–94.

nature of the Godhead involves love and that love is the Holy Spirit, and this can be proved by Scriptures (1 John 4:8, 12–13, 16–18).[76]

In addition, Edwards explains that the Holy Spirit is love, interpreting various metaphors about the Holy Spirit in the Bible: the dove, the oil (in particular, olive oil and holy anointing oil), the fountain of life, the river of life, etc. First, Scripture describes the Holy Ghost as "a dove, which is the emblem of love, or a lover."[77] In particular, much of this can be found in the Song of Songs, such as Canticles 1:15; 2:14; 4:1; 5:2, 12; 6:9.[78] Since only the dove among all birds is a symbol of innocence and love, it can be offered in sacrifice. Thus, this symbol is "love being," which

76. "We may learn by the Word of God that the Godhead or the divine nature and essence does subsist in love. 1 John 4:8, 'He that loveth not knoweth not God; for God is love.' In the context of which place I think it is plainly intimated to us that the Holy Spirit is that love, as in the 1 John 4:12–13: 'If we love one another, God dwelleth in us, and his love is perfected in us. Hereby know we that we dwell in him, because he hath given us of his Spirit.' 'Tis the same argument in both verses: in the 1 John 4:12 the Apostle argues that if we have love dwelling in [us], we have God dwelling in us; and in the 1 John 4:13 he clears the force of the argument by this, that love is God's Spirit. Seeing we have of God's Spirit dwelling [in us], we have God dwelling in [us]: supposing it as a thing granted and allowed, that God's Spirit is God. 'Tis evident also by this verse that God's dwelling in us, and his love—or the love that he hath or exerciseth—being in us, are the same thing. The same is intimated in the same manner in the last verses of the foregoing chapter. The Apostle was in the foregoing verses speaking of love as a sure sign of sincerity and our acceptance with God, beginning with the 1 John 4:18, and he sums up the argument thus in the last verse: 'And hereby do we know that he abideth in us by the Spirit that [he] hath given us.' Again, in the 1 John 4:16 the Apostle tells us that 'God is love; and he that dwelleth in love dwelleth in God, and God in him.' Which confirms not only that the divine nature subsists in love, but also that this love is the Spirit: for it is the Spirit of God by which God dwells in his saints, as the Apostle had observed in the 1 John 4:13, and as we are abundantly taught in the New Testament" (*WJE* 21:121–22). "He that loveth not knoweth not God; for God is love" (1 John 4:8 KJV); "If we love one another, God dwelleth in us, and his love is perfected in us. Hereby know we that we dwell in him, and he in us, because he hath given us of his Spirit" (1 John 4:12–13 KJV); "God is love; and he that dwelleth in love dwelleth in God, and God in him. Herein is our love made perfect, that we may have boldness in the day of judgment: because as he is, so are we in this world. There is no fear in love; but perfect love casteth out fear: because fear hath torment. He that feareth is not made perfect in love" (1 John 4:16–18 KJV).

77. *WJE* 21:126.

78. "*Canticles 1:15*, 'Behold, thou art fair, my love; behold, thou art fair; thou hast doves' eyes,' i.e., eyes of love; and again, *Canticles 4:1*, the same words; and *Canticles 5:12*, 'His eyes are as the eyes of doves'; and *Canticles 5:2*, 'My love, my dove'; *Canticles 2:14*; and *Canticles 6:9*. And this I believe to be the reason that the dove alone of all birds (except the sparrow in the single case of the leprosy) was appointed to be offered in sacrifice" (*WJE* 21:126).

is an offering that God deserves.[79] Moreover, in Matthew 3:17, that the Holy Ghost was descended from the Father in the shape of a dove when Christ was baptized clearly signifies that the Holy Ghost is "the infinite love of the Father and the Son."[80] Edwards explains that the Hebrew word "מְרַחֶפֶה" in Genesis 1:2 signifies "the brooding of a dove upon her eggs" and that both "מְרַחֶפֶה" and its root word "רָחַפ" signify love as well.[81] Second, Scripture delineates the Holy Spirit as "a being poured out and shed forth" and "a being breathed forth," such as "water, fire, breath, wind, oil, wine a spring, a river."[82] Moreover, Edwards argues that these metaphors indicate the affection, love, or joy of the Holy Spirit. For instance, he explains that the type of oil can well represent divine love from its nature, such as smooth, flowing, and diffusive. He representatively uses two aspects of the type of oil as the metaphor of the type of the Holy Spirit. First, the oil comes from olive trees, and olive trees are used to symbolize love and peace. This can be observed in the Noachian deluge: Noah suffered a terrible flood, but he could feel God's love and goodwill through the olive leaves that the dove brought.[83]

79. *WJE* 21:126.

80. *WJE* 21:126.

81. *WJE* 21:126–27. In order to support his interpretation, Edwards quoted Johannes Buxtorf, *Lexicon Hebraicum et Chaldaicum* (1646) on Genesis 1:2: "*Incubare* . . . Quemadmodum columba incumbit pullis suis, neque eos attingit aut lædit alis suis"; Hugo Grotius, *Truth of the Christian Religion* (1729) 1.16: "'In Moses's history we find the spirit or breath, and the darkness; and the Hebrew word Merachepheth, signifies Love . . . Now, because the Hebrew word Merachepheth signifies properly the brooding of a dove upon her eggs, therefore it follows in Sanchuniation, that the living creatures, that is, the constellations, were in that mud, as in an egg; and hence that spirit is called by the name of the dove . . . Lucius Ampelius, in his book to Matrinus, says, 'It is reported that, in the river Euphrates, a dove sat many days upon a fish's egg, and hatched a goddess, very kind and merciful to the life of man'"; Theophilus Gale, *Court of the Gentiles* (1647), and Matthew Poole, *Synopsis Criticorum*, 1, on Leviticus 1:14: "Qu. Cur non de aliis auibus, gallinis, perdicibus, &c? Resp. Cæteræ aves vel sunt magis sylvestres; vel, si sunt domesticæ, vescuntur immundo nutrimento, ut gallinæ, anates, &c. *E turturibus etiam magnis; quia turtur compare mortua nonjungitur alteri: aliter columbe, ideominores tantum aptae.* Vel, quia turtures in matura, columbae in tenera, aetate maxime praestunt. *Quia vero ambas istas aves aliae persequuntur, ideo elegit eas Deus.* Turtur significat Christi castitatem; Columba, quae felle caret, ejus dulcedinem, sive mansuetudinem" (*WJE* 21:126–27nn6–8).

82. *WJE* 21:129.

83. "And the dove came in to him in the evening; and, lo, in her mouth was an olive leaf pluckt off: so Noah knew that the waters were abated from off the earth" (Gen 8:11 KJV).

Second, the oil represents the anointment, and the holy oil is "principal type of the Holy Ghost, well represent the divine love and delight by reason of its excellent sweetness and fragrancy."[84] Next, he explains the Holy Spirt and divine love through the metaphors of water (i.e., water, river, fountain, etc.) in Scripture. Edwards argues that Psalms 36:7–9 reveals that the Holy Ghost is God's love.[85] He exegetes that the English translation of the King James Version Bible of "abundantly satisfied" means "abundantly watered, רָוָה" in Hebrew. He interprets that "precious lovingkindness," "fatness of God's house," "river of his pleasures," "water of the fountain of life," and "God's light" all represent God's love—the Holy Ghost.[86] Moreover, he interprets that "the river of water of life . . . which proceeds out of the throne of God and of the Lamb" in Revelation 22 is the same as the "river of living and life-giving water" in Ezekiel 47.[87] Edwards explains that John 7:38–39[88] demonstrates that the rivers of living water indicate the Holy Spirit, while Christ teaches us the same lesson in John 4:14[89] as well.[90] Therefore, Edwards asserts that the Holy Spirit is the beauty of the divine nature.[91]

The relationship between the existential beauty of the Trinity and divine love (or charity) is likewise evident in Edwards's exposition of 1 Corinthians 13. Edwards explains that the term *charity* in the KJV New Testament, which is "ἀγάπη" in Greek, is better translated into *love*, "for

84. *WJE* 21:127–28. Here, Edwards quoted Psalm 133 to support his explanation. "Behold, how good and pleasant is it for brethren to dwell together in unity! It is like the precious ointment upon the head, that ran down upon the beard, even Aaron's beard: that went down to the skirts of his garments" (Ps 133:1–2 KJV).

85. "How excellent is thy lovingkindness, O God! therefore the children of men put their trust under the shadow of thy wings. They shall be abundantly satisfied with the fatness of thy house; and thou shalt make them drink of the river of thy pleasures. For with thee is the fountain of life: in thy light shall we see light" (Ps 36:7–9 KJV).

86. *WJE* 21:128.

87. *WJE* 21:128.

88. "He that believeth on me, as the scripture hath said, out of his belly shall flow rivers of living water. (But this spake he of the Spirit, which they that believe on him should receive: for the Holy Ghost was not yet given; because that Jesus was not yet glorified)" (John 7:38–39 KJV).

89. "But whosoever drinketh of the water that I shall give him shall never thirst; but the water that I shall give him shall be in him a well of water springing up into everlasting life" (John 4:14 KJV).

90. *WJE* 21:128–29.

91. See chapter 8 in Lovi, *Power of God*.

that is the proper English of it," and this love must be Christian love.[92] For Edwards, God, as revealed in 1 Corinthians 13, is the fountain of love, infinite, unchangeable, and eternal. Thus, God is an "unchangeable and eternal fountain of love."[93] God is a heavenly Father, who "dwells and gloriously manifests himself . . . infinitely lovely. . . . The Father of the family is lovely."[94] Edwards describes Christ as "the Lamb of God, the prince of peace and of love," and "the great Mediator" who expresses all divine love, and the fruits of love "have been purchased" through Him.[95] In terms of the Holy Spirit, Edwards accounts for Him as the fountain of love. Every true Christian's love derives from the Holy Spirit. The Holy Spirit is the Spirit of love, and His attribute is love.[96] Thus, Christian love should be called the "love of the Spirit" or "love in the Spirit," as proclaimed in Romans 15:30; Colossians 1:8; and Philippians 2:1. Furthermore, Edwards argues that a true Christian loves God, and the reason that a Christian can love God is *the excellency of God*. God deserves to be loved because of His love and Holiness, and believers come to love God with holy respect.[97] As a result, through the interpretation of 1 Corinthians 13, Edwards reveals that God's beauty and excellency are well manifested through the trinitarian divine love: "The God . . . is infinitely lovely; gloriously lovely as a heavenly Father, as a divine Redeemer and as a holy sanctifier."[98]

Additionally, in his interpretation of Romans 11:33–36,[99] Edwards explains why God's excellency should be revealed in the divine trinitarian being:

> God's wisdom and omnisciency shines clearest of all in his perfect knowledge of himself, who is the infinite object of his own knowledge. That eternity of his, whereby he was from everlasting to everlasting, which so confounds us miserable worms, is clearly understood by him with the greatest ease, at one simple

92. Edwards, *Charity and Its Fruits*, 2.

93. Edwards, *Charity and Its Fruits*, 468.

94. Edwards, *Charity and Its Fruits*, 470–71.

95. Edwards, *Charity and Its Fruits*, 469.

96. Edwards, *Charity and Its Fruits*, 6.

97. Edwards, *Charity and Its Fruits*, 8–9.

98. Edwards, *Charity and Its Fruits*, 470.

99. "O the depth of the riches both of the wisdom and knowledge of God! how unsearchable are his judgments, and his ways past finding out! For who hath known the mind of the Lord? or who hath been his counsellor? Or who hath first given to him, and it shall be recompensed unto him again? For of him, and through him, and to him, are all things: to whom be glory forever. Amen" (Rom 11:33–36 KJV).

> view; *he also comprehends his own infinite greatness and excellency, which can be done by none but an infinite understanding.*[100]

To summarize, it can be confirmed that Edwards's biblical interpretation of the beauty of God's existence and the trinitarian beauty has the following logical flow: (1) God is the excellent and beautiful being; (2) the beauty should be plural, and the Hebrew term "אֱלֹהִים" indicates God's plural hypostases; (3) the trinitarian beauty is revealed through divine love in the Trinity; (4) God loves His personal idea; (5) Christ is the infinite and prefect idea of God; (6) divine holy energy occurs between the Father and the Son as they love and rejoice each other; and (7) the Holy Spirit is the Spirit of love and the trinitarian divine love per se.

Edwards's Philosophical Examinations on the Beauty of God's Holiness and Moral Perfection

Along with the beauty of God's being and the trinitarian beauty, Edwards's other important theme of God's beauty concerns God's holiness and moral perfection. Michael J. McClymond and Gerald R. McDermott explain that, for Edwards, God's "beauty and holiness were almost interchangeable terms, for 'the beauty of the divine nature does primarily consist in God's holiness.'"[101] In his "The Mind," Edwards argues that the mutual love between the Father and the Son "makes the third, the personal Holy Spirit or the holiness of God, which is his infinite beauty"; in other words, God's holiness is the same as His infinite beauty.[102] By analyzing Edwards's dissertation, "Concerning the End for which God Created the World,"[103] Louis Joseph Mitchell explains that for Edwards, God's

100. *WJE* 10:423 (italics added).

101. McClymond and McDermott, *Theology of Jonathan Edwards*, 95. Edwards quotations are from *WJE* 2:274, 298, 258.

102. *WJE* 6:364.

103. In order to discuss on Edwards's understanding of beauty and holiness, Mitchell quoted Edwards's argument as follows: "Another thing wherein the emanation of divine fullness, that is and will be made in consequence of the creation of the world, is the communication of virtue and holiness to the creature. This is a communication of God's holiness; so that hereby the creature partakes of God's own moral excellency, which is properly the beauty of the divine nature. And as God delights in his own beauty, he must necessarily delight in the creature's holiness; which is a conformity to, and participation of it, as truly as the brightness of a jewel, held in the sun's beams, is a participation, or derivation of the sun's brightness, though immensely less in degree. And then it must be considered wherein this holiness in the creature consists; viz. in love, which is the

"holiness is moral beauty," and this moral beauty "is to be distinguished from God's natural attributes such as power, greatness, knowledge, etc."[104] In the same sense, Edwards argues:

> The moral excellency of an intelligent being . . . is holiness. Therefore, holiness comprehends all true moral excellency of intelligent beings; there is no other true virtue, but real holiness. . . . So the holiness of God is the same with the moral excellency of the divine nature, or his purity and beauty as a moral agent, comprehending all his moral perfections, his righteousness, faithfulness and goodness.[105]

In *The Miscellanies,* Edwards notes beauty, loveliness, and excellency of holiness as follows:

> Holiness is a most beautiful and lovely thing. . . . 'Tis the highest beauty and amiableness, vastly above all other beauties. 'Tis a divine beauty, makes the soul heavenly and far purer than anything here on earth. . . . 'Tis of a sweet, pleasant, charming, lovely, amiable, delightful, serene, calm and still nature. 'Tis almost too high a beauty for any creatures to be adorned with; it makes the soul a little, sweet and delightful image of the blessed Jehovah. . . . How may they[angels] hover over such a soul, to delight to behold such loveliness! How is it above all the heathen virtues, of a more light, bright and pure nature, more serene and calm, more peaceful and delightsome! What a sweet calmness, what a calm ecstasy, doth it bring to the soul! How doth it make the soul love itself; how doth it make the pure invisible world love it; yea, how doth God love it and delight in it. Oh, of what a sweet, humble nature is holiness! How peaceful and, loving all things but sin, of how refined and exalted a nature is it! How doth it clear change the soul and make it more excellent than other beings![106]

For Edwards, holiness is the most beautiful and lovely thing, and it is the highest form of beauty because divine holiness is the highest virtue above all other heathen virtues, and it is the perfect peace and love with no sin. In the following chapters, I will demonstrate that, for Edwards,

---

comprehension of all true virtue; and primarily in love to God, which is exercised in an high esteem of God, admiration of his perfections, complacency in them, and praise of them" (*WJE* 8:442, quoted in Mitchell, "Experience of Beauty," 36).

104. Mitchell, "Experience of Beauty," 36.

105. *WJE* 2:255.

106. *WJE* 13:163–64.

the reason why a human being can be a moral being who has secondary beauty—the reflected beauty of God's primary beauty—is that the human being is an image of God (*imago Dei*), who is the moral perfection and the primary beauty per se; furthermore, this divine attribute affects the justification and sanctification of the human being.[107]

God's holiness is related to His creation and glory. The next chapter discusses this issue in detail, but to describe it briefly, God glorifies himself toward his creatures because revealing and reflecting His beauty into the created world is God's end of creation. In this sense, according to Robert Eugene Colacurcio, in Edwards's understanding, "God exhibits and manifests in man something of his internal fullness and glory. For a man to know God's glory is, therefore, to be implicated in an order constituted by God's holiness."[108]

As Amy Plantinga Pauw explains, for Edwards, the Trinity is "the sum of ontological and moral perfection," and it is "at the heart of Edwards'[s] perception of beauty and excellency."[109] Moreover, according to Roland André Delattre, to know God's beauty, God's moral perfection—in particular, God's holiness—should first be understood because "the divine beauty consists primarily in the beauty of his moral perfections" and "the beauty of all his other attributes is derived from the beauty of his moral perfections."[110]

Edwards's Biblical Interpretations on the Beauty of God's Holiness and Moral Perfection

Edwards argues that the reason Christianity is more excellent and beautiful than all other religions is that it is a significantly holy religion based

107. "'Tis a divine beauty, makes the soul heavenly and far purer than anything here on earth; this world is like mire and filth and defilement to that soul which is sanctified. . . . How doth it[holiness] clear change the soul and make it more excellent than other beings! How is it possible that such a divine thing should be on earth? It makes the soul like a delightful field or garden planted by God, with all manner of pleasant flowers growing in the order in which nature has planted them, that is all pleasant and delightful, undisturbed, free from all the noise of man and beast, enjoying a sweet calm and the bright, calm, and gently vivifying beams of the sun forevermore: where the sun is Jesus Christ; the blessed beams and calm breeze, the Holy Spirit; the sweet and delightful flowers, and the pleasant shrill music of the little birds, are the Christian graces" (*WJE* 13:163–64).

108. Colacurcio, "Perception of Excellency," 227–28.

109. Pauw, "Trinity," 51.

110. Delattre, "Beauty and Sensibility," 207.

on the holy word of God, which is excellent and beautiful.[111] Additionally, the reason why God's moral creatures worship Him is because of the beauty of His holiness.[112]

Edwards states that the Bible proclaims that God's holiness is God's beauty per se. In his *Religious Affections*, Edwards argues that "a love to divine things for beauty and sweetness of their moral excellency is the first beginning and spring of all holy affections."[113] Based on his interpretation of Psalms 29:2; 96:9; and 110:3, Edwards argues that "holiness is in a peculiar manner the beauty of the divine nature."[114]

> By the moral perfections of God, they mean those attributes which God exercises as a moral agent, or whereby the heart and will of God are good, right, and infinitely becoming, and lovely; such as his righteousness, truth, faithfulness, and goodness; or, in one word, his holiness. . . . The moral excellency of an intelligent voluntary being, is more immediately seated in the heart or will of moral agents. That intelligent being whose will is truly right and lovely, he is morally good or excellent. This moral excellency of an intelligent being, when it is true and real, and not only external, or merely seeming and counterfeit, is holiness. Therefore holiness comprehends all the true moral excellency of intelligent beings: there is no other true virtue, but real holiness. Holiness comprehends all the true virtue of a good man, his love to God, his gracious love to men, his justice, his charity, and

111. In order to support his argument, Edwards quoted Psalms 19:7–10; 119:128, 138, 140, 172. "Herein consists the excellency of the Word of God, that it is so holy; *Psalms 119:140*, 'Thy word is very pure, therefore thy servant loveth it.' V. 128, 'I esteem all thy precepts, concerning all things, to be right; and I hate every false way.' V. 138, 'Thy testimonies, that thou hast commanded, are righteous, and very faithful.' And v. 172, 'My tongue shall speak of thy word; for all thy commandments are righteousness.' *And Psalms 19:7–10, 'The law of the Lord is perfect, converting the soul: the testimony of the Lord is sure, making wise the simple: the statutes of the Lord are right, rejoicing the heart: the commandment of the Lord is pure, enlightening the eyes: the fear of the Lord is clean, enduring forever: the judgments of the Lord are true, and righteous altogether: more to be desired are they than gold, yea, than much fine gold; sweeter also than honey, and the honeycomb'*" (*WJE* 2:258). In the same sense, Douglas Sweeney explains that for Edwards, God's holiness is one of aspects that he believes that God is beautiful. Based on Daniel 4:8, 9, and 18, Edwards distinguished God from other gods due to His holiness. Moreover, as following Edwards's interpretation on Psalms 96:9, Sweeney explains Edwards's understanding that "above the greatest, purest beings one could conceive, the Lord shone in the mind of Edwards and the world beyond 'in the splendor of his holiness' (Psalm 96:9)" (Strachan and Sweeney, *Jonathan Edwards on Beauty*, 35–36).

112. Isa 6:3; Rev 4:8, 15:4; Pss 97:11–12, 98:1, 99:2–3, 5, 8–9; 1 Sam 2:2.

113. *WJE* 2:253–54.

114. *WJE* 2:257.

> bowels of mercies, his gracious meekness and gentleness, and all other true Christian virtues that he has, belong to his holiness. So the holiness of God in the more extensive sense of the word, and the sense in which the word is commonly, if not universally used concerning God in Scripture, is the same with the moral excellency of the divine nature, or his purity and beauty as a moral agent, comprehending all his moral perfections, his righteousness, faithfulness and goodness.[115]

Even more, he states that believers' true love of God must be through enjoying His holiness, because when they conceive of God, no attribute of God can be truly beautiful without His holiness, and no attribute in God's nature can be truly loved without the believer's love toward His holiness:

> They that don't see the glory of God's holiness, can't see anything of the true glory of his mercy and grace: they see nothing of the glory of those attributes, as any excellency of God's nature, as it is in itself; though they may be affected with them, and love them, as they concern their interest: for these attributes are no part of the excellency of God's nature, as that is excellent in itself, any otherwise than as they are included in his holiness, more largely taken; or as they are a part of his moral perfection. As the beauty of the divine nature does primarily consist in God's holiness, so does the beauty of all divine things.[116]

Just as Edwards's understanding of God's beauty leads to the trinitarian beauty, his biblical interpretation that God's holiness is His beauty leads to the beauty of holiness of each hypostasis of the Trinity. In his work *Charity and Its Fruits,* which contains Edwards's biblical interpretations of 1 Corinthians 13, Edwards interprets Heaven, which is a world of love and a blessed society full of love; the reason why Heaven can be a land of love is that God, who is a holy sanctifier, is infinitely and gloriously lovely.[117] Moreover, 1 Thessalonians 4:7[118] indicates that "the beauty and excellency of God . . . consist in his holiness."[119] In his sermon "God's Excellencies" regarding Psalms 89:6, Edwards states that God must be

115. *WJE* 2:255–57.

116. *WJE* 258.

117. Edwards, *Charity and Its Fruits,* 470.

118. "For God hath not called us unto uncleanness, but unto holiness" (1 Thess 4:7 KJV).

119. Edwards, *Charity and Its Fruits,* 326.

infinitely praised by all creatures for His glory and excellency, whose excellency is significantly related to His holiness:[120]

> God is infinitely exalted above all created beings in holiness. Holiness is the highest sort of excellency or perfection that ever the creature attains unto; 'tis the highest beauty that shines in the creation. Now God is infinitely holy, and infinitely exalted therein, above the holy angels and all creatures; there is not the least tincture of defilement or pollution in the Deity, but he is infinitely far from it: he is all pure light, without mixture of darkness; he hates and abhors sin above all things, 'tis what is directly contrary to his nature. This, his great holiness, has he made known to us by his justice, truth, and faithfulness in all his dispensations towards us, and by the pure holiness of his laws and commands.[121]

In the same sermon, Edwards directly explains that God's holiness "is the very beauty and loveliness of Jehovah himself," and that holiness is "the excellency of his excellencies, the beauty of his beauties, the perfection of his infinite perfections, and the glory of his attributes."[122] Furthermore, based on Daniel 4:8–9, 18,[123] Edwards interprets that God's holiness is an attribute distinct from other gods to the Israelites, an attribute that instills in His creatures lasting joy, and an attribute that will be praised forever.[124]

Edwards explains that the loveliness and beauty of Jesus Christ comes from His holiness. Jesus Christ is "the Holy One of God (Acts 3:14)," "God's holy child (Acts 4:27)," and "he that is holy, and he that is

120. Edwards presents seven aspects of God's excellency over all creatures: "We shall proceed to show how vastly God is exalted above all the highest and most perfect of created beings: first, in duration; second, in greatness; third, in excellency and loveliness; fourth, in power; fifth, in wisdom; sixth, in holiness; seventh, in goodness and mercy" (*WJE* 10:418).

121. *WJE* 10:423.

122. *WJE* 10:430.

123. "But at the last Daniel came in before me, whose name was Belteshazzar, according to the name of my god, and in whom is the spirit of the holy gods: and before him I told the dream, saying, O Belteshazzar, master of the magicians, because I know that the spirit of the holy gods is in thee, and no secret troubleth thee, tell me the visions of my dream that I have seen, and the interpretation thereof. . . . This dream I king Nebuchadnezzar have seen. Now thou, O Belteshazzar, declare the interpretation thereof, forasmuch as all the wise men of my kingdom are not able to make known unto me the interpretation: but thou art able; for the spirit of the holy gods is in thee" (Dan 4:8–9, 18 KJV).

124. *WJE* 10:423.

true (Revelation 3:7)."[125] The beauty of Christ's human and divine nature is likewise primarily linked to His holiness, and the beauty of Christ's human nature is "the image and reflection" of His divine nature.[126] Christ's beautiful holiness is also related to the gospel. The reason the gospel is beautiful is that it is a holy gospel, and the reason the gospel is holy is that the holy beauty of God and Jesus Christ is revealed in the gospel; in particular, the way of salvation through Jesus Christ is beautiful due to its holiness. In his sermon "True Grace, Distinguished from the Experience of Devils," comparing "truly gracious affections and exercises of mind" with "counterfeit" based on 1 Timothy 3:6; Romans 12:16; and Philippians 2:3,[127] Edwards explains that the sense of holy beauty of God and Christ serves as the foundation of "truly gracious affections and exercises of mind," which "mortifies pride, and truly humbles the soul."[128] In other words, for Edwards's biblical understanding, Jesus Christ is "the holy One of God," who is "possessed of all that holiness which is the infinite beauty and loveliness of the divine nature."[129]

Interpreting Romans 1:4,[130] Edwards explains the holiness of the Holy Spirit, who is the third person of the Trinity, also known as the spirit of holiness. He emphasizes that the expression "holy" in the Holy Spirit does not mean that only this Divine Spirit is holy among the three persons of the Trinity, explaining that this Divine Spirit is conceptually God's holiness itself:

> Hence it is that the Spirit of God, the third person in the Trinity, is so often called the Holy Spirit, as though "Holy" were an epithet some way or other peculiarly belonging to him, which can be no other way than that the holiness of God does consist in him. He is not only infinitely holy as the Father and the Son are, but he is the holiness of God itself in the abstract. The holiness

125. *WJE* 2:258.

126. *WJE* 2:259.

127. "Not a novice, lest being lifted up with pride he fall into the condemnation of the devil" (1Tim 3:6 KJV); "Be of the same mind one toward another. Mind not high things, but condescend to men of low estate. Be not wise in your own conceits" (Rom 12:16 KJV); and "Let nothing be done through strife or vainglory; but in lowliness of mind let each esteem other better than themselves" (Phil 2:3 KJV).

128. *WJE* 25:636–37.

129. Edwards's sermon, "Unbelievers Contemn the Glory and Excellency of Christ," in Edwards, *Works of Jonathan Edwards* [Hickman], 2:61.

130. "And declared to be the Son of God with power, according to the spirit of holiness, by the resurrection from the dead" (Rom 1:4 KJV).

> of the Father and the Son does consist in breathing forth this Spirit. Therefore he is not only called the Holy Spirit, but the "Spirit of holiness."[131]

Moreover, in terms of the holiness of the Holy Spirit, through John 3:6,[132] Edwards explains the holiness of the Spirit of God by comparing the corrupted flesh:

> That the Spirit of God is the very same with holiness (as 'tis in God, 'tis the holiness of God; and as 'tis in the creature, 'tis the holiness of the creature) appears by John 3:6, "That which is born of the flesh is flesh; and that which is born of the Spirit is spirit." Here 'tis very manifest that flesh and spirit are opposed one to another, as two contraries. And 'tis also acknowledged by orthodox divines in general that by the flesh is meant sin or corruption; and therefore by the Spirit is meant its contrary, viz. holiness. And that is evidently Christ's meaning: that which is born of the flesh is corrupt and filthy, but that which is born of the Spirit is holy.[133]

Edwards, in his sermon "A Divine and Supernatural Light," which was preached on Matthew 16:17, explains the relationship between the Holy Spirit and the light. There is a divine and supernatural light that is imparted to the soul of godly men by God. This light is revealed by acts of the Holy Spirit, who "operates in the minds of the godly, by uniting himself to them, and living in them, and exerting his own nature in the exercise of their faculties."[134] Edwards states that this proper nature of the Holy Spirit is holiness.

Finally, in his sermon "God's Excellencies," Edwards proclaims that God's holiness is "the beauty of his beauties" and his "very beauty and loveliness":

> Holiness is the very beauty and loveliness of Jehovah himself. 'Tis the excellency of his excellencies, the beauty of his beauties, the perfection of his infinite perfections, and the glory of his attributes. What an honor, then, must it be to a creature who is infinitely below God, and less than he, to be beautified and adorned with this beauty, with that beauty which is the highest

131. Lovi, *Power of God*, kindle loc. 2.

132. "That which is born of the flesh is flesh; and that which is born of the Spirit is spirit" (John 3:6 KJV).

133. *WJE* 21:123.

134. *WJE* 17:411.

> beauty of God himself, even holiness. The highest honor of angels is their holiness. 'Tis astonishing that God should make even the angels, or any creature, in his own likeness, but how much more admirable is it that God should sanctify sinners—loathsome and abominable creatures—and make them like to himself.[135]

The important fact the quotation reveals is that, as addressed above, God's beauty and holiness are deeply related not only to the Trinity but also to His created world. Therefore, in the theological aesthetics of Jonathan Edwards, the understanding of God's beauty leads to the concern of the beauty revealed in God's work of creation and in His created world.

Conclusion

To Edwards, it is clear that God is the foundation of true beauty. However, it cannot be simply argued that Edwards's understanding of God's beauty was solely the result of his philosophical and aesthetical deliberations. Rather, he developed an theological aesthetics on the being of God based on his interpretations of biblical descriptions of God, through which, he discovered God's excellence and beauty in God's mutual beauty and love of the Trinity. This was not simply a continuation of the tradition of Augustine; Edwards's theological aesthetics is founded on his exegesis of the Bible. He eminently interpreted the passages about the beauty of the trinitarian being in both the Old Testament and New Testament. Through his interpretation, he states that the beauty of God's being is inseparable from the concept of the Trinity. Additionally, through his biblical interpretation, he states how God's holiness—representative attributes of God—and God's moral perfection are related to God's beauty. God's holiness and moral perfection are also revealed in the beauty of each trinitarian personality, and the relationship between God's holiness and beauty is well represented in God's creation and the created world. Therefore, Edwards's theological aesthetics on God led to his understanding of the beauty of His creation and created world, which will be discussed in the next chapter.

135. *WJE* 10:430.

Chapter 5

Jonathan Edwards's Biblical Aesthetics of the Created World

Introduction

FOR JONATHAN EDWARDS, GOD is the Creator who is the primary beauty, and all the beauty of His created world has come from His beauty. Since God is the fountain of genuine beauty, any kind of beauty cannot exist without the light of His beauty. Edwards makes this statement about the relationship between the Primary beauty—God the Creator—and the secondary beauty of His created world:

> For as God is infinitely the greatest being, so he is allowed to be infinitely the most beautiful and excellent: and all the beauty to be found throughout the whole creation, is but the reflection of the diffused beams of that Being who hath an infinite fullness of brightness and glory. . . . God is not only infinitely greater and more excellent than all other being, but he is the head of the universal system of existence; the foundation and fountain of all being and all beauty; from whom all is perfectly derived, and on whom all is most absolutely and perfectly dependent; of whom, and through whom, and to whom is all being and all perfection; and whose being and beauty is as it were the sum and comprehension of all existence and excellence: much more than the sun is the fountain and summary comprehension of all the light and brightness of the day.[1]

1. *WJE* 8:550–51. For more information on primary-secondary beauty, see Mitchell, "Theological Aesthetics."

So, the beauty of the created world is inseparable from the beauty of God. This chapter will reveal how Edwards describes the connection between the beauty of God and the beauty of creation, then explore how humans in particular, created in the image of God, relate to the beauty of God, and finally what Edwards claims about the postlapsarian world and beauty after the Fall.

Edwards's Philosophical Examinations on the Beauty of God's Creation

God's Beauty and His Creation

According to Edwards, "God is infinitely, eternally, unchangeably, and independently glorious and happy: that he stands in no need of, cannot be profited by, or receive anything from the creature; or be truly hurt, or be the subject of any sufferings or impair of his glory and felicity from any other being."[2] This statement of Edwards raises a question: If God does not need to receive anything from His creatures, why did God create the world? Edwards found the answer to this question in God's nature to communicate his beauty.

As we have seen above, God is the greatest Being of beings who "is allowed to be infinitely the most beautiful and excellent."[3] Moreover, God's essence is "to incline to communicate himself."[4] In other words, each person of the Trinity is infinitely and completely beautiful; so, the Trinity communicates in love with His beauty. Edwards emphasizes that God has the disposition to communicate or emanate *ad extra* his infinite excellency, beauty, and fullness.

> As there is an infinite fullness of all possible good in God, a fullness of every perfection, of all excellency and beauty, and of infinite happiness. And as this fullness is capable of communication or emanation ad extra; so it seems a thing amiable and valuable in itself that it should be communicated or flow forth, that this infinite fountain of good should send forth abundant streams, that this infinite fountain of light should, diffusing its excellent fullness, pour forth light all around. And as this is in itself excellent, so a disposition to this in the Divine Being must

2. *WJE* 8:420.

3. *WJE* 8:550.

4. *WJE* 13:277–78.

> be looked upon as a perfection or an excellent disposition; such an emanation of good is, in some sense, a multiplication of it; so far as the communication or external stream may be looked upon as anything besides the fountain, so far it may be looked on as an increase of good. And if the fullness of good that is in the fountain is in itself excellent and worthy to exist, then the emanation, or that which is as it were an increase, repetition or multiplication of it, is excellent and worthy to exist. . . . [I]t appears reasonable to suppose that it was what God had respect to as an ultimate end of his creating the world, to communicate of his own infinite fullness of good; or rather it was his last end, that there might be a glorious and abundant emanation of his infinite fullness of good ad extra, or without himself, and the disposition to communicate himself or diffuse his own fullness, which we must conceive of as being originally in God as a perfection of his nature, was what moved him to create the world.[5]

For Edwards, God is an infinite source of all good, perfection, beauty, and happiness, and He is inherently capable of communicating or emanating these qualities outwardly. Thus, he believes that the end of God's creation is to communicate the fullness of his perfect and infinite goodness.

However, Edwards clarifies that "there is some impropriety in saying that a disposition in God to communicate himself to *the creature*, moved him to create the world."[6] Rather, God's disposition in the fullness of His divinity is "to flow out and diffuse itself."[7] In other words, in His ultimate end in creation, God did not have the diffusive disposition for the end of creation, but for His fullness of divinity and overflowing it. But, Edwards supposes that "a disposition in God, as an original property of his nature, to an emanation of his own infinite fullness, was what excited him to create the world; and so that the emanation itself was aimed at by him as a last end of the creation."[8]

Sang Hyun Lee argues that Edwards's view of creation differs from the Neoplatonic understanding of emanation, which is the concept of overflowing with no purpose, contradicting the claim that Edwards's terms related to emanation seem to be Neoplatonist. According to Lee, in discussing God's creation of the world, Edwards uniquely blends emanationist and teleological concepts. He describes creation as both

5. *WJE* 8:432–34.
6. *WJE* 8:434.
7. *WJE* 8:435.
8. *WJE* 8:435.

an extension of God's inner essence and a purposeful act with a specific objective. Although Edwards's language may evoke Neoplatonic ideas, his perspective on creation diverges from Neoplatonic emanationism, which envisions creation as a non-purposeful overflow. Edwards's choice of words is deliberate, as he perceives creation as a purposeful action and an expansion of God's being. When God exercises divine disposition in the creative process, it results in an ontological growth of God's fullness, converting potentiality into actuality. This explains Edwards's use of emanationist language, as creation serves as an ontological extension of God's prior actuality. As Lee continues, simultaneously, divine disposition functions as a teleological force, with the disposition's aim realized through its exercise. This aspect of Edwards's view of divine creativity sets it apart from Plotinus's Neoplatonic perspective, where necessary emanation leaves no room for teleology. For Edwards, God's emanation is a purpose-driven act. The integration of emanationist and teleological ideas in Edwards's thought is facilitated by his dispositional reinterpretation of the divine being.[9] Furthermore, Walter J. Schultz also challenges the prevailing view in Edwards scholarship that categorizes Jonathan Edwards as a Neoplatonist due to his use of the term "emanation" and its associated metaphors. Schultz believes these judgments are incorrect and lead to a false understanding of Edwards, along with subsequent misinterpretations of Edwards's view of God and creation. Edwards's doctrines of emanationism and dispositionalism are central to this discussion; the former relates to his view of God's action in the universe, and the latter explains God's motivations for creation, highlighting God's self-sufficiency and absolute independence. Schultz argues that understanding these concepts correctly helps to sidestep issues related to the Dionysian Principle, which states that Goodness must diffuse itself. Understanding Edwards's emanationism is also critical to ascertain the applicability of classical notions such as participation, theosis, and divinization to Edwards's view of redemption. Moreover, a proper understanding of Edwards's emanationism sheds light on the specific contents of his idealism, panentheism, continuous creationism, and occasionalism. So, he argues that an accurate interpretation of the concept of emanation, as

9. Lee, "God's Relation to the World," 64–65. See also Lee, *Philosophical Theology*, 172–73. For more information of the view of creation between Jonathan Edwards and Neoplatonism, see chapter 4 in Crisp and Strobel, *Jonathan Edwards*; chapter 1 in Stang, *Our Divine Double*; Helm, "Jonathan Edwards," 43–56; Layton, "One."

used in "End of Creation" can correct errors that have shaped the historical understanding of Edwards's works.[10]

Additionally, what is noteworthy here is that Edwards emphasizes the trinitarian characteristics in externally emanating His beauty and fullness. Edwards stresses that "all the persons of the Trinity do concur in all acts *ad extra*—as the reaction of the world."[11] So, Lee is correct when he argues that Edwards "applied his trinitarianism in his conception of God's activities *ad extra* more rigorously than his predecessors in the Western church."[12]

For Edwards, the emanated beauty of the Trinity through His work of creation is derived from His inward glory. So, in his "Dissertation Concerning the End for Which God Created the World," Edwards argues that God's absolute purpose in creation is His glory; in particular, Edwards believes that "the glorious perfections of God should be *known*, and the operations and expressions of them seen, by *other beings* besides himself."[13] In his *End of the Creation*, Edwards discusses the relationship between God's purpose of the creation and His glory. Here, again, he argues that God's end of the creation is His glory: "God made all things; and the end for which all things are made, and for which they are disposed, and for which they work continually, is that God's glory may shine forth and be received."[14] Edwards continues to state the relationship that God glorifies himself *ad intra* in two ways: the first way is "by appearing or being manifested to himself in his own perfect idea, or, in his Son, who is the brightness of his glory," and the second way is "by enjoying and delighting in himself, by flowing forth in infinite love and delight towards himself, or, in his Holy Spirit."[15] Furthermore, there are also two ways that God glorifies himself *ad extra* regarding His creature: the first way is "by appearing to them, being manifested to their understandings," and the second way is

> in communicating himself to their hearts, and in their rejoicing and delighting in, and enjoying the manifestations which he makes of himself. They both of them may be called his glory in the more extensive sense of the word, viz. his shining forth,

10. Schultz, "Neoplatonist?," 17–21.
11. *WJE* 20:238.
12. Lee, "Editor's Introduction," in *WJE* 21:33.
13. Edwards, "End," in *God's Passion*, 148.
14. *WJE* 13:496.
15. *WJE* 13:495.

> or the going forth of his excellency, beauty and essential glory *ad extra.*[16]

In other words, Edwards asserts, "both these ways of God's glorifying himself come from the same cause, viz. the overflowing of God's internal glory, or an inclination in God to cause his internal glory to flow out *ad extra.*"[17]

This relationship between God's creation and His glory is also related to the attribute of God's communication. The overflow of God's glory is to communicate His glory and beauty with the created world, and the world is created to worship His beauty, excellency, and glory through its reflected beauty of God, who communicates His beauty with the world. This understanding of the relationship between God's creation and His glory is well described in Edwards's confession.

> *God's excellency*, his wisdom, his purity and love, seemed to appear in everything; in the sun, moon and stars; in the clouds, and blue sky; in the grass, flowers, trees; in the water, and all nature; which used greatly to fix my mind. I often used to sit and view the moon, for a long time; and so in the daytime, spent much time in viewing the clouds and sky, to behold the sweet *glory of God* in these things: in the meantime, singing forth with a low voice, my contemplations of the Creator and Redeemer. . . . Formerly, nothing had been so terrible to me. I used to be a person uncommonly terrified with thunder: and it used to strike me with terror, when I saw a thunderstorm rising. But now, on the contrary, it rejoiced me. I felt God at the first appearance of a thunderstorm. And used to take the opportunity at such times, to fix myself to view the clouds, and see the lightnings play, and hear the majestic and awful voice of God's thunder: which often times was exceeding entertaining, leading me to sweet contemplations of my *great and glorious God*. And while I viewed, used to spend my time, as it always seemed natural to me, to sing or chant forth my meditations; to speak my thoughts in soliloquies, and speak with a singing voice.[18]

For Edwards, everything in the world that God created was meant to remind him of God's beauty in various ways. In terms of Edwards's understanding of God's abundant glory and emanation of glory, John Piper notes that this understanding of Edwards is "extremely important" because it shows the

16. *WJE* 13:495.
17. *WJE* 13:495–96.
18. *WJE* 16:794.

explanation of the origin of creation. Piper's observation helps us to trace Edwards's understanding on God's creation and His glory: "(1) *Creation* by God comes from (2) the abundant *diffusion* of God's glory that comes from (3) God's *inclination* to an abundant diffusion of glory that comes from (4) God's infinite *delight* in his glory. The deepest source of it all is the mysterious power of delight in God's being God."[19]

To sum up here, God is the Being who communicates His beauty. The communication of His beauty appears among the three persons of the Trinity (*ad intra*), and in His works of creation *ad extra*. The emanation of God's infinite fullness (beauty) through His creation is also closely related to His glory. God communicates His glory not only in Himself, but also *ad extra* by overflowing it. So, the world is created to worship this overflowing glory and beauty of God and to reveal his own beauty that reflects the Divine beauty.

This perspective on the relationship between God and the world can give rise to an inquiry into the nature of God's communicative attribute and how it pertains to the world. Edwards endeavors to address this inquiry by exploring the interplay between human beings, who are endowed with moral, intellectual, and spiritual faculties as created *Imago Dei*, and the beauty of God.

God's Beauty and the *Imago Dei*

For Jonathan Edwards, in God's work of creation, human beings are the most beautiful creatures who reveal and reflect the Divine's primary beauty as the head of creation and the end of it. The reason why Edwards regards human beings as the head of the secondary beauty is related to the unique nature of humanity created in the *Imago Dei*. Human beings, as they are created in the image of God, reflect His beauty in their moral and spiritual qualities, making them the uniquely beautiful beings in the created world. The beauty of humans is therefore a reflection of God's own beauty, which is the ultimate source and standard of all beauty in the world. This is closely related to their ability to reflect the beauty of God, particularly through their moral and spiritual attributes. Thus, human beings are considered the epitome of beauty in the physical world

19. Piper and Edwards, *God's Passion*, 155.

because of their unique capacity to perceive, appreciate, and express divine beauty through their moral and spiritual qualities.[20]

As we have seen above, Edwards argues that God's ultimate purpose in creation is the communication of His beauty and the manifestation of His glory. In "A Dissertation Concerning the End for Which God Created the World," he posits that God's ultimate end is the emanation and the communication of His goodness, holiness, and joy.[21] The connection between God's attribute of conveying His beauty to the world and human beings as the image of God is a crucial theme in Edwards's theological aesthetics. As bearers of the *Imago Dei*, human beings hold a unique position in receiving and reflecting God's beauty. Being created in God's image, human beings have the necessary faculties to perceive, appreciate, and respond to divine beauty, allowing them to take part in the communication of God's glory. The ability of human beings to communicate with God is based not only on their creation in His image but also in their role as recipients and reflectors of divine beauty. Edwards contends that true virtue's essence lies in the disposition to love and appreciate divine beauty. According to him, true virtue consists mainly of a supreme love for God and a disposition to value and delight in God's beauty above all other things.[22] In the true virtue, there is a "superior kind of beauty," which is "the union of heart to Being in general, or to God the Being of beings" and "benevolence to Being in general."[23] As beings created in the image of God, humans are equipped with the capacity to engage in an authentic and meaningful relationship with their Creator through the appreciation and reflection of His beauty.

In particular, as the image of God, human beings' nature to communicate with the beauty of God are related to their moral, spiritual, and intellectual nature. For Edwards, true virtue is a manifestation of divine beauty. The moral nature of humans, as described in Edwards's thought, reflects God's beauty through their virtuous actions and alignment with

20. For a more comprehensive analysis of Edwards's conceptualization of divine beauty and the *Imago Dei*, see Sweeney, *Edwards the Exegete*, 57–62.

21. *WJE* 8:433.

22. "True virtue most essentially consists in benevolence to Being in general. Or perhaps to speak more accurately, it is that consent, propensity and union of heart to Being in general, that is immediately exercised in a general good will. . . . He that has true virtue, consisting in benevolence to Being in general, and in that complacence in virtue, or moral beauty, and benevolence to virtuous being, must necessarily have a supreme love to God, both of benevolence and complacence" (*WJE* 8:540, 551).

23. *WJE* 8:571.

the general good. As humans pursue moral excellence, they embody and express the divine beauty, which is essential for their happiness and fulfillment. Moreover, Edwards argues that true virtue consists in a love for being in general, an extension of the love for God's beauty, reflecting the believer's recognition of the inherent beauty of all creation.[24] Edwards emphasized the unique moral and spiritual qualities that set human beings apart from other creatures. The beauty and excellency of the soul lie in its spirituality and immateriality, which are manifestations of divine beauty within humans.[25] Furthermore, Edwards asserts that the true excellency of a rational being consists in its knowledge and holiness, emphasizing the significance of these spiritual qualities in mirroring God's beauty.[26] For Edwards, human beings are "the highest order of God's creatures" because they are "intelligent creatures" who are characterized by their uniqueness from other creatures through their genesis in *Imago Dei*; they derive their highest elevated innate nobility through the embodiment of this divine image.[27] The reason why Edwards regards human beings as intelligent beings as the highest creature is related to God's purpose of creation. God created the world to reveal his glory; in the same sense, His creatures should glorify, worship, and meditate upon the Creator. In other words, there should be intelligent beings to enjoy the beautiful world which reflects the Creator's beauty and to glorify the Creator.

> What would this vast universe of matter, placed in such excellent order and governed by such excellent rules, be good for, if there was no intelligence that could know anything of it? Wherefore it necessarily follows that intelligent beings are the end of the creation, that their end must be to behold and admire the doings of God, and magnify him for them, and to contemplate his glories in them.[28]

As a moral, spiritual, and intellectual creature, a human being is capable of knowing, loving, enjoying God's beauty, and glorify God through these abilities. In this sense, Sang Hyun Lee notes that "according to Edwards, God created human beings who can repeat God's internal knowledge and love in their own knowing and loving, as well as the physical universe,

24. *WJE* 8:540.
25. *WJE* 8:548.
26. *WJE* 2:257.
27. *WJE* 23:203.
28. *WJE* 13:185.

which, with the help of human perception of it as the image of God's beauty, can shine forth God's glory in its own way."[29]

Edwards's Biblical Interpretations on the Beauty of God's Creation

God's Beauty and His Creation

Edwards makes it clear that the Trinity created not only the visible but also the invisible world.[30] He devotes a great deal of effort to rational and philosophical approaches to God's creation and His beauty, but never loses sight of the fact that Scripture stands above all rational judgment. In his treatise "The End for Which God Created the World," he concludes the first half of it with a rational consideration of God's end in His creation. Edwards asserts that rational apologetics helps to defend Christian beliefs against rational attacks by providing logical support, and at the same time, ensuring that the teachings of the Bible are not irrational. However, he maintains that human reason has clear limitations, and therefore, the surest guide of revelation is absolutely necessary.

> I confess there is a degree of indistinctness and obscurity in the close consideration of such subjects and a great imperfection in the expressions we use concerning them, arising unavoidably from the infinite sublimity of the subject and the incomprehensibleness of those things that are divine. Hence revelation is the surest guide in these matters.[31]

In this sense, Edwards argues that upon scrutinizing the Scriptures, it becomes evident that God persistently identifies himself as the consummate

29. *WJE* 21:37.

30. "All the glory evidently belongs to God, all is in a mere, and most absolute and divine dependence on the Father, Son, and Holy Ghost. And each person of the Trinity is equally glorified in this work. There is an absolute dependence of the creature on every one for all: all is of the Father, all through the Son, and all in the Holy Ghost. Thus God appears in the work of redemption, as all in all. 'Tis fit that he that 'is, and there is none else' [Deuteronomy 4:35], should be the 'Alpha and Omega, the first and the last' [Revelation 1:11], the all and the only, in this work" (*WJE* 17:212). See also *WJE* 25:63, where Edwards quotes Colossians: "For by him were all things created that are in heaven, and that are in earth, visible and invisible; whether they be thrones, or dominions, or principalities, or powers, all things were created by him and for him" (Col 1:16 KJV).

31. Edwards, "End," 181.

goal in all his works, insinuating that the entity functioning as the "first cause of all things" concurrently represents the "supreme and last end of all things."[32] For Edwards, the most important fact is that "God hath made all things for himself [Prov 16:4], and in the Revelation [Rev 4:11] it is said, they are created for God's pleasure." Moreover, all things "are made that God may in them have occasion to fulfill his good pleasure, in manifesting and communicating himself. In this God takes delight, and for the sake of this delight God creates the world." At the same time, he clarifies the order and relationship between the Creator and creatures: "But this delight is not properly from the creature's communication to God, but in his to the creature; it is a delight in his own act. Let us explain the matter how we will, there is no way that the world can be 'for' God more than [this]; for it can't be so for him, as that he can receive anything from the creature."[33]

In his sermon "God's Excellencies" (1720), interpreting Psalm 89:6, Edwards derives the doctrine that "God is infinitely exalted in gloriousness and excellency above all created beings."[34] Edwards, by interpreting this passage, attempts "to exhibit and set forth the greatness, gloriousness, and transcendent excellency of that God who made us, and whom we worship and adore."[35] God is infinitely exalted for all creatures because of His greatness. His excellency and loveliness are greater than anything else because all other excellencies arise from God. Edwards uses the analogy of the sun and its rays to describe God as the source of all glory and beauty. Just as every single ray comes from the sun, every excellency and

32. Edwards, "End," 183–84. Edwards cited the following biblical passages to support his arguments. God makes himself as the first cause of creation: "Thus saith the Lord, the king of Israel, and his Redeemer the LORD of hosts, I am the first, I also am the last, and besides me there is no God" (Isa 44:6); "I am the first and I am the last" (48:12); "I am Alpha and Omega, the beginning and the ending, saith the Lord, which is, and was, and which is to come, the Almighty" (Rev 1:8); "I am Alpha and Omega, the first and the last" (1:11); "I am the first and the last" (1:17); "And he said unto me, it is done; I am Alpha and Omega, the beginning and the end" (21:6); and "I am Alpha and Omega, the beginning and the end, the first and the last" (22:13). God makes himself as the last end of creation: "For of him, and through him, and to him, are all things" (Rom 11:36); "For by him were all things created, that are in heaven, and that are in earth, visible and invisible, whether they be thrones, or dominions, or principalities, or powers; all things were created by him, and for him" (Col 1:16); "For it became him, by whom are all things, and for whom are all things" (Heb 2:10); and in Proverbs, it is said expressly, "The LORD hath made all things for himself" (Prov 16:4). See *WJE* 8:467.

33. *WJE* 13:496.

34. *WJE* 10:416.

35. *WJE* 10:416.

beauty of the created world comes from God. In the same sense, just as the whole sun is more excellent than each single ray, God is more excellent than all other things.[36]

Edwards recognizes the beauty and excellency of the created world. However, by quoting Job 25:5, "Behold even to the moon, and it shineth not; Yea, the stars are not pure in his sight" (KJV), he argues that all the beauty of the created world, which seems transcendentally excellent, pales in comparison to the excellency of God.[37] He emphasizes that "God's is an infinite excellency, infinite glory, and beauty itself; he is an infinite, eternal, and immutable excellency; he is not only an infinitely excellent being, but a being that is infinite excellency, beauty, and loveliness."[38]

One of the most important terms Edwards uses when addressing biblical passages that make statements about God's end for creation is His glory. In his biblical interpretation of Isaiah 48:11,[39] he emphasizes the fact that God's name and His glory are used interchangeably and the ultimate end of creation is for God Himself.[40] By emphasizing and repeating the statement, "for my own sake," he explains that everything God does is for his own sake and for his own glory. Furthermore, interpreting Romans 11:36,[41] he argues that the way all things exist in relation to God is

36. *WJE* 10:419–20.

37. *WJE* 10:421. "The beauty of trees, plants, and flowers, with which God has bespangled the face of the earth, is delightful; the beautiful frame of the body of man, especially in its perfection, is astonishing; the beauty of the moon and stars is wonderful; the beauty of [the] highest heavens is transcendent; the excellency of angels and the saints in light is very glorious: but it is all deformity and darkness in comparison of the brighter glories and beauties of the Creator of all, for 'behold even to the moon, and it shineth not' (Job 25:5); that is, think of the excellency of God and the moon will not seem to shine to you, God's excellency so much outshines [it]. And the stars are not pure in his sight, and so we know that at the great day when God appears, the sun shall be turned into darkness, shall hide his face as if he were ashamed to see himself so much outshined; and the very angels, they hide their faces before him; the highest heavens are not clean in his sight, and he charges his angels with folly" (*WJE* 10:421).

38. *WJE* 10:421.

39. "For mine own sake, even for mine own sake, will I do it: For how should my name be polluted? And I will not give my glory unto another" (Isa 48:11 KJV).

40. According to David P. Barshinger, "Edwards taught that God's 'name' represents his glory and perfections and that he created the world to make known his name, a teaching to which the Psalms frequently testify (Pss 23:3; 31:3; 109:21; 25:11; 79:9; 106:8; 76:1; 148:13; 135:13)" (Barshinger, *Psalms*, 84). Moreover, he provides various statements from Edwards on passages regarding God's name and glory from his "Blank Bible."

41. "For of him, and through him, and to him, are all things: to whom be glory for ever. Amen" (Rom 11:36 KJV).

for God's glory. God has excellently planned for all things to glorify Him, and God is fulfilling His own purposes for His own glory by caring for all things in His providence.[42]

Edwards elaborates on God's glory (Δοξα, כָּבוֹד) and His creation in his *Miscellanies*. God has a propensity to reveal and communicate Himself, which the Bible describes as His propensity to glorify Himself.

> *A disposition to make an object, that it may be loved and that we may have good will towards*, must be prior to another, and properly distinct from love and goodwill itself. It may be an excellent quality. But it must be [a] quality of some other denomination. If it be called goodness and grace, it must be in a less proper sense. To desire new beings to communicate happiness to 'em, especially without increasing the sum of happiness, don't agree with the notion mankind have of goodness, benevolence, grace, etc. Men may call this disposition in the heart of God by the name of goodness if they please. But 'tis properly referred to another perfection, of which it is one sort of exercise, viz. *the disposition that is in the infinite fountain of good, and of glory and excellency*, to shine forth or to flow out, *which shining forth or flowing out of God's infinite fullness is called God's glory in Scripture.*[43]

Edwards argues that God has a disposition to exert His perfection, and as a consequence of it, He also has a disposition to communicate Himself *ad extra*. However, in that God makes Himself His end, both dispositions are reverted to the single disposition—God's glory, He exerts and communicates Himself.[44]

Furthermore, in his sermon on Exodus 33:18–19, Edwards notes that God's attribute to communicate unites God to His creature.[45] Edwards explains that God's goodness is His love and grace toward His creature. As the Lover, God is united to the beloved by His love. He continues that "by this attribute, God tends to communicate of himself of his own Excellency & happiness to the [c]reature & to bring the [c]reature near to him."[46] This biblical interpretation of Edwards shows that God's attributes

42. Edwards, "End," 195–96.

43. *WJE* 23:151–52 (italics added).

44. *WJE* 23:153.

45. *WJEO* 46.202. "And he said, I beseech thee, shew me thy glory. And he said, I will make all my goodness pass before thee, and I will proclaim the name of the LORD before thee; and will be gracious to whom I will be gracious, and will shew mercy on whom I will shew mercy" (Exod 33:18–19 KJV).

46. *WJEO* 46.202.

to communicate and reveal his beauty (or excellency) are intimately connected to His work of creation.

God's Beauty and the *Imago Dei*

In the biblical interpretation of Jonathan Edwards, three important themes are discovered regarding God's beauty and the beauty of man as *Imago Dei*: intelligence, glory, and holiness. Since the Creator is the communicative Being, He created human beings as intelligent beings to communicate with God. Firstly, man's attribute of intelligence is related to his soul. Edwards reveals that God created both the material and spiritual world.[47] But, human beings are a more special creature than any other creatures. He argues that although God created both human physical bodies and souls, "their souls are in a special and more immediate manner his workmanship."[48] Edwards brings quite a number of biblical passages to reveal the fact that the human soul is one of the masterpieces of God. For instance, he draws upon Ecclesiastes 12:7 to argue that God created the body of human beings with preexisting matter; however, "God is represented as having immediately given or implanted the soul, as in that respect differing from the body, that is of preexistent matter."[49] Moreover, the Bible testifies that God is "Father of our spirits (Hebrews 12:9)," "the God of the spirits of all flesh (Numbers 16:22; 27:16)," and "He that formeth the spirit of man within him (Zechariah 12:1)." He continues, as Genesis 2:7 said, God "breathed into his nostrils the breath of life (whereby something was communicated from an infinitely higher source, even God's own living spirit or divine vital fullness), 'and so man became a living soul.'"[50] In this sense, Edwards claims that due to their souls human beings are infinitely distinguished from all other creatures:

> As the souls of men are more directly from God, by the more special and immediate exercise of his divine power as a creator, and are what he challenges as his by a special propriety, and are the most noble part of the lower creation, and are infinitely

47. *WJE* 25:63–64. "For by him were all things created that are in heaven, and that are in earth, visible and invisible; whether they be thrones, or dominions, or principalities, or powers, all things were created by him and for him" (Col 1:16 KJV).

48. *WJE* 25:64.

49. *WJE* 25:64. "Then shall the dust return to the earth as it was, and the spirit shall return unto God who gave it" (Eccl 12:7 KJV).

50. *WJE* 25:64–65.

> distinguished from all other creatures here below in that they are immortal beings; so they are, above all other creatures which God hath made in this world, the subjects of God's care and special providence.[51]

According to Edwards, God's common providence is provided to all creatures, but His special providence is just for "His intelligent rational creatures, as moral agents."[52] He affirms that only human beings are this kind of creature because reason, intellect, and a capacity of moral agency are directly seated in humans alone.

In his sermon, "The Pure in Heart Blessed (1753)," Edwards notes that one sees God not with physical eyes; rather, it is "an intellectual view by which God is seen."[53] Based on Hebrews 11:27; Colossians 1:15; and 1 Timothy 1:17, he notes that God is invisible. At the same time, he presents biblical passages which testify that God has revealed Himself to His people.[54] Edwards argues that human reason is "an heavenly ray" and "the candle of the Lord" mentioned in Proverbs 20:27, and "it is that wherein mainly consists the natural image of God."[55] Moreover, in his sermon on Job 31:3, he also argues that human reason "is the natural image of God in man," which "is the highest faculty in man and is designed by our maker to ever rule and exalt sense, imagination, and passion, which were made to be servants."[56] Here, Edwards's term "*the natural image*" denotes human intelligence such as reason and understanding. He clearly limits human beings' seeing of God. According to Edwards, in the quest to truly

51. *WJE* 25:65.

52. *WJE* 25:65.

53. *WJE* 17:59–63.

54. "God was wont to manifest himself of old in outward glorious appearances. There was a shining light that was called the glory of the Lord; thus the glory of the Lord was said to descend on the mount and on the tabernacle of the congregation [*Exodus 19:17–19*; *Exodus 33:9–10*]. There was an outward visible token of God's presence; and the seventy [elders], when they saw God in the [mount], they saw a visible shape [*Exodus 24:9–11*]. And it seems [that] when Moses desired to see God's glory, [he stood upon a rock] and he saw God's back parts when God passed by [and covered Moses] with his hand in the hole of the rock (*Exodus 33:18–23*); [Moses] saw some visible glory. But it was so God [might there] condescend to the infant state of the church and to the childish notions that were entertained [in] those days of lesser light; and Moses' request [seems to have been more clearly] answered by God's making his goodness to [pass before] him, and proclaiming his name, and giving [a clear sense] of mind of those things contained in that name, than in showing him [a form of outward] glory" (*WJE* 17:62).

55. *WJE* 17:67.

56. *WJE* 10:195.

understand and apprehend God, it is crucial to recognize that not all forms of comprehension can be considered genuine seeing of God. While education and instruction provide us with foundational knowledge about God's existence, attributes, and deeds, merely accepting this information without further personal exploration fails to deliver the beatific, happifying sight of God as described in Scripture. Similarly, relying solely on speculative reasoning to deduce God's nature as almighty, all-wise, and good is not enough to attain a true spiritual connection with the divine. Rather, the Scripture suggests that a more immediate, experiential form of understanding and viewing is necessary to truly see God and achieve a state of spiritual bliss.

For Edwards, seeing of God is "to have an immediate and certain understanding of God's excellency and love."[57] God granted humans understanding, enabling them to experience delights and happiness through intellectual pleasure and love for God's supreme excellency. The delight of the intellect of humans lies in the observation of spiritual merits and aesthetic qualities; "but the glorious excellency and beauty of God, they are far the greatest." So, Edwards argues that "the pleasure the soul has in seeing God is not only its pleasure, but it is at the same time its highest perfection and excellency."[58]

Edwards goes on to explain how God's eternal beauty relates to human creation. Since "God made men to endure for ever,"[59] God's beauty and excellency should be eternally never-failing. Drawing on Jeremiah 31:3 and Isaiah 26:4; 60:19, he argues that the beauty, excellence, glory, and love of God remain constant and unalterable, allowing humans the opportunity to experience these divine attributes eternally:

> He that has the immediate intellectual views of God's glory and love, and rejoices in that, his happiness is built upon an everlasting rock; *Isaiah 26:4*, "Trust ye in the Lord for ever: for in the Lord Jehovah is everlasting strength." In the Hebrew it is, "in the Lord Jehovah is the rock of ages" The glory of God is a thing subject to no changes or vicissitudes. It will never cease to shine forth. History gives us accounts of the sun's light failing and being more faint and dim for many months together, but the glory of God never will be subject to fade. There never will be any

57. *WJE* 17:64. For a detailed discussion of Edwards's understanding on beatific vision, see chapter 7 of this book.

58. *WJE* 17:68.

59. *WJE* 17:73.

> eclipse or dimness, but it will shine eternally in its strength; *Isaiah 60:19*, "The Lord shall be unto thee thine everlasting light." So the love of God, to [those] that see his face, it will never be subject to any coolings. He loves his saints with an everlasting love; *Jeremiah 31:3*, "I have loved thee with an everlasting love."[60]

Furthermore, in his *Blank Bible,* Edwards reveals the relationship between wisdom (or knowledge) and excellency (or beauty) through his biblical interpretation of Ecclesiastes 7:11–12.[61] He argues that the translation of הַכֶּסֶף בְּצֵל הַחָכְמָה בְּצֵל כִּי is more accurately translated as "wisdom is a shadow, and money is a shadow" rather than "wisdom is a defense, and money is a defense" because God's wisdom is "not only a defense, but a comfort and refreshment."

In an ongoing manner, the succeeding verse elaborates on the premise stated in the prior verse, (namely wisdom is more excellent). This is done by repetitively utilizing words originating from the same root ("יֹתֵר" and "יִתְרוֹן"), thereby underlining the assertion that wisdom holds superiority and is remarkably excellent.[62]

To summarize, Edwards reveals, through a variety of biblical passages, that God created humans in the image of God, with intelligence and wisdom to communicate His beauty. And, human intelligence and wisdom is the most excellent attribute of humans as they reflect the image of God.

Then, the question follows, how does the intellectual ability that humans possess as the image of God relate to God's unique beauty? Edwards finds the answer to this question in the glory of God and man's glorification of God. According to Edwards, the final end for the creation of the good moral world revealed in the Holy Scripture is the glory of God:

> The glory of God is spoken of as the end of God's saints, the end for which he makes them. . . . It is said that God has made and formed them to be his sons and daughters for his own glory, that they are trees of his planting, the work of his hands, as trees of righteousness, that he might be glorified. . . . [T]hey will appear

60. *WJE* 17:73.

61. The original passage in the King James Version reads: "Wisdom is good with an inheritance: and by it there is profit to them that see the sun. For wisdom is a defence, and money is a defence: but the excellency of knowledge is, that wisdom giveth life to them that have it." However, Edwards quotes it as "the excellency of wisdom" instead of "the excellency of knowledge" (*WJE* 24:593).

62. *WJE* 24:593–94.

> rather as promises of making God's people happy, that God therein might be glorified.[63]

Edwards emphasizes the profound connection between the glory of God and mankind. Drawing from various biblical passages, he highlights that the glory of God serves as the ultimate purpose for the creation of the moral world's virtuous aspects. Edwards cites passages such as Isaiah 43:6–7; 60:21; and 61:3 to demonstrate that God created human beings for His glory. He elucidates the relationship between God's promise found in these passages—God will lead His people to exceptional happiness—and God's glory.

> It is said that God has made and formed them to be his sons and daughters for his own glory, that they are trees of his planting, the work of his hands, as trees of righteousness, that he might be glorified. . . . They will appear rather as promises of making God's people happy, that God therein might be glorified. . . . All the preceding promises are plainly mentioned as so many parts, or constituents, of the great and exceeding happiness of God's people; and God's glory is mentioned as the sum of his design in this happiness. . . . The work of God promised to be effected is plainly an accomplishment of the joy, gladness, and happiness of God's people, instead of their mourning and sorrow; and the end in which God's design in this work is obtained and summed up is his glory. This proves, by the seventh position, that God's glory is the end of the creation.[64]

Edwards emphasizes the inseparability of God's glory and human happiness through the examination of various biblical promises. In Isaiah 43, God promises to deliver His people from misery and bring them happiness,[65] ultimately for His own glory. Similarly, in Isaiah 60:21 and

63. Edwards, "End," 192–93.

64. Edwards, "End," 192–94.

65. Edwards states that "happiness is the end of the creation" because it is deeply related into the chief end of man—to glorify God, and to enjoy him forever: "HAPPINESS IS THE END OF THE CREATION . . . For certainly it was the goodness of the Creator that moved him to create; and how can we conceive of another end proposed by goodness, than that he might delight in seeing the creatures he made rejoice in that being that he has given them? It appears also by this, because the end of the creation is that the creation might glorify him. Now what is glorifying God, but a rejoicing at that glory he has displayed? An understanding of the perfections of God, merely, cannot be the end of the creation; for he had as good not understand it, as see it and not be at all moved with joy at the sight. Neither can the highest end of the creation be the declaring God's glory to others; for the declaring God's glory is good for nothing otherwise than to raise joy in ourselves and others at what is declared" (*WJE* 13:199–200).

61:3, God commits to providing future happiness for His people, with His glory as the ultimate objective. Therefore, Edwards asserts, based on biblical passages such as 1 Corinthians 10:31; 1 Peter 4:11; Leviticus 10:3; and Ezekiel 28:22, that the duty of human beings created in the glory of God as their ultimate end.[66] Furthermore, in terms of the relationship between human satisfaction and God's beauty, Edwards interprets Ephesians 3:19 that "the meaning seems to be, that ye might have your souls satisfied with a participation of God's own good, his beauty and joy."[67]

Another attribute that Edwards finds in Scripture that relates to beauty of the *Imago Dei* is the spiritual image of God, i.e., holiness and righteousness. In his sermon on Genesis 3:24, "East of Eden" (1731), Edwards reveals two kind of image of God. One is the natural image of God, which is reason and understanding as we have seen above, and another is the spiritual image of God. Edwards elucidates that in the initial creation of man, his mind embodied the immaculate spiritual image of God, epitomizing unparalleled splendor, unblemished and devoid of any deformity in righteousness and holiness—man's spiritual beauty bestowed by God:

> Man then had excellent endowments. His mind shone with the perfect spiritual image of God, being without any defect in its holiness and righteousness, or any spot or wrinkle to mar its spiritual beauty. God had put his own beauty upon it; it shone with the communication of his glory. And man enjoyed uninterrupted spiritual peace and joy that hence arose. His mind was full of spiritual light and peace as the atmosphere in a clear and calm day.[68]

Edwards makes the same point in another sermon about human holiness and righteousness as a spiritual image of God's beauty. In his sermon, "God Glorified in Man's Dependence (1 Corinthians 1:29–31)" (1731), he argues that man had an original righteousness granted by God in the initial state. God, in His holiness, created man to be holy, and man was totally dependent on God for his holiness.[69]

To sum up, Edwards emphasizes the significance of man as the image of God, showcasing his divine attributes such as intelligence, glory, and holiness and righteousness. Central to this concept is the idea that the pinnacle of God's beauty is holiness, and the highest honor for humans

66. Edwards, "End," 195–98.

67. *WJE* 15:186.

68. *WJE* 17:334.

69. *WJE* 17:204.

is to embody this holiness, conforming to the image of God. This divine image is reflected in the human being's inherent excellency, stemming from God's creation of man as an understanding creature. According to Edwards, man's reason and intelligence form the natural image of God, granting him the capacity for intellectual delight and the ability to appreciate God's glory and beauty. The human mind, in its original state, was adorned with the perfect spiritual image of God, characterized by unblemished holiness and righteousness, reflecting the divine glory. In other words, as the image of God, the natural image of man represents the faculties of reason and understanding, while the spiritual image of man refers to man's initial holiness and righteousness, embodying the essence of divine beauty.

Edwards's Studies on Beauty and the Fall

As with Augustine in his *Confessions,* Edwards does not try to find beauty in human depravity and sinfulness per se.[70] In the light of previous discussion, it can be postulated that God is the pinnacle of true beauty. Correspondingly, the sin committed by human beings, which reflects a conscious choice to sever ties with God and pursue their lives disconnected from Him, signifies a deviation from this sublime beauty and excellency inherent in God. So, Edwards's primary focus does not revolve around the connection between sin and beauty; instead, he ponders the resilience of beauty in the aftermath of the Fall. This understanding of Edwards channels his thoughts into two principal streams: Firstly, his understanding of the typology addressing the persisting fragments of the beauty of the created world. Secondly, the beauty of the redemptive work of Jesus Christ, who recovers the beauty of God's beautiful creatures corrupted by sin. Furthermore, Edwards regards the redemption of Christ

70. Reflecting upon the transgression of theft, an act he was guilty of in his youth, Augustine humbly admits that there was a complete absence of beauty in the sin. Delving into specifics, he articulates that his sin was devoid of any splendor pertaining to justice or wisdom. Moreover, this transgression did not uphold the beauty innate to the human soul, memory, and sensory apparatus, nor did it respect the physical existence of life. It neglected the enchanting beauty of the cosmos, exemplified by the radiant stars, each resplendent in its designated position. It overlooked the allure of the terrestrial world and the oceans, teeming with myriad forms of life, constantly undergoing the cyclical process of creation and destruction. Furthermore, Augustine emphasizes that the sin did not even possess a semblance of imperfect or shadowy beauty. See Augustine, *Confessions* 2.6.12.

as not merely the restoration of broken beauty, but the culmination of beauty that allows God's beauty and glory to shine more brightly. Therefore, in the final part of this chapter we will examine Edwards's biblical interpretation of human depravity and beauty, as well as the connection between his typology and beauty, before turning to the beauty of the Redeemer, Jesus Christ, in the next chapter.

Edwards's Philosophical Examination of the Beauty and the Fall—Typology[71]

As we have seen above, Edwards does not find beauty in the Fall itself. Furthermore, his statements about the Fall and beauty are mostly based on biblical interpretation, so it is not easy to see his rational philosophical work on the subject. His typology is also largely based on biblical interpretation. Nevertheless, Edwards's statements about beauty as a type left in general revelation after the Fall are noteworthy. Therefore, in this section, we will briefly examine his typological understanding of beauty left in the postlapsarian world before moving on to his testament of Scripture to explore this topic in more detail.

Edwards has no doubt that God has retained His beauty in the postlapsarian world after the Fall. In *The Miscellanies,* he asserts that our reason tells us of our fallen human state and, at the same time, of God's desire for reconciliation. God's continual generosity serves as evidence of this. This is seen in the world through structures designed for our well-being and an outpouring of divine wisdom and power. If God were against mankind, the continuous application of wisdom and power for humanity's benefit over millennia would seem inconsistent. Furthermore, evidence of God's benevolence isn't confined to the Bible but is evident in natural phenomena. Hence, Edwards argues that through nature, God has provided tangible proof of his benevolent intention and desire to reconcile with humanity.[72] In this sense, for Edwards, the tangible proof of God's favor exists in the postlapsarian world as types.

71. The purpose of this section is not to present Edwards's typology in its entirety, but to cover some of the aspects of Edwards's theological aesthetics that are revealed in his typology. See the following primary and secondary sources on Edwards's typology: *WJE* 11; Knight, "Typology," 190–209; McClymond and McDermott, *Theology of Jonathan Edwards,* 116–29; Nichols, "Typology," 575–77; Batschelet, "Use of Typology"; Kloosterman, "Use of Typology," 59–96; McDermott, "Types in Nature," 271–83.

72. *WJE* 13:280–81.

Edwards believes that "the whole universe, heaven and earth, air and seas, and the divine constitution and history of the holy Scriptures, be full of images of divine things, as full as a language is of words."[73] As can be verified from this statements, Edwards not only goes beyond finding the meaning of the New Testament with types that appear in the Old Testament, but is also convinced that there are types in the created world to convey God's excellency, beauty, glory, and favor. According to Edwards, in the natural world, God employs a method where inferior entities are molded in alignment and analogy with their superior counterparts, thereby serving as their representations. This implies that the less prominent and somewhat obscure aspects of His works are imbued with the capacity to symbolize those elements that are more substantial, superior, spiritual, and divine. In essence, these representations provide a direct reflection of Himself and the most elevated facets of His work.[74]

Since God is a communicative Being who has an attribute to share His perfection, and fallen humans perceive beauty and feel joy and pleasure through what they sense with their physical sensory organs, and experience, God teaches them through types.[75] It is noteworthy that McClymond and McDermott introduce the aesthetic evidence as one of four important rationales of Edwards's belief. "The world was almost as full of evidence for this system of correspondences as it was of the types themselves," they note. "Edwards connected types to the arts. Both, he explained, appeal to the same aesthetic and erotic capacities. Each uses the principle of *mimesis* and fulfills human desires for the dramatic and the beautiful. Types, then, are a part of the divine aesthetic, the way in which God unites pedagogy and aesthetics."[76]

73. *WJE* 11:152.

74. *WJE* 13:434; 11:55.

75. *WJE* 11:191; 14:140.

76. The four reasons are as follows: the system in scripture, the natural world itself, the teleological reason, and the aesthetic evidence. Examining *The Nature of True Virtue,* McClymond and McDermott analyze that Edwards proposes that *secondary beauty*, visible in things like plants, architecture, and music, arises from the harmony or union of different elements. Moreover, they continue, Edwards equates this to the spiritual unity seen in a celestial society of diverse minds, united by benevolence, and although this doesn't conclusively establish the typological nature of secondary beauty, it supports the possibility of its existence. Thus, they explain that Edwards suggests it would be logical for this typological system to exist if all secondary beauty's origin and pattern is beauty itself. See McClymond and McDermott, *Theology of Jonathan Edwards*, 119–22, 124.

In short, although the world has lost its initial excellency and beauty as the world created by God, there are still inferior beauties in the post-lapsarian world that is representative of far superior beauties.

Edwards's Biblical Interpretations on Beauty and the Fall

In his various sermons, in particular, the second sermon of his book *A History of the Work of Redemption* and his sermon "East of Eden," Edwards delineates the stark contrast between the created world before and after the Fall. By conducting an exegetical analysis of Genesis 1–3, he construes that the world prior to the Fall was suffused with the light of the knowledge, glory, and favor of God.[77] Furthermore, prior to the Fall, humanity basked in the perpetual radiance of God's countenance, with divine providence amply furnishing all that was necessary to satiate the needs of the soul. Beyond spiritual sufficiency, mankind was also endowed with impeccable beauty, both in terms of intellectual capacity, symbolized by reason, and in physical body:

> Man was rich in a fullness of outward blessings. Everything around him poured in delight and gladness into his soul. The visible world and all the fullness of it was contrived to cheer and delight his senses. And the senses themselves and all the organs of the body were without doubt in a perfect vigor and sprightliness, and the form of the body exquisitely beautiful. And his soul was in a very perfect state, the faculties of it in full strength, not broken, impaired, and weakened and ruined, as they are now. The soul of man with regard to the quickness and clearness of its faculties was then like the heavenly intelligences—as a flame of fire. The natural image of God that consists in reason and understanding was then complete. And man then had excellent endowments. His mind shone with the perfect spiritual image of God, being without any defect in its holiness and righteousness, or any spot or wrinkle to mar its spiritual beauty. God had put his own beauty upon it; it shone with the communication of his glory. . . . Man enjoyed the favor of God and smiles of heaven; there were smiles without any frowns. He had communion with God; God was wont to come to him and converse as a friend and father.[78]

77. *WJE* 9:133.

78. *WJE* 17:333–34.

Humanity in a prelapsarian status, has cognitive capabilities reflecting divine intelligence and righteousness. This ideal existence was characterized by an intimate, harmonious relationship with God, filled with divine favor and friendship.

However, subsequent to mankind's Fall, this luminescence was extinguished, leading to the world being shrouded in an encompassing darkness. This condition of profound gloom exceeded the initial state of the world described in Genesis 1:2, representing a state of despair so severe that neither angel nor human had the capacity to alleviate it. Edwards elaborates that before the faintest flicker of divine light emerged from God's Word in Genesis 3:15, the world existed in a state of profound darkness, devoid of the slightest comfort or semblance of hope.[79] Moreover, following the Fall, humans suffered a severe estrangement from God, culminating in the loss of divine grace, magnificence, and favor, metaphorically described as God's smile.[80] As mankind forfeited God's love, they concurrently lost their love for holiness, resulting in the cessation of deriving joy and happiness from practicing holiness and enjoying communion with God. Consequently, the beautiful creation lost its beauty and became "sinful and loathsome."[81]

This interpretation of Genesis, when viewed in the light of Edwards's theological aesthetics, can be interpreted as a cessation of God-supplied spiritual light after the Fall, which in turn can be interpreted as a cutoff of all spiritual beauty supplied by a communicating God. In other words, the reason the world is beautiful is due to the secondary beauty that abundantly reflects the beauty provided by God. However, with human corruption came complete spiritual darkness, causing the created world to lose the light of beauty it once reflected in its vibrant colors. This loss of beauty also means a loss of man's beauty that he has as the *Imago Dei*. Edwards explains that after the Fall, man is not only devoid of any true excellence, but he is also an entirely polluted being who is infinitely offensive, and thus man is the object of God's displeasure.[82] Furthermore,

79. *WJE* 9:133.

80. "The earth lost its beauty and pleasantness. There was a curse brought upon it; there was, as it were, a deathly darkness brought upon things here below. The tokens of the presence and blessing of God were taken away. His smiles were gone and the tokens of his anger were everywhere seen. That bloom and beauty and joy that all nature seemed to [be] clothed with was gone" (*WJE* 17:334).

81. *WJE* 17:336.

82. See his sermon, "God Glorified in Man's Dependence (1 Corinthians 1:29–31)," in *WJE* 17:204.

"man lost the soundness and vigor and luster of his own body" and lost "his highest excellency and the proper glory of human nature, viz. his original righteousness and the spiritual image of God."[83] Edwards continues to explain that this loss of human beauty led to a loss of communion with God and His favor, blessing, and love.[84]

> We are little, despicable creatures, and mean worms of the dust, as nothing and less than nothing before God. Such a sense Abraham expressed, Genesis 18:27, "Abraham answered and said, Behold now, I have taken upon me to speak unto the Lord, which am but dust and ashes." . . . Man had this sort of comparative littleness before the Fall; he was then infinitely little and mean in comparison with God. But his natural meanness is become much greater since the Fall. That moral ruin under which his nature has fallen has greatly impaired his natural faculties, though it has not extinguished them. . . . Fallen man is infinitely different from God in both these respects; both as little and as filthy.[85]

Therefore, humans have become unable to rejoice in God's excellence, beauty, and glory as abundantly and clearly as they could before the fall.[86]

Based on the biblical interpretation of Deuteronomy 28:63 and Ezekiel 5:13, Edwards states that the Bible reveals that God takes pleasure in punishing sin.[87] Nevertheless, he continues that what is intrinsically pleasing to God is to do good to creatures, to be merciful to them, and that, in other words, creature misery is intrinsically inconsistent with God's pleasure. Citing numerous biblical passages, Edwards argues that they support the idea that God delights to show His mercy toward His creatures.[88] However, this mercy of God is predicated on one clear light—

83. *WJE* 17:334.

84. *WJE* 17:335.

85. *WJE* 8:234–36.

86. *WJE* 17:68.

87. Edwards, "End," 221. "The Lord will rejoice over you, to destroy you" (Deut 28:63 KJV); "Then shall mine anger be accomplished, and I will cause my fury to rest upon them, and I will be comforted" (Ezek 5:13 KJV).

88. Edwards quotes the following passages to support his explanation: "Thou art a God ready to pardon, gracious and merciful, slow to anger, and of great kindness" (Neh 9:17); "The LORD is merciful and gracious, slow to anger, and plenteous in mercy" (Ps 103:8); "The LORD is gracious and full of compassion, slow to anger, and of great mercy" (Ps 145:8). We have again almost the same words: "Who is a God like unto thee, that pardoneth iniquity, &c. He retaineth not his anger for ever, because he delighteth in mercy" (Jonah 4:2; Mic 7:18); "I have no pleasure in the death of him that dieth, saith the LORD God; wherefore turn yourselves, and live ye" (Ezek 18:32); "He doth

the revelation of the gospel to man after the Fall. Edwards explains that this revelation of salvation in the gospel was designed by God in His love so that humans would not be left without hope because of the verdict of condemnation in Genesis 3:16–24.[89] With the Fall of man, the light of excellency and beauty that the created world had received from God was lost, but God preserved the world from losing its beauty by giving it the light of the revelation of redemption (the covenant of redemption).[90] According to Edwards, "from the fall of man till the incarnation of Christ, God was doing those things that were preparatory to Christ's coming and working out redemption and were forerunners and earnests. . . . Soon after [the Fall] the custom of sacrificing was appointed to be a standing type of the sacrifice of Christ till he should come and offer up himself a sacrifice to God."[91] At this point, Edwards's overarching understanding of the beauty which left in the postlapsarian world is revealed in his understanding of typology.

Edwards goes beyond simply interpreting the types of Christ in the Old Testament (for example, seeing King David as a foreshadowing of Christ) and believes that glimpses of God's beauty can be found in nature. In order to support his argument, Edwards cites a number of biblical passages; for example, he uses passages like Jeremiah 17:8; Psalm 1:3; and Numbers 24:6 to argue that an ever-flowing river represents the goodness of God and the abundance of the saints:

> And so likewise are rivers which are ever-flowing, that empty vast quantities of water every day and yet there is never the less to come. The Spirit communicated and shed abroad, that is to say, the goodness of God, is in Scripture compared to a river; and the trees that grow and flourish by the river's side through the benefit of the water, represent the saints who live upon

not afflict willingly, nor grieve the children of men" (Lam 3:33); "As I live, saith the LORD God, I have no pleasure in the death of the wicked, but that the wicked turn from his way and live: turn ye, turn ye from your evil ways; for why will ye die, O house of Israel!" (Ezek 33:11); and "Not willing that any should perish, but that all should come to repentance" (2 Pet 3:9). See Edwards, "End," 221.

89. As Edwards puts is, the Fall has led to "banishment from the garden, sorrow, subjection, toil, etc." (*WJE* 9:133n7).

90. The loss of beauty does not refer to the complete absence of beauty. Rather, it speaks of the loss of the true beauty that humans possessed as the spiritual image of God before the Fall (e.g., true virtue). While the primary beauty was lost due to the fall, the secondary beauty remained, albeit in an imperfect and corrupted form.

91. *WJE* 9:134.

> Christ and flourish through the influences of his Spirit. *Jeremiah 17:8, Psalms 1:3, Numbers 24:6.*[92]

He also argues that natural phenomena such as storms, waves, and thunder reveal God's wrath and majesty; moreover, in the same way some kinds of created things reveal God's mild attributes.

> The waves and billows of the sea in a storm and the dire cataracts there are of rivers have a representation of the terrible wrath of God, and amazing misery of [them] that endure it. Misery is often compared to waters in the Scripture—a being overwhelmed in waters. God's wrath is compared to waves and billows (*Psalms 88:7, Psalms 42:7*). *Job 27:20* "Terrors take hold as waters." *Hosea 5:10*, "I will pour out my wrath upon them like water." In *Psalms 42:7*, God's wrath is expressly compared to cataracts of water: "Deep calleth unto deep at the noise of thy waterspouts." And the same is represented in hail and stormy winds, black clouds and thunder, etc. As thunder, and thunder clouds, as they are vulgarly called, have a shadow of the majesty of God, so the blue sky, the green fields and trees, and pleasant flowers have a shadow of the mild attributes of goodness, grace and love of God, as well as the beauteous rainbow.[93]

This wrath of God burns away the sin and evil of the world and purifies the saints in Jesus Christ, which Edwards explains is illustrated by the refining of metal with tremendous heat, as described in Matthew 13:41–42.[94]

Edwards quotes many biblical passages and uses his typology to explain the beauty that remains in the postlapsarian world due to the light given by God, in spite of human sin and utter darkness. However, for this explanation by Edwards—that while God has gathered all the light

92. *WJE* 11:54–55. "For he shall be as a tree planted by the waters, and that spreadeth out her roots by the river, and shall not see when heat cometh, but her leaf shall be green; and shall not be careful in the year of drought, neither shall cease from yielding fruit" (Jer 17:8 KJV); "And he shall be like a tree planted by the rivers of water, That bringeth forth his fruit in his season; His leaf also shall not wither; And whatsoever he doeth shall prosper" (Ps 1:3 KJV); "As the valleys are they spread forth, As gardens by the river's side, As the trees of lign aloes which the LORD hath planted, And as cedar trees beside the waters" (Num 24:6 KJV).

93. *WJE* 11:58.

94. WJE 11:58–59. See note 8 above. "The Son of man shall send forth his angels, and they shall gather out of his kingdom all things that offend, and them which do iniquity; And shall cast them into a furnace of fire: there shall be wailing and gnashing of teeth" (Matt 13:41–42 KJV).

of excellency and beauty and after the Fall of mankind the utter darkness has covered the created world, beauty still remains in this world due to the revealed one light—a single obvious premise should be required: the identity of the revealed light—the redemptive work of Jesus Christ.[95]

Conclusion

In Jonathan Edwards's theological perspective which intertwines the concepts of divine glory and human happiness, God's glory is multifaceted, consisting of an intrinsic aspect seated in His will—holiness and happiness—and an extrinsic one which involves the dissemination of His self-knowledge to created beings. Edwards posits that God's self-enjoyment of His full glory and its external communication to intelligent beings are inseparable phenomena. He insists that humans find joy and fulfillment in the manifestation of God's perfection, thereby glorifying Him.

Edwards asserts that God's primary purpose in creating the world was to display His glory, which is conveyed to His creation and reverberated back to Him through the happiness of the *Imago Dei*. This happiness, in essence, derives from a profound union with God, which is fostered by an understanding and recognition of His holiness, glory, and beauty. Furthermore, Edwards designates humans as the most splendid of all God's creations. In his view, humans embody and mirror divine primary beauty, establishing them as the crown of creation and its culmination. He ascribes humanity's preeminence in secondary beauty to the distinctive human characteristic known as the *Imago Dei*. In being fashioned in God's image, humans reflect His beauty in their moral and spiritual characteristics, rendering them uniquely beautiful within creation. Human beauty, in this light, becomes a mirror of God's beauty, which is deemed the absolute source and benchmark of all beauty. This aspect is intricately tied to their capacity to echo God's beauty, predominantly via their moral and spiritual qualities. Consequently, humans stand as the epitome of beauty in the physical world, due to their unique ability to perceive, appreciate, and express divine beauty through their moral and spiritual traits.

Following humanity's Fall, this radiant beauty was extinguished, resulting in the world being enshrouded in pervasive darkness. While Edwards does not find beauty in the Fall or in sin itself, he does affirm the

95. *WJE* 9:133–34.

beauty that remains in the postlapsarian world. He argues, not through rational reasoning, but through his interpretation of Scripture and the typology that is based on that interpretation, that there is a glimmer of beauty in the fallen world. According to Edwards, there is only a glimmer of light in the world, where the light of beauty is lost because God has withdrawn the light. The light is the revelation of the redemptive work of Jesus Christ, and it is in this light that God's beauty can be found in the world.

Chapter 6

Jonathan Edwards's Biblical Aesthetics on the Work of Redemption

Introduction

THE CULMINATION OF EDWARDS's theological aesthetics is found in his understanding of the beauty of Christ as revealed in the context of redemptive history. This is because the spiritual beauty lost due to human fallibility is more gloriously restored through Christ's work of redemption. However, Edwards was active during a period when the essence of Christian beauty was assailed. The philosophical climate of Enlightenment and Rationalism, along with deistic religious views, assailed the fundamental articles of orthodox Christianity. Edwards not only actively responded to these attacks on Christianity but was also compelled to defend the true Christian faith. Specifically, he focused on revealing the beauty and excellence of the redeemer and his redemptive work, Christ, based on a robust interpretation of the Bible rather than on philosophical or rational reasoning. Therefore, this chapter will concentrate on exploring Edwards's theological aesthetics by first examining the philosophical backdrop of his era before engaging fundamentally with his extensive biblical exegesis.

Philosophical Assailment on the Beauty of Jesus Christ as the Redeemer in Edwards's Time

Edwards's studies on the beauty and excellency of Jesus Christ, the Mediator and Redeemer, have mostly evolved as a defense of proper Christology against the attacks of deists. According to Gerald McDermott, the deists rejected "the notion of a mediator (Christ) who atoned for human sin—a doctrine shared by Calvinists and other orthodox" and also opposed the satisfaction doctrine of atonement, which claims the need for the Mediator's sacrifice to obtain God's forgiveness.[1] This is clearly seen in the thought of many English deists, including Thomas Chubb and Matthew Tindal. The English Deist Thomas Chubb (1679–1747) asserted that while the New Testament contains expressions suggesting Christ redeemed us through his blood, these phrases are metaphorical and should not be the foundation for certain doctrines. He believed that these doctrines regarding Christ as Redeemer are contrary to reason; furthermore, he contended that these arguments did not negate the idea that reason can guide religious matters. So, he argued that God's forgiveness is appropriately grounded in repentance and reformation, rather than the sacrifice of a mediator.[2] The Deist Matthew Tindal (1657–1733) argued that if God required reparation, it would mean He could be hurt, which contradicts the idea of a perfect God. He emphasized that humans do not violate divine laws out of contempt for God, and God, being all-sufficient, is not affected by whether His laws are followed or not. Human understanding sometimes mistakenly projects our emotions and motives onto God, assuming He wants satisfaction or reparation. Such assumptions wrongly humanize God, ascribing to Him our flaws like anger, jealousy, or desire for recognition. Reason indicates that such emotions are fitting only for imperfect beings, not an unlimited and perfect deity. If God could feel anger or dissatisfaction from human actions, He would be perpetually distressed, which would go against His nature of complete perfection. Thus, Tindal also rejected the orthodox understanding of the doctrine of the atonement of Christ.[3]

1. McDermott, *Confronts the Gods*, 26.

2. Chubb says, "It is true, Christ is said to redeem us to God by his blood, and many like expressions are contained in the New Testament; but then these are plainly figures of speech, which were not intended to be a foundation and support for the doctrines I have now been considering" (Chubb, *Discourse Concerning Reason*, 20–22).

3. Tindal, *Christianity*, 38–39.

Eighteenth-century English deists also rejected the sacrificial system presented in the Old Testament. They argued that the Jewish law has no relation to the gospel, and that the Jewish religion is barbaric and cruel, tainted with "priestcraft," and thus detestable. Furthermore, they contended that the sacrificial rituals of Judaism resemble the rites of barbaric pagans. In detail, English deists critiqued Judaism for its perceived emphasis on the "letter of the law," likening this to pagan practices of idol worship.[4] The argument was that both Judaism and paganism were bound to materialistic worship—whether of the written law or of lifeless objects and animals—instead of recognizing the spiritual essence of a deistic God. Moreover, English deists noticed parallels between Jewish rituals and those of various indigenous cultures from East India, America, and West Africa. These similarities were used to suggest the idea of a universal religious instinct. Instead of seeing diverse religious practices as fundamentally distinct, deists saw them as stemming from a shared religious impulse that various cultures expressed in different ways.[5] Frank Edward Manuel explains that for English deists, Judaism was "a progenitor of Christian zealotry" and "spawned one of the cruelest religions that had ever enslaved mankind."[6] They even posed the following cynical question: "Since miracles were exposed as frauds and prophecies shown to be superstitions or errors, what was the point of studying the texts of the Jewish prophets to find evidence that Christ's coming had been predicted?"[7]

Edwards recognizes that the assumption of deists would be a deadly poison to the Reformed faith. In his critique, Edwards highlights their ignorance of true Christianity, insisting that they dismiss the Bible and all divinely revealed religion, believing instead that *the Bible* is merely a manmade artifact and that *the Christ* was "a cheat; [that] God never gave any revelation of his mind any otherwise than by the light of nature."[8] He warns that many have been deceived by the argument of deists, and have come to regard themselves as deists, having lost the true Christian faith; thus, this shift has led to public scorn towards the Bible, and blatant disrespect for Christ.[9] Therefore, against these deists' blasphemies and distortion of

4. Manuel, *Broken Staff*, 191.
5. Manuel, *Broken Staff*, 166, 179.
6. Manuel, *Broken Staff*, 191.
7. Manuel, *Broken Staff*, 191.
8. *WJE* 19:719.
9. *WJE* 19:719.

the Bible and the redemptive work of Christ, Edwards emphatically states what genuine Christianity is: the necessity of the divine revelation and the excellency and beauty of the redemptive work of Christ.

Edwards's Biblical Interpretations on the Beauty of the Divine Work of Redemption and Christ

As addressed in the previous chapter, Edwards states that a glimmer of light was given to humanity who lost the light of spiritual beauty coming from God, and that light of spiritual beauty is the light of the covenant of the redemption revealed in Genesis 3:15. Based on his typological interpretation of the Bible, he interprets sacrificial offerings as a type of Christ's crucifixion. Furthermore, his biblical exegesis serves as a basis for explaining how Christocentric redemption possesses manifold excellencies, and how glory and holiness—synonyms for beauty as previously examined—are discovered in the work of redemption.

Sacrifice as a Type of Jesus Christ's Crucifixion

In various sermons, Edwards speaks of Christ's offering of Himself as a sacrifice. Edwards assert that by offering Himself as a sacrifice, He has presented the strongest incentive for individuals to seek, embrace, and be united in heart with the Divine. This act of self-sacrifice represents a pinnacle of righteousness and obedience to the Father in Christ, providing God with the utmost inducement to accept humanity. Concurrently, it furnishes the most compelling motivation for people to receive and love God. Edwards would argue that this act serves as the most persuasive appeal to secure divine love and remains the most splendid and appealing display of God's mercy and love ever revealed.[10]

> 'Tis thus especially that the sacrifice Christ offered is said to be a sweet smelling savor to God. 'Tis as there was a righteousness in it. It was as Christ in offering up this sacrifice offered up to God, a heart fall of divine and holy love and respect to God's authority and command. He expresses such a love by his voluntary bearing or going through those sufferings. This made Christ's sacrifice not only satisfactory or to appease his anger, but it was a sweet smelling savor to merit his favor. Ephesians

10. Edwards, "Great Mediator," 321–22.

> 5:2 says, "Christ also hath loved us and given himself for us, an offering and a sacrifice to God for a sweet smelling savor." By this especially it was that God was well pleased with his Son. He was not only well pleased with our surety so far that his anger was appeased, but so that he infinitely delighted in him for his righteousness' sake. Isaiah 42:21 says, "The Lord is well pleased for his righteousness." If Christ by his being slain merited for himself his own exaltation, then doubtless he has thereby merited glorious things for us. For it was for ourselves that he was slain. It was upon our account that he laid down his life. And if that act of Christ was so excellent and meritorious as to merit such a glorious reward as his exaltation, a being exalted at God's right hand.[11]

Christ's sacrifice "was of infinite value, his blood infinitely precious" and "a savor infinitely sweet to God and of power sufficient to appease His anger."[12]

In the second sermon of *A History of the Work of Redemption,* Edwards argues against deists who claim the futility of sacrifice in the context of the Old Testament, explaining the significance of the sacrifice in the Old Testament in the context of redemptive history. Edwards illuminates the profound depth and symbolism ingrained in the ancient custom of sacrifice, emphasizing its pivotal role in foreshadowing the ultimate sacrifice of Christ for humanity's salvation. Contrary to some beliefs, Edwards asserts that these rites predate the Levitical laws introduced by Moses, tracing them instead back to the very dawn of God's visible church. Notable figures like Abraham, Isaac, Jacob, and even earlier personalities like Noah and Abel, in Edwards's view, are testaments to this age-old custom. Referencing Isaiah 29:13, he accentuates the necessity of divine mandate for such practices, emphasizing that only divinely sanctioned rituals possess the verity and foundation for faith and divine acceptance. Drawing on Hebrews 11:4 and Genesis 4:4, Edwards points to Abel's offerings as evidence of the rite's antiquity and its basis in unwavering faith. He also connects this to the genesis of sacrificial practices and the divine promise noted in Genesis 3:15, arguing that this covenant represents the first step in God's elaborate plan for salvation.

> And 'tis very probable that it was instituted immediately after God had revealed the covenant of grace in Genesis 3:15, which

11. Edwards, "Worthy of His Exaltation," 355–56.
12. Edwards, "That the Son of God," 177.

> covenant and promise was the foundation on which the custom of sacrificing was built. That promise was the first stone that was laid towards this glorious building the Work of Redemption which will be finished at the end of the world. And the next stone which was laid upon this was the institution of sacrifices to be a type of the great sacrifice.[13]

In his interpretation, the act of God adorning Adam and Eve with animal skins resonates far beyond mere functionality.[14] With references to Genesis 3:18 and Exodus 25:5, he perceives this act of God as a powerful allegory, with the skins pointing toward the righteous protection of Christ and the divine grace not man-made but conferred by God. Edwards paints the sacrificial practices as a nocturnal beacon, a reflection heralding the impending arrival of the Messiah, the true "sun of righteousness."[15] To him, this beacon takes shape both in prophecies announcing Christ's advent and in typologies that prefigure His redemption. He places sacrifices at the heart of this typology, instilling the idea of requisite appeasement to God and atonement for sin. Furthermore, Edwards marvels at the global ubiquity of sacrificial customs, seeing them not as mere coincidence but as a testament to the authenticity of Christian doctrine. He believes that such rites, widely accepted as crucial for atonement of sin, are traced back from ancestral all the way to Noah and his lineage, setting the stage for the gospel's quintessential message of Christ's redemptive sacrifice.[16]

Edwards emphasizes the significance of the sacrificial offering for soteriology in two respects: (1) The system of sacrificial offerings is the initial manifestation of Christ to His visible church as part of the soteriological process after the Fall, in accordance with His priestly office. (2) As evidenced by God clothing them in animal skins, it demonstrates that Christ commenced His intercessory ministry immediately after human

13. *WJE* 9:135.

14. Edwards interprets the skins as the skins of sacrificial offerings, not just any animal skin. "God made them coats of skins and clothed them; which by the generality of divines is thought to be skins of beasts slain in sacrifice. For we have no account of anything else that should be an occasion for man's slaying beasts but only to offer 'em in sacrifice till after the flood. Men were not wont to eat the flesh of beasts as their common food till after the flood. The first food of man in paradise before the fall was the fruit of the trees of paradise, and when he was turned out of paradise after the fall, then his food was the herb of the field, Genesis 3:18. The first grant that he had to eat flesh as his common food was after the flood. So that 'tis very likely that these skins that Adam and Eve were clothed [in] were skins of their sacrifices" (*WJE* 9:135–36).

15. *WJE* 9:136.

16. *WJE* 9:134–37.

transgression.[17] In other words, in Edwards's theology, the significance of the sacrifice as the beginning of redemptive history, which began immediately after the Fall, is that Jesus Christ is the center of God's redemptive covenant for humanity and its historical realization. This is the unifying theme of Edwards's thirty sermons in his *A History of the Work of Redemption.*[18] This Christocentric interpretation of redemptive history reveals that the restoration of the divine spiritual beauty of the world lost due to human depravity must ultimately be understood in the light of the excellency and beauty of Jesus Christ manifested within redemptive history.

Christocentric Work of Redemption

Through his biblical interpretation, Edwards examines the implications of Christ's redemptive work in terms of his theological aesthetics. Edwards emphasizes the beauty of Christ's redemptive work by contrasting the "excellency of the great things that the Word of God teaches about Christ and the way of any saved by [H]im" with the "misery" of sinners who are ignorant of their need for salvation, contrasting the excellence/beauty of Christ's salvation with the misery/ugliness of sinners.[19] Edwards says, "if Adam had never sinned, he will have been made happy for his own goodness" and "if Adam had, never fallen, he would have had eternal life on his own account and on his own goodness"; however,

17. *WJE* 9:136–40.

18. John Wilson, the editor of *A History of the Work of Redemption,* analyzes the 30 sermons of Jonathan Edwards as follows: "We have noted that Edwards' text and doctrine are both fully explicated in the course of the first of the thirty sermons. Thereafter he devotes eleven preaching occasions to a close discussion of the dispensations through which redemption was advanced from the fall of man to the coming of Christ. This development of God's Work of Redemption takes place under the general text and doctrine, with additional 'observations' about the last dispensation. Their improvement or application is concentrated in the thirteenth sermon. Nevertheless, the eleven sermons stand as a rational statement that has a distinctively historical cast. Under the same text and doctrine, three more sermons offer a rational theological analysis (rather than a historical discussion) of the period of Christ's humiliation or life; improvement of this section is made in Sermon Seventeen. With Sermon Eighteen, Edwards begins to discuss the Work of Redemption from Christ's resurrection to the end of the world and its eventual return to God. The same text from Isaiah and the same doctrine frame this section. A short concluding section of Sermon Twenty-one is explicitly an improvement or application, as is all of Sermon Twenty-five. The last part of Sermon Twenty-nine and all of Sermon Thirty are set out as an improvement of the whole" (Wilson, "Editor's Introduction," in *WJE* 9:36).

19. Edwards, "What Is Meant," 239.

"now since we have fallen and lost our goodness . . . we can be saved only by believing in Christ."[20] Based on Mark 16:16—"He that believeth not shall be damned," Edwards argues that those who do not believe in Christ will be damned, which means "to be damned is to be deprived of all good and to suffer misery to all eternity, the fruit of the wrath of God for sin."[21] In other words, the happiness, beauty, excellency, goodness, and eternal life that man possessed in the prelapsarian world were lost with the Fall, and now these aesthetic attributes can only be restored by the salvation of Christ. In this sense, Edwards uses the analogy of light to describe Christ and the proclamation of His redemptive work: "Christ was the Light of the world . . . The preaching of the gospel was like the rising of the sun in the morning that shone away all darkness and filled the world with light."[22] Based on his interpretation, Edwards argues that the defining characteristic of a saved person who believes in Jesus Christ is the opening of the eyes "to see the glorious excellency of Jesus Christ."[23] Edwards's various contrasts, such as darkness and light, excellency and misery, happiness and unhappiness, and curse and glory, further reveal the stark difference between the beauty lost by sin and the beauty restored by Christ's redemptive work.[24]

Edwards discovers His infinite excellency in Christ's passion and obedience as the center of redemptive work. He argues that as depicted in Ephesians 2:6–9,[25] Christ's act of obedience in redemption demonstrated His infinite excellency, love, and respect for the Father's honor, surpassing any human or angelic act, and was characterized by infinite humility, self-denial, and holiness to uphold God's glory. The depth of Christ's mercy and love for humanity, inherent in His nature, exemplified His infinite excellency and earned Him an infinite reward, achieving immeasurable good for God's glory and mankind, exceeding the combined contributions of all creatures. This act of redemption, in which the glory of God's grace was infinitely manifested, deemed Christ worthy of reverence and praise, as

20. Edwards, "What Is Meant," 241–42.

21. Edwards, "What Is Meant," 242–43.

22. Edwards, "What Is Meant," 239.

23. Edwards, "What Is Meant," 245.

24. Edwards, "Worthy of His Exaltation," 353–54.

25. "And hath raised us up together, and made us sit together in heavenly places in Christ Jesus: That in the ages to come he might shew the exceeding riches of his grace in his kindness toward us through Christ Jesus. For by grace are ye saved through faith; and that not of yourselves: it is the gift of God: Not of works, lest any man should boast" (Eph 2:6–9 KJV).

celebrated by the redeemed in Revelation 5:9, acknowledging His worthiness, sacrifice, and redemptive power across all peoples and nations.

His sermon series—*A History of the Work of Redemption*—provides a richer understanding of Edwards's theological aesthetics. In all thirty sermons in *A History of the Work of Redemption,* Edwards states the same doctrine: "The Work of Redemption is a work that God carries on from the fall of man to the end of the world."[26] Edwards bifurcates the interpretation of the work of redemption into two pivotal aspects, both intrinsically interwoven with Christ's public life and mission. The narrower interpretation accentuates the immediate redemptive work of Christ during His time on earth—His passion, crucifixion, and resurrection, which stand as the direct instruments of human salvation. Conversely, the broader scope encapsulates all divine actions, which while encompassing Christ's earthly ministry, extend both backwards into divine preparations and forwards into the ongoing results of Christ's work of redemption.

In his view, while certain preparatory actions pertinent to redemption began prior to humanity's fall, they were always Christocentric. This is illustrated by his reference to the eternal covenant of redemption—agreed upon within the Holy Trinity—where Christ was preordained to be the savior of humanity. Additionally, Edwards posits that the effects of Christ's redemptive work, although culminating in a temporal sense, bear fruit that will perpetuate throughout eternity. In order to capture the magnitude of Christ's redemptive act, Edwards presents two points: (1) On an individual scale, Christ's redemption is evidenced through the transformative journey of souls: from their conversion and justification to sanctification, culminating in their eternal glorification. This personal redemption begins after the Fall and continues until the very end of time. (2) On a more cosmic scale, Edwards envisions Christ's redemption as a series of divine interventions and actions throughout human history. These actions, though multifaceted, share a unified objective: the materialization of the grand salvific plan orchestrated by Christ.

In short, Jonathan Edwards's theological reflection paints a vivid portrait of Christ's central and enduring role in the Work of Redemption. For Edwards, Christ is not merely a transient agent but the very fulcrum upon which the entirety of redemption pivots, spanning the course of human history and extending into eternity. Next, in order to delve deeper into Edwards's understanding of the beauty of Christocentric redemptive work, it

26. *WJE* 9:116.

is essential to examine both beauty inherent in Christ as the redeemer at the core of the redemptive work and the beauty of the work itself.

The Conjunction of Excellencies of Jesus Christ

As Louis Mitchell has observed, in Edwards's thought, it is through the person and work of Christ that God's beauty is most dramatically and intimately revealed.[27] In his sermon "The Excellency of Christ" (1738), interpreting Revelation 5:5–6,[28] Edwards focuses on the two distinctive titles by which the text refers to Christ: "the Lion of the tribe of Judah" and "a Lamb as it had been slain."[29] He derives a doctrine from the fact that two beings with extreme personalities—the powerful predator lion, and the weakest prey lamb—describe the one person, Jesus Christ: "There is an admirable conjunction of diverse excellencies in Jesus Christ."[30] He explains the diverse excellencies in Jesus Christ in two ways: (1) He illustrates how these excellencies are beautifully combined within Christ, and (2) he describes how this magnificent combination of excellencies manifests in Christ's work.

Conjunction of Diverse Excellencies in Jesus Christ

Again, Edwards categorizes how these excellencies are combined within Christ into three distinct ways: Firstly, Christ exemplifies a union of excellencies that, in human perception, seem distinct from one another. Secondly, He embodies a blend of diverse attributes that we would typically view as entirely irreconcilable within a singular being. Lastly, these varied excellencies are directed by Him towards humanity in ways previously thought unimaginable for one entity.

27. Mitchell, "Experience of Beauty," 81.

28. "And one of the elders saith unto me, Weep not: behold, the Lion of the tribe of Juda, the Root of David, hath prevailed to open the book, and to loose the seven seals thereof. And I beheld, and, lo, in the midst of the throne and of the four beasts, and in the midst of the elders, stood a Lamb as it had been slain, having seven horns and seven eyes, which are the seven Spirits of God sent forth into all the earth" (Rev 5:5–6 KJV).

29. *WJE* 19:564.

30. *WJE* 19:565.

In Christ, We Observe a Union of Qualities That, in Our Understanding, Appear Entirely Different from One Another

Edwards contends that in Christ, an awe-inspiring blend of infinite eminence and condescension is evident. Christ, embodying God's nature, stands supremely above all—sovereign over earthly and celestial realms. He is described as "King of Kings, and Lord of Lords" and His majesty is referenced in Proverbs 30:4, "What is his name, and what is his Son's name, if thou canst tell?" and Job 11:8, "It is high as heaven, what canst thou do?" His omnipotence, boundless wisdom, and immeasurable riches make even the grandest kings seem insignificant. Yet, this same exalted figure showcases an unparalleled humility. According to Edwards, Christ's attention is not reserved for the elite; he graciously acknowledges even the most downtrodden, with James 2:5 highlighting God's regard for the "poor of the world." Christ's humility is further emphasized in Matthew 19:14, where He says, "Suffer little children to come unto me." Remarkably, His humility does not end at mere recognition; He aligns Himself with humanity, even enduring shame, suffering, and death. This juxtaposition of immense stature and profound humility in a single being is, according to Edwards, extraordinary. Edwards emphasizes that Christ is both the embodiment of perfect righteousness and infinite mercy. While His divine nature upholds the utmost standards of justice, punishing sin, He simultaneously exudes a boundless grace that extends even to the most grievous offenders. This is not a passive grace; Christ took on immense sufferings to ensure that these blessings were bestowed to us.[31]

Christ Embodies a Blend of Characteristics That, to Our Perception, Would Have Appeared Irreconcilably Different within a Single Entity

Edwards reveals that in Christ a variety of mutually incompatible excellencies are combined:

> Infinite glory and the lowest humility, infinite majesty and transcendent meekness, the deepest reverence toward God and equality with God, infinite worthiness of good and the greatest patience under suffering of evil, an exceeding spirit of obedience with supreme dominion over heaven and earth, absolute

31. *WJE* 19:566–67.

> sovereignty and perfect resignation . . . self-sufficiency and an entire trust and reliance on God.[32]

Edwards quotes numerous Scripture passages to illustrate each of Christ's excellencies, vividly showing how the revealed Word reveals His beauty. Edwards emphasizes that neither created entities (like humans or angels) nor other divine entities exhibit the coexistence of infinite glory and humility.[33] Created beings lack the capacity for infinite glory, and while divine nature inherently opposes pride, the virtue of humility cannot be ascribed to entities like God the Father or the Holy Ghost.[34] This is primarily because humility signifies a sense of one's insignificance in comparison to God, a virtue that cannot be attributed to God Himself. However, Edwards stresses that, in Jesus Christ, this seeming paradox is resolved. Being both human and divine, Christ transcends these boundaries. His divine nature is underscored as Philippians 2:6 states that Christ, in His divine form, equated Himself with God. Furthermore, John 5:23 underlines that Christ deserves the same honor as the Father, and Hebrews 1:8 echoes God's affirmation of Christ's eternal dominion. Even the angels, the highest of created beings, accord Him the same reverence as God the Father, as highlighted in Hebrews 1:6.[35] Edwards continues by contrasting Christ's exaltation with his humility. No other being, whether human or angel, exemplified humility as profoundly as Jesus did. His acute awareness of His relative position to God the Father is evident in verses like Matthew 11:29. His earthly life was a testament to this humility, reflected in His decision to lead a modest life in the household of Joseph and Mary, His humbling act of washing the feet of His disciples, and His ultimate submission to being crucified.[36]

32. *WJE* 19:567–71.

33. He says, "such as are conjoined in no other person whatever, either divine, human, or angelical" (*WJE* 19:567).

34. Edwards argues, "They meet in no created person; for no created person has infinite glory: and they meet in no other divine person but Christ. For though the divine nature be infinitely abhorrent to pride, yet humility is not properly predicable of God the Father, and the Holy Ghost, that exist only in the divine nature; because it is a proper excellency only of a created nature; for it consists radically in a sense of a comparative lowness and littleness before God, or the great distance between God and the subject of this virtue; but it would be a contradiction to suppose any such thing in God" (*WJE* 19:568).

35. *WJE* 19:568.

36. *WJE* 19:567–68.

Edwards explains that in the multifaceted nature of Christ, being both human and divine, He exhibits both immense majesty and unmatched meekness. With respect to Christ's infinite majesty, he quotes Psalms 45:3 which paints an image of Him as an almighty figure girded in glory and honor.[37] His mightiness is described as one that dominates the heavens and displays excellence beyond the skies. He is depicted as a formidable force in Psalms, causing even the earth to quake and reducing all its inhabitants to mere grasshoppers in His presence. In Edwards's thought, the scriptures further illustrate His unparalleled power, eternal reign, and infinite dominion, making it evident that His majesty knows no bounds. On the other hand, Edwards also reveals that despite His grandeur, Christ showcases an unmatched meekness. In his interpretation of Mathew 21:4–5, Edwards states that His meekness symbolized by His choice to ride an ass.[38] According to Edwards, Christ Himself proclaimed his meek and humble nature in Matthew 11:29.[39] His earthly life and interactions provide tangible evidence of this. He consistently demonstrated meekness, especially in the face of accusations, insults, and adversities. His capacity for forgiveness was unparalleled, even extending to those who sought to harm Him. Notably, even when surrounded by mocking soldiers, Christ chose silence, embodying the prophecy of going to His fate like a lamb to the slaughter.[40]

Edwards states that His excellency can be found in the fact that Jesus Christ embodies a unique blend of deep reverence towards God and an inherent equality with Him. During His time on Earth, Christ displayed a profound sense of respect and devotion towards God the Father. Edwards suggests that Luke 22:41 provides evidence of the manner in which He worshipped, notably by adopting reverent postures such as kneeling during prayer. This behavior is particularly significant considering Christ's human form and the humility inherent to it. Simultaneously, Edwards argues that Christ's divine nature signifies His inherent equality with God the Father. The Father has all the attributes or perfections that Christ has, and unlike any other being, Christ has an equivalent magnitude and splendor that the Father has. This establishes that while Christ's earthly

37. *WJE* 19:569.

38. *WJE* 19:569.

39. *WJE* 19:569.

40. *WJE* 19:568–69.

manifestation showed reverence to the Father, His intrinsic nature, being divine, makes Him coequal with God in all aspects.[41]

Edwards proclaims that Jesus Christ exemplifies an unparalleled union of intrinsic worthiness and profound patience in the face of adversity. Citing Hebrews 12:2, Edwards argues that despite the immense challenges, Christ endured the excruciating pain of the cross, undeterred by the shame associated with it. As cited in 1 Peter 2:20–24, Christ's response to torment was neither retaliatory nor resentful. Instead, He chose to commit Himself to the righteous judgment of God. By bearing our sins and undergoing such hardships, Christ set forth a beacon of hope, guiding humanity towards righteousness.[42]

Edwards finds the unique complexity between Christ's unwavering obedience to God's will and His inherent sovereignty over creation. On one hand, Christ stands as the supreme ruler over all creation, both in heaven and on earth. This dominion arises from two distinct aspects of His being. First, in His role as the God-man and Mediator, His authority is designated by the Father, making Him act as a representative or vice-gerent of the Father. Second, in His intrinsic divine nature, He possesses an inherent right to lordship, making Him coequal with the Father. Thus, His reign over the world is not merely derivative or delegated, but it is innately His. Contrary to the Arian belief, Christ is not a subordinate deity but is, in all facets, the Supreme God. Yet, this supreme ruler demonstrated a spirit of obedience that remains unmatched in its depth and fervor. Throughout His earthly life, Christ consistently abided by the will and commandments of God. Edwards finds this unwavering obedience in John 14:31 and John 15:10.[43] The pinnacle of His obedient nature can be discerned in His acceptance of the daunting task ordained by God—His crucifixion. Moreover, Edwards points to two more passages. As highlighted in John 10:18, Christ willingly surrendered to the immense sufferings that was set before Him, a command that arguably presented the highest challenge to obedience. This unparalleled submission to God's will, even to the point of death, as referenced in Philippians 2:8, sets Christ apart as the quintessential model of obedience.[44] Thus, Edwards argues that such an act remains unparalleled, even more so

41. *WJE* 19:569–70.

42. *WJE* 19:570.

43. *WJE* 19:570–71.

44. *WJE* 19:571.

considering that the one exhibiting this obedience is simultaneously the sovereign lord of all existence.

In Edwards thought, Christ holds unchallenged sovereignty over the entire cosmos from the perspective of His divinity. He is the central orchestrator of every event, the mastermind behind divine decrees, and the force behind all of creation and providential actions. His dominion over all things is reflected in scriptural affirmations like Colossians 1:16–17, which attests that everything exists through Him and for Him.[45] Similarly, John 5:17 underscores the harmonious work between the Father and the Son, echoing their collaborative efforts in directing the course of the universe. Christ's command to the leper in Matthew 8:3, "I will, be thou clean," further exemplifies His authoritative power. However, Edwards also mentions that juxtaposed against this backdrop of omnipotent authority is Christ's profound sense of resignation. Despite His omnipotence, Christ displayed a level of submission to God's will that is unparalleled throughout history. Edwards argues that this is most aptly illustrated in His earthly moments of extreme anguish, as He grappled with the imminent horrors of His crucifixion. As revealed in Matthew 26:39–42, He showed the most amazing obedience in the most terrible moments of suffering.[46]

Finally, in terms of a blend of characteristics that would have appeared irreconcilable within a single entity, Christ shows a blend of self-sufficiency and a profound trust in God. On the one hand, in His divine essence, Christ is the epitome of self-sufficiency. He does not require anything outside of Himself; all creation hinges on Him while He remains uninfluenced by anything or anyone. This is the core of what it means to be absolutely independent. His eternal generation from the Father does not imply any kind of dependency. It is not a capricious act but an intrinsic and necessary aspect of His divine nature. On the other hand, Edwards explains that despite this autonomous nature, Christ, during His earthly ministry, showcased an unwavering trust and dependence on God. This is evident when His adversaries pointed out that He had put His trust in God, hoping God would rescue Him, as mentioned in Matthew 27:43. Moreover, the Apostle Peter reinforces this notion in 1 Peter 2:23, noting that Christ wholly "committed himself" to God.[47]

45. *WJE* 19:571.

46. *WJE* 19:571.

47. *WJE* 19:571–72.

In Christ, There Are Diverse Excellencies That Are Thought to Be Inapplicable to The Same Object: Justice, Mercy and Truth

Edwards asserts that Christ displays a harmonious blend of characteristics, such as justice, mercy, and truth, that would otherwise appear impossible to coexist when directed at humanity. He references Psalms 85:10, highlighting how these qualities meet in Christ. While God's strict and vengeful justice is thoroughly manifested in Christ, so is His incredible mercy towards sinners. Christ upholds God's justice and righteousness, ensuring sinners face judgment. Yet, He remains the redeemer, demonstrating unparalleled love and grace. Edwards cites Romans 3:25–26, emphasizing how Christ serves as the propitiation, showcasing God's righteousness and mercy, ensuring justice while justifying believers. Additionally, Edwards underscores the immutable truth of God as evidenced in Jesus Christ. Christ's sufferings stand testament to the unalterable truth of God's law and its threats against humanity's sins. The severity of this truth was most significantly tested when sin was imputed to Christ. While He wholly respects this truth, Christ also brings forth promises of deliverance from the law's penalty, offering eternal life, as all God's promises find fulfillment in Him.

In short, through extensive biblical exegesis, Edwards demonstrates that the various excellencies in Jesus Christ are a remarkable combination. Some excellencies are of a very different nature, others have features that seem incompatible with each other, and still others are attributes that cannot be applied to the same person, but all of them are mysteriously harmonized in Christ being the creator and redeemer.

Conjunction of Excellencies Revealed in the Acts of Jesus Christ

Secondly, Edwards describes how this magnificent combination of excellencies manifests in Christ's acts: (1) His incarnation, (2) His public life, (3) His Passion, (4) His exaltation, and (5) His final judgment.

Excellencies in Christ's Incarnation

In Edwards's perspective, Christ's taking on human form is a monumental display of both his infinite condescension and his divine dignity. His condescension is evident in the manner of his incarnation: He, who was God, became man, and not just any man, but one born into poverty. He was conceived in the womb of a young woman so poor that she could only afford the sacrifice allowed for those in poverty, as noted in Luke 2:24 and Leviticus 12:8. His birth in a stable, wrapped in swaddling clothes and laid in a manger, further underlines this humbling act. But, Edwards argues that despite these humble circumstances, Christ's divine dignity was not diminished. His conception by the Holy Spirit, as stated in Luke 1:35, preserved his divine nature. He was conceived and born without sin, even though he was born of a human mother. Furthermore, the purpose of his birth—to conquer Satan, to restore peace, and to bring glory to God—was proclaimed by a choir of angels, affirming his divine status. Thus, in the event of Christ's birth, Edwards sees an extraordinary juxtaposition of divine dignity and human humility, of the infinite lowering itself to the finite, while still maintaining its infinitude. This duality captures the essence of Christ's character and mission.[48]

In his letter "To Lady Mary Pepperrell," Edwards also states the beauty of Christ's incarnation. Edwards articulates the unique splendor of Christ as a manifestation of divine glory in a form that is both awe-inspiring and approachable to human beings. He is the eternal light of the world, sent by God to illuminate the full beauty of the Deity to mankind.[49] Edwards notes that Christ's incarnation serves as a lens through which the ineffable glory of God is made accessible to human beings. In becoming flesh, Christ brings the divine down to a level that is comprehensible and relatable to us, tempering His majesty with qualities of meekness and humility. Edwards appeals to various biblical references like Isaiah 24:23; Matthew 24:29; and Revelation 6:12 to point out that

48. *WJE* 19:573–74.

49. The view of Edwards on the beauty of Christ's incarnation is well revealed in *The Miscellanies*: "This end is obtained by Christ's incarnation, viz. that the saints may see God with their bodily eyes as well as by an intellectual view. They may see him in both ways of seeing which their natures, being body and spirit, are capable of; they may see him as they see one another, which shall not only be spiritually but outwardly. The saints in heaven will have two sorts of sight, intellectual and corporeal; it is the will of God that he himself, or a divine person, should be the principal entertainment of both those kinds of sight. Thus God saw it meet that it should be, and therefore assumed a body that appears with that transcendent visible majesty, glory and beauty, that is exceeding expressive of the divine greatness, holiness and grace. This is a much more perfect and real way of seeing God with bodily eyes, than to behold some glorious preternatural representation, as God sometimes appeared under the old testament. Job comforted himself, that he should see God with his bodily eyes" (*WJE* 13:501–2).

Christ's glory is so overwhelming that it makes even the natural sun appear dark. Yet, Christ as the "Lamb of God" radiates this intense light in a way that is not harsh but healing, thanks to His humanity. The light is gentle and restorative, like the rising sun with healing in its wings (Mal 4:2), a nurturing rain to a parched earth, or a balm for wounded spirits (Ps 72:6). In essence, through the incarnation of Jesus Christ, Edwards captures the dual nature of Christ's glory: awe-inspiring yet intimately accessible, infinitely majestic yet deeply humble, a glory that brings both deep reverence and loving familiarity. The glory of Christ is the ultimate revelation of God's nature, tailor-made to engage, captivate, and heal the human soul.[50]

In addition, Edwards argues that Christ's incarnation also has the ultimate divine glory. Jonathan Edwards emphasizes the angelic proclamation at the birth of Christ as recorded in Luke 2:14: "Glory to God in the highest, and on earth, peace and good will towards men." Edwards argues that the angels have insight into God's cosmic plans. Therefore, their proclamation serves as a strong affirmation of what Edwards sees as the ultimate objective of Christ's coming into the world: the glory of God.[51]

Excellencies in His Public Life

Edwards finds Christ's excellence and beauty in the various events of his life; in particular, in relation to Christ's redemptive work, Edwards focuses on the humility and gentleness, majesty and glory of Christ in His public life. Jesus chose to live in modest circumstances, so much so that he had no permanent place to sleep and relied on the charity of his followers for sustenance (Luke 8). He treated his disciples with a fatherly affection, speaking to them as friends and companions. He also endured criticisms and hardships from the scribes and Pharisees with patience and humility, thereby displaying the meekness of a "lamb." However, at the same time, Edwards focuses on the fact that Jesus demonstrated his divine majesty through his miracles, showing his omnipotent power as the "Lion of the tribe of Judah." His ability to heal the sick, restore sight to the blind, open the ears of the deaf, and raise the dead exhibited his control over nature. Edwards cites various Bible verses to support these claims, such as Job 9:8, which refers to

50. *WJE* 16:415–17.

51. *WJE* 8:486.

God "treading on the waves of the sea," and Psalm 65:7 and 107:29, which describe God's power to calm the seas.[52]

Edwards cites John 2:11 to highlight how Jesus manifested his divine glory even in the midst of earthly limitations. In special instances, Jesus allowed his divine majesty to be visibly manifested, such as during his transfiguration. Moreover, he also mentions that Peter recounts this in 2 Peter 1:16–17, describing himself as an "eye-witness" to Christ's majesty when God declared, "this is my beloved Son in whom I am well pleased."[53] In summary, Edwards discovers that Jesus perfectly balanced meekness and majesty, appearing simultaneously as the "Lamb of God" and the "Lion of the tribe of Judah," showcasing his unique blend of human humility and divine authority in His public life.

Excellencies in the Passion of Christ

Jonathan Edwards argues that the most extraordinary display of Christ's dual nature—as both the "Lamb of God" and the "Lion of the tribe of Judah"—is evident in his act of sacrificing himself for sinners during his Passion. Edwards states that this act is the pinnacle of Christ's redemptive work. According to Edwards, Christ's role as a "lamb" is most visible during his crucifixion. He cites Isaiah 53:7, which describes Christ as going "like a lamb to the slaughter," to emphasize the extreme humility and meekness that Christ exhibited when he was slain. This self-sacrifice identified Christ with the sacrificial lamb of the Passover, as mentioned in 1 Corinthians 5:7: "Christ our Passover sacrificed for us." Edwards suggests that in this act, Christ is the antitype of the Lamb of the Passover, a fulfillment of the symbolism inherent in the Old Testament ritual. However, Edwards also maintains that it is in this very act of meek sacrifice that Christ most profoundly manifests his majestic, lion-like qualities. While he does not detail these aspects as thoroughly in this segment, the implication is that Christ's act of sacrifice also displays his divine authority, power, and majesty. The submission to death as a sacrifice is the ultimate act of authority over life and death, as well as a demonstration of divine love and justice.[54]

52. *WJE* 19:575.
53. *WJE* 19:575.
54. *WJE* 19:576.

Edwards finds seven excellencies in the passion of Christ. First of all, Jonathan Edwards delves deeper into the paradox of Christ's dual nature of meekness and divine majesty in the context of Christ's ultimate act of sacrifice, emphasizing that it was in the greatest depth of his humiliation that Christ's divine glory shone the brightest. Edwards argues that although Christ was born in lowly circumstances, subjected himself to his human parents, lived in poverty, and suffered manifold indignities, it was his Passion, beginning with his agony in the Garden of Gethsemane and culminating in his crucifixion, that represented the pinnacle of his humiliation. This act, according to Edwards, had Christ enduring unprecedented physical pain, emotional sorrow, and social disgrace. Despite this extreme low point, or perhaps because of it, Edwards states that Christ's divine glory was never so clearly manifested as it was in his willingness to undergo these sufferings. The "fruit" or outcome of this act revealed its purpose and therefore its glory. The magnitude of Christ's sacrifice and its profound impact on redemption became fully visible afterward. Edwards references Revelation 5:9–12, where heavenly hosts praise Christ for his redemptive act, declaring him "worthy" because he was slain and redeemed humanity with his blood. In essence, Edwards argues that the crucifixion represents a supreme "conjunction of excellencies" in Christ's character, manifesting both his utter humility and his divine glory. The act is both the ultimate humiliation and the ultimate display of divine authority, and this paradox is celebrated by heavenly beings as the most glorious act ever performed.[55]

Secondly, Jonathan Edwards accentuates the profound paradox in Christ's ultimate act of sacrifice: that it simultaneously represents the pinnacle of Christ's love for both God and humanity, even those who were enemies of God. Edwards argues that Christ's willingness to lay down his life under unimaginable suffering was the ultimate manifestation of his love and obedience to God the Father. It served to vindicate the honor, authority, and majesty of God in a way that no mere creature could ever do. However, this very act of ultimate obedience to God also represents Christ's supreme expression of love towards sinful humans, who were enemies and estranged from God. Edwards cites Romans 5:10 to point out that it was while humanity was in a state of enmity with God that Christ's sacrificial death occurred. His willingness to endure physical torment and emotional anguish was driven by a desire to save human

55. *WJE* 19:576–77.

souls from eternal damnation and to secure for them eternal glory. For Edwards, the crucifixion is the pinnacle of a "dying love," a love so profound that it willingly embraces death and suffering for the sake of the beloved. It is a love that sweats blood, endures shame and spitting, and bears excruciating sorrow. This act, Edwards says, reveals Christ's regard for God's honor most eminently because it offered him up as a victim to "revenging justice" to vindicate God's honor. Simultaneously, this very act also manifested his love even for those who dishonored God, a love so deep that only the shedding of his own blood could atone for such guilt. Therefore, according to Edwards, the crucifixion embodies a supreme and astonishing union of seemingly contradictory excellencies: love for God and love for fallen humanity.[56]

Edwards's third point on this matter delves into another profound paradox surrounding Christ's sacrifice: that in the very act of suffering from divine justice, Christ also stood for divine justice. Christ's unimaginable sufferings reveal his deep regard for the honor of God's justice because he willingly humbled himself to undergo these sufferings in fulfillment of divine law and justice. And yet, paradoxically, during these very moments of supreme humiliation and suffering, Christ himself was also the direct object of this very divine justice he sought to uphold. Edwards argues that when Christ undertook to save sinners by substituting himself in their place, he essentially took upon himself the wrath of God's justice in place of humanity. Divine justice was then fully expressed upon him, not sparing him in any way, but expending "all its force" upon him. Edwards refers to various Biblical passages, such as Psalms 22:14, to emphasize the visceral, physical toll this took on Christ, describing it in terms that suggest a brutal, bodily breakdown. Yet, this was the means by which Christ upheld the honor of God's justice. By suffering its "terrible executions," he satisfied the requirements of divine justice, demonstrating its non-negotiable importance. This act, therefore, according to Edwards, epitomizes the "diverse excellencies" that converge in the person of Christ: an "infinite regard" for the justice of God and an incomprehensible love for sinful humanity. In sum, Christ displayed a harmonious integration of seemingly contradictory qualities: upholding the honor of God's justice while also suffering under it to save humanity.[57]

56. *WJE* 19:577.

57. *WJE* 19:577–78.

Fourthly, Edwards points out that Christ's holiness was never more vividly displayed than during his final sufferings. His decision to willingly endure such torment serves as an act of supreme obedience to God. Christ's holiness shines forth precisely because He continues to uphold God's honor and obeys His divine will, even when faced with unimaginable suffering. His holiness is tested and revealed to be pure, akin to gold or silver refined in the furnace. Furthermore, Edwards observes that Christ's death is the highest manifestation of his hatred against sin. His sacrifice serves to negate the dishonor that sin has brought upon God. By doing so, he fully aligns himself with the divine justice and holiness of God. However, the paradox is that, in fulfilling this role, Christ becomes subject to the full extent of God's wrath against sin. He is "made a curse for us," taking on the punishment and the divine displeasure that should have been directed at sinful humanity. Therefore, in this singular act of sacrifice, Christ demonstrates a harmonious integration of attributes that might seem contradictory: unyielding holiness and the most profound obedience to God are displayed alongside a willingness to be treated as sinful and bear the terrible wrath of God. In doing so, he manifests both love for God and grace for sinners, again highlighting the "diverse excellencies" that Edwards sees as converging uniquely in the person of Christ.[58]

Edwards's Fifth point highlights another paradox inherent in Christ's crucifixion: Christ is treated as utterly unworthy during His final sufferings, and yet it is precisely these sufferings that make Him deemed worthy of exaltation and glory. In His final hours, Christ is subjected to extreme humiliation. The crowd cries for His death and even prefers Barabbas, a criminal, over Him. The Father subjects Him to a death that seems as if it is a response to infinite offenses, because of the sins of humanity that are laid upon Him. He is treated as unworthy to live, let alone as a person of infinite worth and dignity. However, Edwards notes that it is primarily for this act of supreme sacrifice and obedience that Christ is considered worthy of the highest honor and exaltation. His humiliation becomes the pathway to His glorification. As Paul writes in Philippians 2:8–9, it is because He humbled Himself to the point of death that God has "highly exalted" Him. This is the song of the heavenly beings in the apocalyptic vision of Revelation; they declare Him worthy because He was slain. So, in the very act where Christ is treated as the least worthy, He performs the deed that makes Him supremely worthy. This is another

58. *WJE* 19:578.

example of the "diverse excellencies" Edwards sees in Christ: infinite dignity combined with infinite condescension, the highest worth manifest through apparent unworthiness, and supreme love shown to those who are infinitely unworthy of it. Edwards stresses that these paradoxes are not contradictions but profound complements that reveal the unique person and work of Christ. His worthiness comes not in spite of His humiliation and suffering but precisely through them. In this way, Christ embodies an extraordinary synthesis of qualities that would seem to be mutually exclusive but in Him exist in perfect, harmonious union.[59]

Sixthly, Christ endured the most extreme suffering from those to whom He displayed His love most vividly. This apparent contradiction reveals another layer of the "admirable conjunction of excellencies" in Christ's character and work. Regarding His relationship with God the Father, Christ experiences an excruciating moment of abandonment or forsakenness on the cross.[60] This is not because God the Father had animosity towards the Son, but because Christ was bearing the weight of human sin, and God's justice required that sin be fully punished. Yet it is at this very moment of apparent divine abandonment that Christ's love for the Father is most clearly displayed:

> Christ in his last sufferings suffered most extremely from those that he was then in his greatest act of love to. He never suffered so much from his Father (though not from any hatred to him, but from hatred to our sins), for he then forsook him (as Christ on the cross expresses it), or took away the comforts of his presence.[61]

Finally, in His final moments of suffering, Christ was most vulnerable to his enemies, yet it was through this vulnerability that He achieved ultimate victory over them. Edwards argues that during the crucifixion, Jesus Christ was seemingly at his most vulnerable, completely in the hands of his enemies. This moment is encapsulated by the verse Luke 22:53, where Jesus himself acknowledges, "this is your hour and the power of darkness." Despite this apparent defeat, it is precisely through these sufferings that Christ triumphs over evil. Drawing on Colossians 2:14–15, Edwards explains that Christ used the very instrument of his torture, the cross, to achieve ultimate victory. In being crucified, Christ

59. *WJE* 19:578–79.

60. "My God, My God, why have you forsaken me?" (Matt 27:46 KJV).

61. *WJE* 19:579.

"blotted out the handwriting of ordinances" against humanity and "made a show" of evil powers, triumphing over them. Edwards makes use of vivid Biblical analogies to illustrate his points. Like David defeating Goliath with his own sword, or Samson's riddle in Judges 14:14 ("Out of the eater came forth meat, and out of the strong came forth sweetness"), Jesus turns the tables on Satan and defeats him using the very means by which Satan hoped to conquer Jesus. The crucifixion, which seemed like Satan's victory, became his downfall. In this sense, Edwards emphasizes the dual nature of Christ as both the sacrificial "Lamb" and conquering "Lion of the tribe of Judah." In his moment of greatest weakness, Christ displayed his greatest strength, defeating his enemies not in spite of his sufferings, but through them. Thus, Edwards captures the profound paradox that in his seeming defeat, Christ was victorious; in his vulnerability, he was most powerful.[62]

Excellencies in His Exaltation

How does Christ continue to manifest both lion-like and lamb-like qualities, even in His exalted state in heaven? Edwards cites Revelation 14:1, which portrays Christ as a Lamb standing on Mount Zion, to emphasize that even though Christ is in a position of majesty and dominion He still embodies the qualities of a lamb. Edwards argues that Christ's exalted status does not negate His humility; in fact, it enhances it. The reason is that "though the man Christ Jesus be the highest of all creatures in heaven, yet he as much excels them all in humility, as he doth in glory and dignity; for none sees so much of the distance between God and him, as he does."[63] This deep awareness does not result in arrogance but in profound humility. He is above all other creatures in heaven not just in glory but also in humility. Even in His interactions with the saints in heaven, Christ maintains His lamb-like qualities of mildness, sweetness, and condescension. Edwards cites Revelation 7:17 to emphasize that Christ, even while seated on the throne of the universe, continues to act as a shepherd, leading His flock to "living fountains of waters" and wiping away their tears. Edwards also stresses that Christ's lamb-like qualities extend to His ongoing interactions with believers on Earth. He exhibits love, gentleness, forbearance, and compassion, making intercessions for

62. *WJE* 19:579–81.

63. *WJE* 19:581.

them, comforting them, and inviting them into sweet communion with Him. Finally, Edwards notes that Christ's sacrificial marks are eternally present, as if to remind all of creation that He is a lamb that was slain, even as He enjoys His exalted status. The book of Revelation expresses this most vividly in depicting Christ opening a book sealed with seven seals, a task only He is worthy to do, in part because He is both the Lion of Judah and the slain Lamb.[64] In short, Edwards argues that Christ's qualities of majesty and humility, power and gentleness, are not mutually exclusive but are perfectly united, both in His earthly ministry and in His heavenly reign. Even in His exalted state, Christ maintains a balance of being both a lion in majesty and a lamb in humility and love.

Excellencies in His Final Judgment

Edwards discusses how the union of Christ's seemingly contrasting attributes—lion-like and lamb-like—will be made evident during the Last Judgment. At this time, more than any other, Christ will manifest His lion-like characteristics of "infinite greatness and majesty." Edwards argues that to the wicked, His appearance will be terrifying. Edwards cites Revelation 20:11 to describe the grandeur and power of Christ's judgment seat, before which even heaven and earth will "flee away." He portrays a vivid image of all types of men—kings, rich men, bondmen, and free men—seeking refuge from the overwhelming presence of Christ, in fear of His wrath. This imagery captures the "Lion of the tribe of Judah" aspect of Christ, one of infinite justice and majestic fury. However, he argues that in contrast, to His saints, Christ will manifest His lamb-like characteristics. For them, the Last Judgment is not a day of terror but a day of consummation, akin to a wedding day. He will receive them as friends and family, treating them with "infinite mildness and love."[65] For the saints, Christ's lion-like attributes are not terrifying but comforting, as they signify the ultimate triumph of good over evil, justice over injustice. In this sense, Christ will "clothe himself wholly with sweetness and endearment" for His saints, inviting them to inherit the Kingdom and reign with Him eternally.[66] To sum up, Edwards argues that the Last Judgment will be the ultimate manifestation of Christ's dual nature. For

64. *WJE* 19:581–82.
65. *WJE* 19:582.
66. *WJE* 19:582.

the wicked, He will be the Lion of infinite justice and majesty, while for the righteous, He will be the Lamb of infinite mildness and love. Both these aspects will be present, and each will be experienced differently depending on one's relationship with Him, highlighting the "admirable conjunction of excellencies" in Christ.[67]

Various Excellencies Found in the Diversity of the Names of Jesus Christ

Jonathan Edwards focuses on the rich tapestry of names and representations used in Scripture to describe Jesus Christ. He underscores the multifaceted nature of Christ's character and essence by drawing attention to the array of titles and images ascribed to Him. Edwards observes that these varying titles and representations are not just random selections or mere poetic devices. Instead, they serve a higher purpose of conveying the diverse and sometimes seemingly contrasting qualities that coexist in Christ. By providing a variety of images and names, Scripture captures the breadth and depth of the excellencies of Christ's nature and work.

For instance, Isaiah 9:6 is pointed out as a singular verse that contains multiple titles for Christ. It illustrates the paradox and mystery of Christ's nature—He is both a child and the everlasting Father, both human and divine. Edwards uses the title "Wonderful" as an epitome for this union of diverse excellencies.[68] Moreover, Christ is described as a "sun" in Malachi 4:2, illuminating and guiding, and as a "star" in Numbers 24:17. Specifically, He is likened to the "morning star" in Revelation 22:16, which outshines all other stars and heralds the dawn. In Canticles 2:1, Christ is likened to a rose and a lily, both sweet and beautiful, while in the next verse, He is compared to a tree bearing sweet fruit. Lastly, He is described as a "root out of a dry ground" in Isaiah 53:2, indicating His humble origins, and as the "tree of life" in Revelation 2:7, which is in "the midst of the paradise of God," denoting His life-giving, eternal nature.[69]

The wide range of comparisons from Scripture that Edwards mentions are intentionally chosen for their distinct attributes. Christ is likened to both the sun and the star—sources of light, guidance, and hope. He is a lion, symbolizing strength and majesty, and yet also a lamb, signifying

67. *WJE* 19:582.

68. *WJE* 19:582.

69. *WJE* 19:583.

gentleness and sacrifice. Such comparisons help believers grasp the fullness of who Christ is. To Edwards, these descriptions also showcase the grandeur of Christ. By drawing attention to the multiplicity of His excellencies, Edwards aims to evoke awe, admiration, and worship among believers. For in recognizing the vastness of Christ's nature, believers are called to a deeper reverence and love for Him. The multifaceted imagery used in Scripture to describe Christ serves to deepen believers' understanding of Him, drawing them closer in relationship and deepening their faith. Edwards's exposition emphasizes the richness of Christ's character and the profound depths of the Scriptures in conveying it.

Beauty of the Redemption

Glory and the Redemption

Edwards sees the beauty of redemption in the glory of God and the holiness of the saints. Jonathan Edwards argues that Christ sought the glory of God as His ultimate aim or end. According to Edwards, when Christ says he did not seek his own glory in John 7:18, it should not be understood as him having no regard for his own glory. Rather, Christ's ultimate aim was not his own glory but the glory of God, the one who sent him. This is supported by John 12:27–28, where Christ, faced with the terrible prospect of his imminent crucifixion, seeks solace and support in the glory that will come to God as a result of His sufferings.[70] Edwards believes that in moments of extreme difficulty, one naturally seeks support in one's ultimate aim, and Christ's ultimate aim was God's glory. Moreover, in John 17:1, in the last prayer that Christ made with his disciples before His crucifixion, He says, "Father, the hour is come, glorify thy Son, that thy Son also may glorify thee." Edwards contends that this request to glorify the Son so that the Son may glorify the Father represents Christ's supreme desire and aim.[71]

Continuing this discussion, Edwards argues that the ultimate end of the work of redemption, led by Jesus Christ, is to glorify God. Starting with the Gospel of John, Edwards focuses particularly on several key verses.[72] In John 7:18, Jesus is clear about his intentions: "He who speaks

70. *WJE* 8:483–84.

71. *WJE* 8:484.

72. *WJE* 8:485.

on his own does so to gain personal glory, but he who seeks the glory of the one who sent him is a man of truth; there is nothing false about him." Jesus explicitly states that his actions and ministry are aimed at glorifying God the Father. Edwards sees this as an unambiguous statement on the ultimate end of Jesus's work. Edwards's idea is further developed in John 12:27–28, where Jesus, contemplating his imminent crucifixion, finds consolation in the purpose behind his suffering: the glory of God.[73] The heavenly response, "I have both glorified it, and will glorify it again," signifies divine affirmation of this objective. Edwards also draws attention to John 12:29–31 where Jesus says, "Now is the judgment of this world; now the ruler of this world will be driven out." In this narrative, Jesus appears to be rejoicing in the impending success of his redemptive work, a success measured in terms of divine glory.

In John 17, often referred to as Jesus's 'High Priestly Prayer,' Jesus prays not just for himself but also for his disciples and all believers. He explicitly asks for the glory of both the Father and the Son. Edwards emphasizes that Jesus presents his ministry and imminent sacrifice as a finished work aimed at glorifying God, fulfilling the very mission for which he was sent. Edwards then broadens his theological vision to include other New Testament texts. Philippians 2:6–11 is discussed as a Pauline reflection on the self-humbling of Christ, who became obedient unto death, with the resulting glorification being directed toward God. In Ephesians 1, Paul describes the spiritual blessings and predestination of believers as designed to culminate in the "praise of the glory of His grace."[74] Additionally, Edwards incorporates Old Testament texts like Psalms 79:9 and prophetic books like Isaiah 44; 48; and 49 to reveal a long-standing biblical tradition that views the deliverance and redemption of God's people as avenues for God's glorification.[75] Edwards connects these individual observations to assert a cohesive biblical theology: both the Old and New Testaments consistently and coherently signal that God's glory is the ultimate and final objective of the redemptive narrative.[76]

In his sermon "God Glorified in the Work of Redemption (or God Glorified in Man's Dependence)"[77] (1730), on 1 Corinthians 1:29–31,

73. *WJE* 8:485.

74. Edwards goes on to present other passages in the same manner as Phil 2:6–11, e.g., John 12:4–5, 23, 28; 13:31–32; 17:1. See *WJE* 8:486.

75. *WJE* 8:488.

76. *WJE* 8:487–88.

77. The full title of the sermon is "God Glorified in the Work of Redemption, By the Greatness of Man's Dependence upon Him, in the Whole of it" (*WJE* 17:199).

Edwards makes specific statements about redemptive work and glory. Edwards argues that the goal of the work of redemption revealed in the passage—"that no flesh should glory in his presence . . . that, according as it is written, He that glories, let him glory in the Lord"—is that God alone should be glorified.[78] According to Edwards, all the positive attributes and virtues that humans possess are given through Christ, who serves as the conduit for divine grace. Edwards identifies four key areas of human goodness that are addressed and fulfilled through Christ: wisdom, righteousness, sanctification, and redemption. So, Edwards argues that all redeemed people must be absolutely dependent on God for all good and excellent things, and when they are totally dependent on God, God is exalted and glorified in the work of redemption.[79]

Edwards explains that the reason why the redeemed must depend on God for all goodness and excellency is that "the redeemed have all of the grace of God" and "it was of mere grace that God gave us his only begotten Son."[80] According to Edwards, this grace is multi-dimensional, encompassing various aspects of the divine-human relationship and revealing the incalculable worth of what has been given to humanity. Firstly, Edwards asserts that the grace bestowed is enormous in proportion to the dignity and excellency of the gift itself—Christ. The person of Christ is infinitely worthy and glorious, and His proximity to God makes this gift even more invaluable. This gift is not just any gift; it is a divine act, a bestowal of the very essence of God's own nature and presence. Secondly, Edwards discusses the grace in relation to the benefits accrued to humanity. In Christ, we are saved from an infinite and eternal misery and are recipients of eternal joy and glory. The stakes could not be higher; we are delivered from endless suffering and granted eternal happiness. This makes this grace not just large, but infinite. Thirdly, Edwards points out that the grace is made even more significant by the unworthiness of its recipients. Humans do not merit this divine favor; in fact, humans have "merited infinitely ill of God's hands."[81] The grace, then, is not just a gift but an unmerited favor, a demonstration of divine munificence that directly challenges the notion of human unworthiness. Fourthly, the manner in which this grace is given contributes another layer to its greatness. Christ was given to humanity in a form we could understand and

78. *WJE* 17:200–201.

79. *WJE* 17:202–3.

80. *WJE* 17:203.

81. *WJE* 17:203.

relate to: in human flesh, beset with the "infirmities" that characterize our fallen state. Furthermore, He was given in a "low and afflicted state," ultimately being "slain" so that He could spiritually nourish us.[82]

Additionally, Edwards emphasizes that the redeemed "are also dependent on God for all, as they have all through him": "Wisdom, and the pardon of sin, deliverance from hell, acceptance into God's favor, grace and holiness, true comfort and happiness, eternal life and glory."[83] Even more, based on Hebrews 7:27 and 9:26, he repeats the reason for our dependence on God:

> Our blessings are what we have by purchase; and the purchase is made of God, the blessings are purchased of him, and God gives the purchaser; and not only so, but God is the purchaser. Yea, God is both the purchaser and the price; for Christ, who is God, purchased these blessings for us, by offering up himself as the price of our salvation. He purchased eternal life by the sacrifice of himself; Hebrews 7:27, "He offered up himself"; and Hebrews 9:26, "He hath appeared to take away sin by the sacrifice of himself." Indeed it was the human nature that was offered; but it was the same person with the divine, and therefore was looked upon as an infinite price: it was looked upon as if God had been offered in sacrifice.[84]

In other words, all the blessings we have come from God because redemption was accomplished by God through the payment of Christ for our salvation.

Edwards examines how the glory of God is manifested through the redemption of humanity and emphasizes the notion of a dependence of the redeemed on God. Firstly, Edwards posits that humanity's dependence on God illuminates God's divine qualities, such as his all-sufficiency, power, and grace. This dependence serves as an obligation for humans to recognize and acknowledge God's attributes. It is not just that we need God, but that our need for Him is so complete that it draws our attention inescapably toward Him. It is a type of dependence that not only situates God's attributes in our view but compels us to take notice of them, contemplating God as the ultimate source and sustainer of all goodness. Secondly, Edwards argues that this dependence underscores the chasm between the Creator and the created, affirming God's infinite superiority.

82. *WJE* 17:203.

83. *WJE* 17:206–7.

84. *WJE* 17:207.

Our utter dependence on God manifests our emptiness and God's complete fullness. This gap clarifies the incalculable difference between our limited capacities and God's infinity, urging us to ascribe to God the glory that is rightfully His. It serves as a corrective to any human arrogance that may try to claim attributes or virtues as originating from anywhere other than God. Lastly, Edwards suggests that humanity's all-encompassing dependence on God directs our "whole souls" to Him, preventing the division of our attention or loyalty. If we were to depend partly on God and partly on another entity, our focus and devotion would be fragmented. However, because all good things come solely from, through, and in God, our attention and devotion should focus undividedly on Him. This universal dependence ensures that God remains the "object of our undivided respect."[85] In summary, Edwards elaborates that the dependency of the redeemed serves a threefold purpose: it obligates us to recognize God's attributes, accentuates God's comparative glory by highlighting our emptiness, and ensures our complete and undivided devotion to God. It is a cyclical relationship where our dependence shines a spotlight on God's glory, and God's glory, in turn, validates our dependence. This all converges to fulfill God's ultimate design—He should appear all and man nothing, reinforcing the divine intent to be the singular focus of our lives.

Edwards argues that the privilege of the saved is "knowing that Christ is our Redeemer." According to Edwards, Job's confession in Job 19:25[86] "implies not only that we know that Christ is a divine and glorious person but that he with all his glory is ours."[87] In detail, those who can affirm, "I know that my Redeemer lives," perceive Christ as transcending all, recognizing Him as the Son of the living God, whose glory and excellency surpass all things, fulfilling the deepest desires of the soul.[88] This divine beauty is so immense and enlightening that it brings unparalleled peace and joy to the soul, making any form of sorrow inconsistent. The sight of the Son of God, who is full of grace and truth, brings comfort to the soul, rendering the adversities posed by Satan or any other entity ineffective. Furthermore, Edwards emphasizes that the soul, while basking in the divine glory and recognizing the superior excellency of Christ, also understands the intimate, unbreakable relationship with Him, as stated in the biblical passage,

85. *WJE* 17:210–12.

86. "I know that my redeemer liveth" (Job 19:25 KJV).

87. Edwards, "It Is a Matter," 45–70.

88. Edwards, "It Is a Matter," 54.

"My beloved is mine, and I am his" (Song 2:16).[89] Thus, Edwards argues that regardless of any worldly deprivations, the believer experiences tranquility and confidence, knowing that the glorious and excellently beautiful Christ is ever-present with them, a bond that cannot be broken.

In Edwards's sermon, "Jesus Christ Is the Shining Forth of the Father's Glory," focusing on Hebrews 1:1–4, he delves deep into Christ's divine glory, excellency, and beauty, elucidating how Jesus is the brightness of His glory and the express image of His person.[90] In this sermons, Edwards discusses the mysteries of the incarnation and the eternal procession of the Son from the Father, emphasizing the transcendent dignity and excellency of Jesus Christ. Edwards delves deep into the mystery of the incarnation, elucidating the nature of Christ's relationship with the Father. He asserts that Christ is not merely a part or attribute of the Father but possesses all the glory of the Father, having the same divine essence. The Son, he contends, shines forth in the Father's glory both in Himself and in His eternal proceeding from the Father, as stated in Philippians 2:6 and Zechariah 13:7. Edwards transitions to discuss the work of redemption, portraying it as the most glorious manifestation of God's power, wisdom, holiness, and grace. He relates this work to a new creation, referencing Isaiah 65:17, and declares it to be a masterpiece of divine works, surpassing all others in glory and excellency.

> Here is the most glorious discovery of God's power. The work of redemption is a glorious discovery of God's power. A work of creation spoken of in Scripture as a new creation. In some respects a more glorious discovery of power than the first creation. Greatness of power to be judged of by the greatness and gloriousness of the effect. Effect in new creation more glorious thing, more excellent, former not be mentioned nor come (Isa 65:17). Effect may be looked upon greater because in this work the terms from which and to which more distant. Power more manifested because not only great effect produced but great opposition overcome of sin and Satan, the powerful adversary.[91]

To sum up, for Edwards, in the work of redemption, Christ unveils the most radiant revelation of God's glory ever witnessed in this world, embodying the pinnacle of divine works and constituting the core subject of the Bible.

89. Edwards, "It Is a Matter," 54–55.
90. Edwards, "Shining Forth," 223–44.
91. Edwards, "Shining Forth," 230–31.

Holiness and Redemption

For Edwards, the work of redemption was "Brightest discovery of the holiness and justice of God."[92] Christ's redemption was "the contrivance and scheme in all respects holy," and He was "Holy Savior," "Holy goodness," and "Holy means."[93] Christ's obedience for His work of redemption was "was an infinitely holy act on account of the infinite respect to God's authority and glory of his majesty as it in compliance with his authority and as it was in repair the injury that man had done to the honor of God's majesty where he had a mind to save sinners."[94] So, Edwards asserts that "never so great a manifestation of holiness as in the death of Christ."[95]

In his sermon, "Grace Tends to Holy Practice" (1738), Edwards argues that Christ's redemptive acts were not an end in themselves but aimed at transforming the lives of the redeemed, pushing them toward holy practices. Firstly, Edwards highlights that Christ sanctified himself so that the elect might also be sanctified, as articulated in John 17:19. In essence, Christ's self-sanctification laid the groundwork for the grace that enables believers to live sanctified lives. This is not just about obtaining salvation but about leading a life that mirrors Christ's holiness. Secondly, Edwards points to Colossians 1:21–22, emphasizing that Christ reconciled believers to God explicitly to transform them from individuals tainted by "wicked works" into those who are "holy and unblamable and unreprovable" in God's eyes. The act of reconciliation is thus deeply connected to the transformation of ethical conduct. Thirdly, Edwards underscores the idea, found in multiple scriptural passages like Titus 2:14 and 2 Corinthians 5:15, that Christ's redemption aims to create a people "zealous for good works," who do not "live unto themselves" but unto Christ. It is not just about individual salvation; it is about a communal ethos of holiness and good works. Finally, Edwards cites Hebrews 9:14 to reinforce that Christ's redemptive act has a cleansing effect, purging believers' "consciences from dead works to serve the living God." Here, Edwards stresses the transition from a life preoccupied with "dead works" to one engaged in service to God.[96]

92. Edwards, "Shining Forth," 235.
93. Edwards, "Shining Forth," 235.
94. Edwards, "Worthy of His Exaltation," 353.
95. Edwards, "Shining Forth," 235.
96. *WJE* 8:295–96.

Furthermore, in Edwards's theological framework, the concept of "effectual calling" or saving conversion is not an end in itself but serves the higher purpose of enabling believers to live in "holy practice." Citing Ephesians 2:10 and 1 Thessalonians 4:7, Edwards argues that the grace granted through conversion is specifically aimed at preparing individuals for a life of good works and holiness.[97] The Apostle Paul's statement in Ephesians 2:10 that "We are created in Christ Jesus unto good works" is central to Edwards's argument. Edwards brings attention to 1 Thessalonians 4:7, in which Paul tells the Thessalonians that God's calling is towards holiness and not uncleanness. This, Edwards suggests, makes it abundantly clear that the process of conversion is aimed not merely at saving souls from damnation but at consecrating them for a life that reflects divine holiness.

In Edwards's view, spiritual knowledge and understanding are not just intellectual or theoretical concepts; they are fundamentally practical and deeply connected to how one lives. He distinguishes between "speculative knowledge," which one might equate with mere intellectual or theoretical understanding, and "saving knowledge," which is practical and transformative.[98] Citing passages from both the Old and New Testaments, Edwards argues that a true, saving knowledge of God naturally leads to a life of holiness. Pharaoh's refusal to obey God in Exodus 5:2 is attributed to his lack of knowledge about who God is. On the other hand, the Apostle John, in 1 John 2:3–4, states emphatically that knowing Christ is inextricably linked with keeping His commandments. Essentially, knowing God is not just about having facts or doctrinal points about Him; it is about experiencing a transformative relationship that has a tangible impact on one's behavior. Edwards goes further to say that this transformative, practical knowledge reveals the beauty and excellence of God's holiness, making the ugliness and destructiveness of sin more apparent. If one genuinely knows God, one understand why He is worthy of obedience and why the ways of sin are not just wrong but utterly repulsive. Edwards refers to Psalms 14:4 and Jeremiah 22:16 to emphasize that the absence of spiritual knowledge is the reason why wicked men engage in sinful practices. It is not just about not knowing God in the abstract; it is about not knowing Him in a way that changes how you live.[99] In summary, for Edwards, a true understanding of God which is given to the

97. *WJE* 8:296.

98. *WJE* 8:296–97.

99. *WJE* 8:297.

redeemed is far from passive; it is an active, dynamic knowledge that inevitably leads to a life of holiness. If you genuinely know God, it will show in your behavior and disposition, underscoring the view that spiritual knowledge is, at its core, deeply practical. Therefore, Edwards proclaims "that man that is sanctified and made holy, has more excellency than all the wicked men in the world, and is more honorable, and will be honored more, than all the rich and powerful men upon earth, put together, that are destitute of holiness."[100]

Conclusion

Edwards's work on the beauty and excellency of Jesus Christ as Redeemer and of the work of redemption serves primarily as a defense against the deistic critiques prevalent in his era. Deists like Thomas Chubb and Matthew Tindal challenged traditional Christian understandings of atonement and redemption, arguing that such doctrines contradict reason and misrepresent the nature of a perfect God. Eighteenth-century English deists also dismissed the Old Testament and Jewish laws as irrelevant or even detestable, suggesting they were rooted in materialistic worship similar to paganism. Edwards viewed these deistic claims as a severe threat to the Christian faith. In his rebuttal, he accuses deists of fundamentally misunderstanding true Christianity and the Bible, warning that their views could lead to a loss of faith and public contempt for Christian doctrine. Edwards emphasizes the necessity of divine revelation and underscores the beauty and excellency of Christ's redemptive work as central features to orthodox Christianity.

In Jonathan Edwards's theological exploration, he argues that Jesus Christ embodies a unique and harmonious blend of diverse excellencies that are often perceived as mutually exclusive or irreconcilable in any singular being. As we have shown, Edwards organizes these into three main categories. First, Christ combines seemingly opposite qualities such as infinite majesty and profound humility, perfect righteousness and boundless grace. His character reconciles the immense stature of a divine being with the profound humility of one who serves humanity, even to the point of suffering and death. Second, Edwards outlines multiple pairs of seemingly incompatible attributes in Christ—like infinite glory and humility, deep reverence toward God and equality with God, supreme

100. *WJE* 10:430.

dominion and utter obedience—to show that Christ transcends these contradictions. In Christ, these attributes are not only reconciled but also harmoniously united. Third, Christ displays a mix of characteristics, such as justice, mercy, and truth, that are usually considered impossible to coexist when applied to humanity. Yet, in Him, these attributes are seamlessly integrated. Edwards substantiates his points through extensive biblical exegesis, concluding that these varied excellencies are miraculously harmonized in Christ, who serves as both the creator and the redeemer of humanity. Thus, according to Edwards, Christ is a unique entity that defies human categorization, embodying a union of attributes and roles that would otherwise seem contradictory.

Edwards argues that this unique and harmonious blend of diverse excellencies can also be revealed in the acts of Christ. First, Edwards perceives Christ's incarnation as a powerful blend of divine dignity and human humility. While Christ's humble birth underlines his human side, his conception by the Holy Spirit upholds his divine essence. Through his incarnation, Christ reveals God's glory in a manner both grand yet intimately relatable, offering a vision of divinity that is both deeply reverent and warmly familiar. Second, in Christ's public life, Edwards sees a perfect fusion of humility (as portrayed in his modest lifestyle and interactions) and divine majesty (demonstrated through his miracles). While Christ lived humbly, moments like his transfiguration revealed his divine grandeur. Third, the crucifixion, according to Edwards, is the apex of Christ's redemptive work, manifesting both his lamb-like humility and lion-like majesty. Through this ultimate sacrifice, Christ exhibited both profound humility and unmatched divine authority. Fourth, even in his heavenly exalted state, Christ exemplifies the virtues of both the lion and the lamb. While he holds supreme power, he still extends boundless love, gentleness, and humility towards his followers, both in heaven and on Earth. Fifth, Edwards emphasizes that during the Last Judgment, Christ's dual nature will be paramount. He will be a fierce lion, delivering justice to the wicked, yet also a gentle lamb, showering boundless love on the righteous.

His theological aesthetics of redemption centers around the glory of God and the transformative impact it has on the believer. Humanity's complete dependence on God not only serves as a recognition of His glory but also ensures undivided devotion towards Him. Additionally, redemption is not just about saving from sin but also about sanctification—leading a life that reflects Christ's holiness. According to Edwards, this sanctification is the natural result of having a saving knowledge of God, which is deeply practical and life changing.

In conclusion, we have ascertained that Edwards's biblical interpretation of Christ as the Redeemer and His redemptive work consists of statements that reveal the abundant and awe-inspiring excellencies inherent in Christ and His ministry. Consistent with orthodox Christian theology, the understanding of redemption is integrally linked with Jesus Christ, who is the Redeemer and the head of the Church. This understanding also extends to the final judgment. Both heaven and hell will materialize as a result of redemption on the final day. Therefore, the subsequent chapter will examine how Edwards's aesthetic interpretation of the Bible addresses ecclesiological and eschatological themes.

Chapter 7

Jonathan Edwards's Biblical Aesthetics of the Church and Heaven

Introduction

In the preceding chapter, we explored Jonathan Edwards's biblical interpretation of Christ as the Redeemer and His redemptive work which highlights the abundant and awe-inspiring excellencies inherent in Christ and His ministry. Importantly, it also lays the foundation for understanding the church as a divine institution with an essential role in God's redemptive plan—a role that extends to the final judgment. While Edwards's thoughts on Christ as the Redeemer offered intricate and insightful revelations, the scope of this chapter broadens to explore Edwards's ecclesiological aesthetics and biblical interpretations concerning the church, as well as the beauty of heaven.

In particular, while philosophical studies of Edwards's theology have shed light on his conception of the beauty of the church, the way his biblical interpretation illuminates areas that cannot be fully captured by philosophical inquiry remains fascinating but under-explored. Studies of the beauty of heaven also tend to focus on Edwards's sermon "Heaven is a World of Love." Therefore, this chapter will explore Edwards's broader biblical understanding of the beauty of the church and heaven through a variety of texts and sermons.

Jonathan Edwards's Philosophical Examination of the Beauty of the Church

As Douglas Sweeney has insightfully pointed out, despite Jonathan Edwards's extensive work in pastoral ministry, his ecclesiology, or doctrine of the church, has largely been overlooked by academic scholars.[1] The scarcity of research on this topic is partially because Edwards never published a standalone book or pamphlet specifically focusing on it. Sweeney further notes that Jonathan Edwards extensively wrote on church membership, particularly during Northampton's "communion controversy," but his writings focus mainly on local church issues rather than offering a broad doctrine of the church.[2] Edwards's lack of direct reference to his ecclesiology also creates difficulties in tracing his philosophical approach to the beauty of the church.

In order to overcome these difficulties, Krister Sairsingh attempts to discover the philosophical approach of Edwards's ecclesiological aesthetics in his essay "The Nature of True Virtue."[3] He extensively analyzes the relationship between Jonathan Edwards's concept of true virtue and his understanding of the church, proposing that Edwards's notion of a "community of consent" essentially aligns with his ideal vision of the visible church.[4] According to Sairsingh, Edwards does not explicitly say that this community created through the exercise of true virtue is the church, but the natural progression of his ideas strongly suggests this conclusion. In Edwards's view, true virtue is underlined by general benevolence, or a deep-seated love and goodwill for all of existence. Edwards posits that when individuals exercise this form of benevolence, they form a union of hearts, especially with those who also share the same benevolent nature. This is different from a simple, natural morality which is driven by self-interest. Edwards, according to Sairsingh, argues that the visible church should be seen as a gathering of individuals who are united by

1. For more studies on Edwards's ecclesiology, see Sweeny, "Church," 167–89; Schafer, "Conception of the Church," 51–66; Bibber, "Concepts of Church"; Sairsingh, "Idea of Divine Glory"; Hall, "Editor's Introduction," in *WJE* 12:1–90; Pauw, "Church as Mother"; "Jonathan Edwards' Ecclesiology"; Bezzant, *Jonathan Edwards and the Church.*

2. Sweeney, "Church," 167.

3. Sairsingh, "Divine Glory," 217.

4. Sairsingh, "Divine Glory," 217.

this general benevolence, not just by the virtue of being part of an institutionalized religion.[5]

Sairsingh highlights Edwards's categorization of beauty into two types: primary and secondary.[6] Primary beauty is intrinsically tied to true virtue and relates to spiritual qualities, whereas secondary beauty is tied to natural morality and aesthetics. In Edwards's thought, the church, in this regard, would be a community that identifies with the primary beauty—consisting of people united by their genuine love for God and each other:

> The significance of Edwards' distinction between primary and secondary beauty, between the beauty of true virtue and the morality of natural conscience is that it affords Edwards a means of distinguishing the church as the community of true beauty is comprised of those whose hearts are united in love to God and to one another. This community is to be distinguished from the natural community whose object of consent and love is not being in general but a private and a limited system.[7]

As George Marsden argues, this community of true virtue is distinct from a community that appears to be virtuous. According to Marsden, Jonathan Edwards argued that many qualities praised as true virtue are actually expressions of private interests extended to larger groups. For example, while familial love is universally admired, it often manifests as a form of private benevolence rather than public goodwill, as families can be selfish toward others. Similarly, love for one's community or nation, although commendable within those contexts, does not qualify as universal benevolence. Edwards cited the Romans, whose patriotic love was praised but led to the detriment of other nations. His general principle was that the larger the group to which a private affection extends, the more likely people are to mistake it for true virtue, due to the limitations of their perspective.[8] Jonathan Edwards posited that benevolence within private systems, such as family or nation, is admired because it exhibits secondary beauty. In contrast to the community motivated by natural conscience and self-interest, which is driven by secondary beauty, the church is the community of primary beauty, where hearts are united in

5. Sairsingh, "Divine Glory," 217–18.

6. For an explanation of Edwards's understanding of primary and secondary beauty, see chapter 3 of this book.

7. Sairsingh, "Divine Glory," 250. See Sairsingh, "Divine Glory," 242–49.

8. Marsden, *Jonathan Edwards*, 468–69.

love to God and to each other.[9] In sum, for Edwards, the concept of true virtue is not merely an isolated moral idea but serves as a foundational principle for his ecclesiology. The church, as Edwards sees it, is a community bound by a shared profound love for God and the entire system of being, as opposed to communities that are guided by self-interest and a limited view of morality.

Edwards's understanding of God's end of the creation and its connection to the true and beautiful community supports the appropriateness of Sairsingh's analysis. Edwards argues that "God made the world that he might communicate, and the creature receive, his glory."[10] As previous chapters addressed, Edwards states that the end of God's creation is to express and communicate His glory, i.e., excellency and beauty. In Jonathan Edwards's theological framework, the purpose of intelligent creatures is not merely to passively receive the benefits of God's attributes such as justice, wisdom, and goodness. Instead, these creatures are envisioned as active participants in a cosmic drama whose ultimate purpose is to promote God's glory. Edwards notes that God's glory is essentially the external expression and communication of His intrinsic attributes. When God created the world, His aim was not dual (to make creatures happy and to exhibit His perfections) but singular ("to shine forth or flow out" His essential glory and "infinite fullness").[11] Intelligent creatures are uniquely positioned to be concerned in these effects, as Edwards puts it. They are capable of understanding, loving, and enjoying God, thereby actively participating in the realization of God's glory. In other words, humans have a role in manifesting or making evident the glory of God through their actions, decisions, and even their capacity for intellectual and emotional experiences like understanding and joy. This is not a one-sided relationship where God simply bestows His goodness or justice upon His creations. Rather, it is a dynamic interaction, where intelligent creatures contribute to the unfolding of God's attributes. This is a profoundly participatory view of existence. It places a certain kind of cosmic responsibility on intelligent creatures to actively seek and promote God's glory. Their ultimate end, in

9. Sairsingh notes that Edwards acknowledges the difficulty in distinguishing between these two types of communities. This is because the external forms of moral and spiritual life can be imitated. Edwards's later writings, like *The Religious Affections*, aim to address this issue by providing criteria to distinguish between true and false forms of religious affection. Sairsingh, "Divine Glory," 251–52.

10. *WJE* 13:495.

11. *WJE* 23:152.

everything they do, should align with this higher purpose. They are participants in the divine act of making God's intrinsic qualities known and felt, thereby fulfilling the ultimate purpose for which they were created: to contribute to the manifestation of God's glory:

> It seems to be a thing in itself fit and desirable, that the glorious perfections of God should be known, and the operations and expressions of them seen by other beings besides himself. . . . As God's perfections are things in themselves excellent, so the expression of them in their proper acts and fruits is excellent, and the knowledge of these excellent perfections, and of these glorious expressions of them, is an excellent thing, the existence of which is in itself valuable and desirable. 'Tis a thing infinitely good in itself that God's glory should be known by a glorious society of created beings. And that there should be in them an increasing knowledge of God to all eternity is an existence, a reality infinitely worthy to be, and worthy to be valued and regarded by him, to whom it belongs in order that it be, which, of all things possible, is fittest and best.[12]

In other words, for Edwards, the knowledge of God's inherent attributes and their manifestations is not only intrinsically good but also eternally desirable. This ever-expanding understanding within a community is infinitely good, forming a reality that is the fittest and best of all possible existences.

However, the glorious obligations of humanity to God as a holy community made in the image of God were lost after the Fall. Men have lost the light of spiritual beauty that was supplied by God, and they have lost the privilege of rejoicing and enjoying the glory of God that they had when they were created. This loss was restored through the redemptive work of Christ. Edwards argues that "the church is everywhere spoken of, as being so nearly united to Christ that she is one with him; and Christ, as having an inclination that believers should be partakers of his glory."[13] Sweeny and Strachan's statement about Edwards's aesthetic ecclesiology is a good description of how the role of the church implies beauty: "The church, as with all the created order, existed to reflect the holiness and goodness of God in a world cursed by sin. It represented the lasting physical manifestation of God on earth, an outpost exhibiting the beauty

12. *WJE* 8:430–32. See also *WJE* 23:151–53.

13. *WJE* 13:272–73.

of the Lord in a darkened world."[14] Thus, the church is a community of holy beauty that, through the merits of Christ, regains the duties and privileges of humanity—as a holy community—lost due to the Fall.

In short, Jonathan Edwards's ecclesiological aesthetics, as elucidated by Krister Sairsingh and George Marsden, offer an understanding of the church as a community of consent grounded in true virtue and primary beauty. In contrast to communities animated by self-interest or limited moral perspectives, Edwards conceptualizes the church as a gathering of individuals united by a general benevolence—a deep-seated love for all of existence. This love extends beyond mere institutional affiliation, elevating the church to a community that embodies primary beauty, which is intrinsically connected to true virtue and spiritual qualities. Edwards argues that other communities often represent secondary beauty, shaped by narrower forms of morality and self-interest. Only the church, as a community imbued with primary beauty, exemplifies hearts united in love for both God and all of creation. Edwards's theology, moreover, outlines a participatory cosmology in which intelligent creatures are not mere passive recipients of God's glory but active contributors to its manifestation. This active engagement was compromised after the Fall, but was restored through the redemptive work of Christ, transforming the church into a community of holy beauty. Through Christ, the church reclaims its original, exalted purpose: to serve as an embodiment of God's glory, drawing its members into a profound and holistic love for God and the entire system of being. In this way, true virtue becomes not an isolated moral concept, but a foundational principle for understanding the church as a space where the holy and the beautiful converge, fulfilling humanity's ultimate purpose in the cosmic drama of divine glory.

Jonathan Edwards's Biblical Interpretations on the Beauty of the Church

Edwards's Biblical Understanding of the Church

Based on the interpretation of 1 Corinthians 15,[15] Edwards sees the church as the entire body of believers, headed by Christ, bound together

14. Strachan and Sweeney, *Jonathan Edwards on Beauty*, 98.

15. "For since by man came death, by man came also the resurrection of the dead. For as in Adam all die, even so in Christ shall all be made alive" (1 Cor 15:21–22 KJV); "And as we have borne the image of the earthy, we shall also bear the image of the heavenly" (15:49 KJV).

in the covenant of grace just as humanity, headed by Adam, was bound by the covenant of work.[16] In his sermon "Christians a Chosen Generation" (1731),[17] Edwards states that Christians "are under the same government. They are one society, one body politic, and therefore as here the church is represented by a nation, so oftentimes [it] is called a city. They are subject to the same king, Jesus Christ. He is the head of the church; he is the head of this body politic."[18] In detail, Jonathan Edwards conceptualizes the church as a singular society under Christ, their celestial Head. He expounds upon four key aspects that unite this divine society: native country, language, governance, and communal interests. Firstly, supported by references to the saints being 'born from above' and aligning with the idea that "they are near akin to the inhabitants of the heavenly world" (Heb 12:22–23), Edwards argues that Heaven serves as the church's "native country," with its members born anew from celestial principles and divine guidance.[19] Consequently, although they are temporarily earthly sojourners, they long for their ultimate celestial abode. Secondly, Edwards identifies a doctrinal and spiritual "common language" among the church members that transcends mere linguistic commonality.[20] This language includes adherence to foundational doctrines and uniformity in prayer and praise. He draws upon 2 Timothy 1:13, which mentions holding "fast the form of sound words," and Jude 3, which speaks of the faith "once delivered to the saints," to argue that this spiritual vernacular unifies their religious expression and practice. In the third segment on governance, Edwards asserts that the church is ruled by Jesus Christ, the spiritual King, substantiated by passages like Psalms 110:3, which describes people being "willing in the day of thy power."[21] All members willingly subject themselves to Christ's rule, guided by universal laws and disciplined through both external and internal means. Christ's mode of governance is unique, exerting immediate influence on the wills of his subjects to ensure compliance with divine ordinances. Lastly, Edwards emphasizes the unity of public interests and

16. *WJE* 3:323–25.

17. The main passage is 1 Peter 2:9: "But ye are a chosen generation, a royal priesthood, an holy nation, a peculiar people; that ye should show forth the praises of him who hath called you out of darkness into marvelous light" (*WJE* 17:276).

18. *WJE* 17:304.

19. *WJE* 17:303.

20. *WJE* 17:303–4.

21. *WJE* 17:304–5.

concerns within the church.[22] Just as citizens of a nation share common laws, enemies, and socio-political goals, members of Christ's body are knit together by shared covenants, adversaries, and ultimate objectives. The flourishing of the church corresponds to the spiritual well-being of its individual members, and they collectively engage in spiritual warfare under Christ, their supreme Commander. Thus, Edwards portrays the church as a homogeneous, divinely guided society distinctively characterized by its heavenly origin, unified spiritual language, Christ-centric governance, and collective spiritual interests. This organic union of the church with Christ is closely tied to Christ's redemptive work on the basis of the covenant of grace.

The Redemptive Unity and Shared Glory between Christ and the Church

For Edwards, in the intricate narrative of Christ's relationship with His church, His redemptive work plays a pivotal role, underpinning the unity between Him and His believers. This unity is not merely symbolic, but is deeply entrenched in the idea that the rewards and merits Christ achieved through His sacrifice are shared with His church, making them co-participants in His glory. Here, Edwards raises and addresses critical questions regarding the distribution of Christ's merits and rewards. It queries how believers can benefit from Christ's merits if He sought them for Himself, and conversely, how Christ benefits if the merits were for the believers.[23] Edwards resolves this conundrum by presenting Christ as a "public person," representing and acting for the entirety of the body of believers, thereby ensuring that the merits were for both Him and the believers.[24] Drawing upon Colossians 1:18–19, Edwards underscores Christ's role as the head of the church and His excellency in all things.[25] He elucidates that while all fullness and excellencies dwells in Christ, the benefits and glory He merited are shared with the church, forming a

22. *WJE 17*:305.

23. Edwards, "Worthy of His Exaltation," 359.

24. Edwards, "Worthy of His Exaltation," 359.

25. Here, Edwards uses the term "preeminence" instead of excellency (Edwards, "Worthy of His Exaltation," 360).

unity termed by Edwards as "one mystical Christ"—a collective body of all believers unified under Christ.[26]

Referencing 1 Corinthians 12:12, Edwards further explores this unity, demonstrating that the church, despite its diverse membership, forms one body in Christ. He contends that Christ's actions and merits were for the benefit of this unified body, comprising both Christ and the believers, thereby sharing the glory of His redemptive work. In order to illustrate the communion of benefits within this mystical body, Edwards employs the metaphor of the head and body, explaining that while benefits flow from the head (Christ) to the members (believers), they are also retained in the head. He draws analogies with a king and the head of a family, representing and sharing in the prosperity of their respective domains, to illuminate this concept.[27] Edwards also expounds on the idea that by taking on human nature and becoming our surety, Christ extended His person to include all believers, making them parts or members of Him. This unity signifies that the entire body, head and members alike, share in the rewards and righteousness of Christ's work. Moreover, citing 1 Timothy 3:16, Edwards explains that Christ needed satisfaction for the imputed guilt He took upon Himself, emphasizing that this does not diminish the glory of Christ's love but rather showcases His love in uniting Himself with us.

> Though he had no guilt of his own that needed to be satisfied for, yet he had imputed guilt and he needed satisfaction for this. After he was once become our surety and took our guilt upon him if he had not satisfied, justice and the law would have stood against him and so is said to be justified (1 Tim 3:16). This doesn't at all derogate from the glory of Christ's law to us in doing and suffering he has benefit as well as we of what he did and suffered and was to be rewarded for it. For this doesn't at all argue against the freeness of the love of Christ in making himself one of us, in becoming the head of this body when he had no need of anything, nor was capable of any addition to his happiness. It shows his love that he would thus unite himself to us.[28]

In short, Edwards delves into the complex relationship between Christ and His church, elucidating how the glory of Christ's redemptive work is shared with believers through a communion of benefits within the

26. Edwards, "Worthy of His Exaltation," 360–61.

27. Edwards, "Worthy of His Exaltation," 360–61.

28. Edwards, "Worthy of His Exaltation," 361.

mystical body of Christ. And, he addresses the dichotomy of merit for Christ and believers, resolving it through the understanding of Christ's role as a public person representing the whole body, thereby emphasizing the shared nature of His glory and rewards with His church.

The Happiness of the Church and Divine Righteousness

The significance Edwards placed on the relationship between the redemptive work and the church can also be discerned in his sermon series, *A History of the Work of Redemption* (1739), which takes Isaiah 51:8 as its focal text.[29] In the first sermon of the series, Edwards reveals the relationship between the work of redemption and the church. He posits that the work of redemption is a divine operation that spans from the fall of man to the end of the world. In order to expose this doctrine,[30] Edwards interprets the passage (Isa 51:8) relating to the happiness of the church. Edwards provides a theological framework that centers on the church's enduring happiness as a manifestation of God's immutable attributes of mercy and faithfulness. He argues regarding the church that these divine qualities will see the church safely through all the challenges and changes the world may offer, leading it to a state of eternal victory and deliverance. According to Edwards, this enduring happiness of the church is rooted in the eternal attributes of God's righteousness and salvation.[31]

Edwards compares the happiness of the church in God's righteousness and salvation to the power and prosperity of the church's enemies. He argues that the seemingly beautiful things that the church's enemies have, such as glory, power, and prosperity, which are described as "the finest and most glorious apparel," are cursed by God and will diminish and eventually disappear.[32] In his exegesis of Nehemiah 9:8, he argues that the word "righteousness" is very often used in the Bible to refer to God's "faithfulness in fulfilling his covenant promises to his church."[33] He also draws on Psalms 24:5; 36:10; 51:14; and Daniel 9:16 to show that God's righteousness

29. "For the moth shall eat them up like a garment, And the worm shall eat them like wool: But my righteousness shall be for ever, And my salvation from generation to generation" (Isa 51:8 KJV).

30. "Doctrine—The Work of Redemption is a work that God carries on from the fall of man to the end of the world" (*WJE* 9:116).

31. *WJE* 9:114.

32. *WJE* 9:113–14.

33. *WJE* 9:114.

and "covenant mercy" are the same.[34] Moreover, Edwards argues that the phrases "forever" and "from generation to generation" used in Isaiah 51:8 confirm the continuity of God's salvation for the church.[35] Edwards's description of the church as forever and from generation to generation for the happiness of the church is in clear contrast to the term "shortlived" used to describe the prosperity and glory of the church's enemies.[36] In short, Edwards's comparison of the eternal happiness of the church and the perishable glory of the church's enemies illustrates the beauty of what God's righteousness has bestowed upon the church.

Edwards's argument that the happiness of the church belongs to the righteousness of God is closely tied to the nature of the beauty that the church possesses. As we have seen in previous chapters, before the Fall, the world was imbued with divine light, representing the knowledge, glory, and favor of God. Humanity existed in a state of spiritual and intellectual fulfillment, graced by both divine providence and intrinsic beauty. However, the Fall led to a catastrophic dimming of this divine light, plunging the world into profound darkness and despair, a state more dire than the initial condition described in Genesis 1:2. This spiritual void was so intense that neither angelic nor human intervention could remedy it. Edwards describes the post-Fall condition as one of extreme alienation from God, marked by the loss of divine grace and favor. This resulted in humanity losing its love for holiness and, consequently, its source of joy and happiness. The creature that was once beautiful in its spiritual essence became sinful, epitomizing the loss of divine favor and the degradation of human nature.[37] In outlining his entire sermon series on the work of redemption, Edwards states that God revealed himself from time to time from the Fall until the coming of Christ, and that in the meantime the church has seen the light of revelation in the word of God, and this light was a sign of the true light, like the sun shining from Christ as the light of the world. Just as he states that the light of spiritual beauty, which was given to the prelapsarian world, was taken away with the Fall, and began to shine a glimmer of light of revelation, like moonlight (reflected from the sun), has been given to the church, and that it has been given to

34. *WJE* 9:114–15.

35. *WJE* 9:115–16.

36. *WJE* 9:113.

37. In terms of Edwards's aesthetic understanding on the Fall, see chapter 5 of this book.

the church progressively, according to the progressiveness of the revelation of the Redeemer.[38]

> God did soon after the fall begin actually to save the souls of men through Christ's redemption. In this Christ who had newly taken upon [himself] the work of mediator between God and man did first then begin that work wherein he appeared in the exercise of his kingly office, as in the sacrifices he was represented in his priestly office, and in the first prediction of redemption by Christ he had appeared in the exercise of his prophetical office. In that prediction the light of Christ's redemption first began to dawn in the prophecies of it; in the institution of sacrifice it first began to dawn in the types of it; in this, viz. his beginning actually to save men, it first began to dawn in the fruit of it.[39]

The created world, deprived of the light of spiritual beauty by sin, is again enlightened with the light of divine spiritual beauty by the imputed righteousness of Christ, and the church is made the possessor of eternal happiness by the righteousness of God.[40]

The Progressive Beauty of the Church

In Edwards's theological aesthetics, the church's excellency is not fixed, but has an increasing and developing quality. He argues that the church's

38. "God revealed himself of old from time to time from the fall of man to the coming of Christ. The church during that space of time enjoyed the light of divine revelation in God's word. They had in a degree the light of the gospel, but all these revelations were only so many forerunners and earnests of the great light that he should bring who came to be the light of the world. That whole space of time was as it were the time of night wherein the church of God was not indeed wholly without light, but it is like the light of the moon and stars that we have in the night, a dim light in comparison of the light of the sun and mixed with a great deal of darkness. 'No glory by reason of the glory [that excelleth],' 2 Cor 3:10. The church indeed had the light of the sun then but it was but as reflected from the moon and stars. The church all that while was a mirror, Gal 4:1–2" (*WJE* 9:129).

39. *WJE* 9:137–38.

40. By understanding Edwards's concept of union with Christ as an ontological concept, Anri Morimoto interprets not only Edwards's soteriology but also the entirety of Reformed soteriology as still within the scope of Catholic theology; however, Edwards's understanding on the doctrine of the justification is thoroughly based on the imputation of Christ's righteousness. In his sermon "Justification by Faith Alone," based on his exegesis of Romans, Edwards makes it clear that salvation is granted because of the accomplishments and righteousness of Christ, not as a reward for obedience. See *WJE* 19:147; Morimoto, *Jonathan Edwards*; Cho, *On Justification*; Kang, "Justified by Faith."

glory develops as it battles its enemies and experiences God's deliverance in times of hardship.

> By each of them God delivers his church. Each of them is accompanied with a glorious advancement of the state of the church. The first, which ended in the destruction of Jerusalem, was attended with bringing the church into the glorious state of the gospel, a glorious state of the church very much prophesied of of old, whereby the church was advanced into far more glorious circumstances than it was in before under the Jewish dispensation.[41]

For instance, Edwards emphasizes that although Satan was filled with intense fury, aiming to dismantle God's church just before the biblical flood, his efforts were in vain. Edwards points out that the global deluge might have overthrown the world, but it failed to disrupt God's ongoing Work of Redemption. Instead of collapsing, this divine enterprise continued to be fortified, serving as a precursor to the forthcoming arrival of the Savior who would accomplish the redemptive work for his people. He continues that the church's resiliency and ongoing role in God's plan demonstrate its ultimate triumph over the forces that aim to destroy it.[42] In addition to the flood, Edwards asserts that historically, the church has often found itself outmatched by its enemies in terms of strength. Yet, the church rarely resorts to forcible resistance; instead, it entrusts itself to divine protection. Edwards highlights various epochs when the church faced severe persecutions—from the Jewish antagonisms before Rome's destruction of Jerusalem to the heathen persecutions before Constantine and the oppression under Papal authorities. Despite these existential threats, the church has remarkably endured. What makes this resilience especially astonishing, according to Edwards, is the frequency with which the church has teetered on the brink of annihilation, only to be miraculously saved each time. He cites Biblical examples like the flood during the time of Noah and the escape at the Red Sea as divine interventions that preserved the church when all seemed lost. Similarly, in historical instances such as the last heathen persecution, the Arian heresy, and attempts by papal powers to dismantle the churches of the Reformation, divine intervention has repeatedly thwarted the apparent triumph of the church's enemies. Edwards says, "after the darkest times

41. *WJE* 9:352.
42. *WJE* 9:148–50.

of the church God has made his church most gloriously to flourish."[43] Finally, Edwards emphasizes that Christ gives grace to His church and leads it into glory.[44] By citing Isaiah 26:17 and 42:10–12, he concludes that the church has suffered as a woman in labor to establish the glorious kingdom of Christ in the world, and that in the end the church will rejoice and give glory to Jehovah.[45] To sum up, the glory possessed by the church has progressively developed because of the church's suffering at the hands of her enemies, her struggles against them, and her eventual preservation and deliverance by God.

The Holy Spirit and the Church

In Edwards's ecclesiology, if the church is organically united and headed by Christ, then the way God communicates Himself to the church is through the Holy Spirit.[46] He interprets 1 Corinthian 13:8 and derives the doctrine—"That great fruit of the Spirit in which the Holy Ghost shall not only for a season but everlastingly be communicated to the church of Christ is divine love." Edwards emphasizes that the divine or Christian love is not just one among many fruits of the Spirit, but the very epitome of the Spirit's unfailing, eternal influence on the church. This divine love is unique in that it neither fails nor ceases, making it a defining characteristic of both individual members and the collective body of the church. It is the cornerstone that underpins both individual faith and collective spirituality.[47] He distinguishes between other gifts and love given to the church and saints. Other gifts are means to promote holiness and the building up of Christ's kingdom, but divine love is the sum of all holiness, the end goal itself. Hence, when other gifts have served their purpose and cease to be, divine love persists eternally. It is not merely another aspect of spiritual life but the ultimate aim of the Christian faith, the enduring testament to the Holy Spirit is an eternal influence on the church.

Drawing on 1 Corinthians 2:14–15 and Jude 1:19, Edwards argues that the first sign that identifies a member of the church as a true saint is

43. *WJE* 9:448–49.
44. *WJE* 9:371–72.
45. *WJE* 9:477–78.
46. *WJE* 8:158.
47. *WJE* 8:358–60.

the indwelling of the Holy Spirit.[48] Noting that the word ψυχικοί used in Jude 1:19 is the same as the word translated "natural" in 1 Corinthians 2, he argues that "the Spirit of God is given to the true saints to dwell in them, as his proper lasting abode; and to influence their hearts, as a principle of new nature, or as a divine supernatural spring of life and action."[49] The Holy Spirit, given to dwell among the true saints, makes them partakers in the divine nature. Since the essential nature of the Holy Spirit is holiness, the saints who have received His special grace become partakers in His holiness. Edwards argues that the most extraordinary work God accomplishes is one that involves a deep, intimate fellowship with human beings. This is a fellowship in which individuals, though creatures, come to participate in the divine nature—not in essence but in a manner that is profoundly intimate and reflective of God's own attributes. Edwards emphasizes that the Scripture provides ample evidence for this. For instance, the notion of believers being "partakers of divine nature" is explicitly mentioned in 2 Peter 1:4. Other passages, such as 1 John 4:12, 15–16; Romans 8:10; and John 17:21, point to God and Christ dwelling within the believer. This is not a superficial relationship; rather, it is one of remarkable closeness, wherein the believer becomes the "temple of the living God" (2 Cor 6:16). Moreover, there are scriptural indications that believers live through Christ's life (Gal 2:20), they are made partakers of God's holiness (Heb 12:10), they experience the love of Christ dwelling in them (John 17:26), and they are filled with a unique joy that is fulfilled in them (John 17:13). Clearly, for Jonathan Edwards, this is not about becoming divine in essence—a notion that is not only heretical but also blasphemous. Rather, it is about partaking in God's spiritual fullness, beauty, and happiness to the extent that a creature can do so (Eph 3:17–19; John 1:16).[50]

The True Saints and the Beauty of the Church

According to Edwards, true saints, who are members of the church, love God, Jesus Christ, and His word and work, and that this love is motivated by "the divine excellence and glory of God," not by any benefit or gain for

48. *WJE* 2:197.

49. *WJE* 2:197–200.

50. *WJE* 2:203.

themselves.[51] Drawing on 2 Corinthians 3:18 and 4:3–6, he argues that the believer is convinced of the divine things in the gospel by seeing and feeling the glory and beauty of God.[52] It is the "new spiritual sense" given to the true saints that enables them to comprehend the divine beauty and moral excellency.[53] Edwards makes it clear that this "new sense" is only possessed by true saints:

> So that the spiritual perceptions which a sanctified and spiritual person has, are not only diverse from all that natural men have, after the manner that the ideas or perceptions of the same sense may differ one from another, but rather as the ideas and sensations of different senses do differ. . . . This new spiritual sense, and the new dispositions that attend it, are no new faculties, but are new principles of nature. . . . the Spirit of God by his common influences may assist men's natural ingeniosity, as he assisted Bezaleel and Aholiab in the curious works of the tabernacle [Exodus 36:1–2]: so he may assist men's natural abilities in political affairs, and improve their courage, and other natural qualifications; as he is said to have put his Spirit on the seventy elders [Numbers 11:25], and on Saul, so as to give him another heart [I Samuel 8:9]: so God may greatly assist natural men's reason, in their reasoning about secular things, or about the doctrines of religion, and may greatly advance the clearness of their apprehensions and notions of things of religion in many respects, without giving any spiritual sense.[54]

Edwards says that only saints having this sense can see or know the beauty of holiness. Edwards even stresses,

> By this men understand the true glory of heaven, which consists in the beauty and happiness that is in holiness. By this is seen the amiableness and happiness of both saints and angels. He that sees the beauty of holiness, or true moral good, sees the greatest and most important thing in the world, which is the fullness of all things, without which all the world is empty, no better than nothing, yea, worse than nothing. Unless this is seen, nothing is seen, that is worth the seeing: for there is no other true excellency or beauty.[55]

51. *WJE* 2:240.
52. *WJE* 2:297.
53. *WJE* 2:205–6.
54. *WJE* 2:205–7.
55. *WJE* 2:274.

For Edwards, true saints have a true sense of taste, given to them by the Holy Spirit, that enables them to discern what is truly spiritually holy beauty.

Another thing that is emphasized in Edwards's understanding of the beauty of the church is that just as there is a "beautiful symmetry and proportion" in Christ, there is also this beauty in the true saints.[56] In Edwards's view, true religious affections display a sense of beautiful symmetry and proportion, which is a natural outcome of genuine sanctification. He contrasts this true beauty to the glaring imbalances often seen in the false religiosity of hypocrites. While even true saints may have imperfections due to various factors like inadequate education or natural temperament, their affections and virtues lack the disproportion seen in hypocrites.[57] Edwards argues that for true saints, their affections are a reflection of the full image of Christ, based on the idea that "of his fullness we have all received, grace upon grace" (John 1:16). Each grace found in Christ is correspondingly found in the believer, creating a harmonious spiritual profile. This harmony includes a balanced coexistence of hope and fear, joy, and godly sorrow, which is scripturally supported (Pss 33:18; 147:11; Matt 28:8; Ezek 20:42–43). On the other hand, Edwards notes that hypocrites often display an uneven spiritual life, similar to "Ephraim" in Hosea 7:8—described as "a cake not turned," or half-baked. Their affections are partial, lacking balance and proportion.[58]

In Edwards's interpretation, Christ is not just the provider of all good and perfection to the elect in both heaven and earth, but He Himself is fulfilled by the church. The church serves as Christ's glorious and beautiful ornament, much like a virtuous wife serves as a crown to her husband. Edwards draws from multiple biblical references to substantiate this: he mentions John 17:5 to talk about Christ filling all things and being filled by the church; John 19:23 to describe the church as Christ's seamless garment, symbolic of the unity of its diverse members; Exodus 28:2 and Psalm 133:2 to discuss the church as a garment made for glory and for beauty; Isaiah 62:3 and Zechariah 9:16–17 to portray the church as a crown of glory and a royal diadem in God's hand.[59] Moreover, Edwards suggests that Christ finds "exceeding and satisfying delight and joy" in the church, citing Isaiah 62:5 where it states, "As the bridegroom

56. *WJE* 2:365–66.

57. *WJE* 2:365.

58. *WJE* 2:365–67.

59. *WJE* 15:186.

rejoices over the bride, so shall your God rejoice over you." Edwards argues that the ultimate purpose of creation, accomplished through and for Christ, was for Him to obtain a spouse—the church—upon whom He could pour His love and find eternal delight. This relationship completes Christ, much like Adam was completed by Eve, as cited from Genesis 2:20.[60] In summary, Edwards asserts that the church is not just the recipient of Christ's love and perfection but also serves as the entity that completes and delights Him.

Edwards's theological aesthetic interpretation of the church does not just stop at an understanding of the earthly church; it extends to an interpretation of the church's twofold state. Interpreting 1 Corinthians 13:8–10, he states the twofold state of the church and its relationship to love. Edwards highlights the distinction between the imperfect and perfect states of the Christian church.[61] He posits that the church has two imperfect states: the early days of the church when it was not fully established and its entire time on earth until the end of days, both compared to a state of childhood. In contrast, the church's perfect states are likened to stages of maturity: one when the church has fully evolved in its worldly existence and the other when it reaches its heavenly state, achieving its full stature in Christ. Central to these states is the enduring nature of divine love or charity, which persists even when other spiritual fruits fade. Edwards's discussion on this issue expands the aesthetic interpretation of the church to include a study of heaven.[62]

Jonathan Edwards's Philosophical Examination of the Beauty of Heaven

Kin Yip Louie addresses Edwards's aesthetic eschatology stating Edwards's list of five kinds of glory "enjoyed by separated souls"[63]: (1) they dwell "in the same blessed abode with the glorified human nature of

60. *WJE* 15:187.

61. *WJE* 8:366–67.

62. This line of reasoning that connects the church and heaven is also consistently present in Edwards's other works. For instance, in his sermon series "A History of the Work of Redemption," Edwards explains that the praise spoken of in Isaiah 42:10–12 will not just fill the earth, but will also fill the heavens, and that the earthly and heavenly churches will praise God in unison and in glory. See *WJE* 9:477–78.

63. Regarding this expression, Louie notes that "a term employed by Edwards to describe the soul in the intermediate state, after the death of the physical body but before the bodily resurrection at eschaton" (Louie, "Theological Aesthetics," 141).

Christ"; (2) "they go to be with Christ, to dwell in the immediate, full, and constant view of him"; (3) "the souls of true saints, when absent from the body, go to be with Jesus Christ, as they are brought into a most perfect conformity to, and union with him"; (4) "they enjoy a glorious and immediate intercourse and converse with him"; and (5) "they are received to a glorious fellowship with Christ in his blessedness."[64] As Louie's work reveals, Edwards understands heaven as a world of divine love filled with beauty and excellency. For Edwards, as addressed above, God is the communicative Being, and the Being eternally delivering His excellency.[65] He argues that heaven is a progressive state as the created world has been developed through the progress of the revelation:

> It seems to me probable that that part of the church that is in heaven have been, from the beginning of the world, progressive in their light and in their happiness, as the church on earth has; and that much of their happiness has consisted in seeing the progressive wonderful doings of God with respect to his church here in this world.[66]

In detail, since God's excellency and beauty are infinite, His attribute is unceasingly and eternally communicated and delivered to the finite creatures not only in the earth but also in heaven.

Edwards argues that in heaven, the saints will be focused on Christ's love and glory. He posits that the mutual love among saints in heaven will be so great that the fact that Christ Jesus loves other saints will bring them immense joy. Seeing Christ express His love towards them will fill them with delight.

They will also find joy in observing other saints who are pleased that Christ loves and rejoices in them.[67] In describing the heavenly happiness enjoyed by the saints after the resurrection, Edwards states that the physical beauty of the saints in heaven will be most beautifully and excellently transformed.[68] The senses, such as sight and hearing, are much more sophisticated in the post-resurrection saints, allowing them to see each

64. Louie, "Theological Aesthetics," 141–46. He cites Edwards's statements of the five kinds of glory from the Banner of Truth Trust edition of Edwards, *Works of Jonathan Edwards*, 2:27–29.

65. *WJE* 8:533–34.

66. *WJE* 13:478. For more study on the progressiveness of heaven in Edwards's thought, see Paul Ramsey, "Heaven Is a Progressive State," in *WJE* 8:706–38.

67. *WJE* 13:303.

68. *WJE* 13:301.

other's beauty more clearly and to have more enjoyable and intimate conversations. Here, Edwards stresses seeing Christ in heaven. For Edwards, of the senses, sight is the most noble and will be the source of immense pleasure and delight, far surpassing our current capacities. He states that the illumination in the heavenly realms will primarily come from the radiance of glorified bodies, particularly their faces, and most importantly from Jesus Christ in His glorified form, as well as potentially any visible manifestation of God's presence. The luminosity emanating from Christ's face will be incomparably more excellent and pleasing than any light found in the earthly realm.[69] In other words, the ultimate source of this sensory delight will be God, specifically in the vision of Christ's external glory. This visible glory serves as a conduit for perceiving divine spiritual glory; it is not an end in itself. Edwards contends that this sensory experience will be wholly subordinate to spiritual experiences and delights. The visible manifestation of God's glory will thus act as a supplement to, rather than a substitute for, the spiritual perception of the same. In essence, Edwards situates the *visio beatifica* (beatific vision) in a framework where both body and spirit are harmoniously integrated, each enhancing the experience of divine glory. The external senses, rather than detracting from spiritual engagement, facilitate a fuller, richer experience of God's glory, without any risk of inordinacy or overshadowing spiritual experience.[70] According to McClymond and McDermott, "heavenly vision was a basic theme in Edwards's treatment of heaven."[71] Edwards's views on the *visio beatifica*—the divine sight of God experienced by saints in heaven—appear to have evolved over time, demonstrating a subtle shift from a more Platonic skepticism about the physical body to a viewpoint that incorporates bodily experience. Initially, Edwards emphasized the ineffable, invisible nature of God and suggested that the divine is known primarily through intellectual or spiritual understanding, not through physical sight. McClymond and McDermott note that his early writings resonate with the theological ideas of Aquinas, emphasizing that God, being a spiritual entity, is understood through intellectual means, with the eye of the soul deemed superior to the physical eye. But somewhat in contrast to their interpretation, Ramsey interprets Edwards's understanding of the *visio beatifica* to contrast with the medieval concept of God's vision or *summum bonum* (the highest good), particularly in relation to

69. *WJE* 13:369–70.

70. *WJE* 18:350–51.

71. McClymond and McDermott, *Theology of Jonathan Edwards*, 300.

Christ's eternal intercessory role. In other words, as Ramsey interprets, unlike the understandings of Dante and Aquinas, Jesus Christ, the incarnate God-man, continues to play a central role in communion even after completing his redemptive work on Earth and ascending to heaven.[72] These divergent interpretations regarding Edwards's understanding of the *visio beatifica* converge on the point that, while Edwards never abandoned the concept of intellectual vision, he shifted to a more moderate perspective in his later writings. McClymond and McDermott point out that Edwards did not abandon his initial focus on the intellectual perception of God. Instead, he integrated it with an increasingly refined understanding that also involves a bodily vision of the glorified humanity of Christ in heaven. Thus, while maintaining the importance of intellectual or spiritual apprehension, Edwards came to include the corporeal aspect in his conception of how the divine is experienced in the afterlife.[73] Hans Boersma's interpretation of Edwards's understanding on the *visio beatifica* is a good synthesis of the arguments of McClymond and McDermott and Ramsey. According to Boersma, drawing on Neoplatonist metaphysics, Jonathan Edwards's interpretation of the *visio beatifica* represents a shift from the dominant views in the Western Church that emerged through Thomas Aquinas's articulation of Aristotelian anthropology. In Edwards's perspective, the resurrection of the body holds significant, even indispensable, value for experiencing the deifying vision of God. Boersma notes that Edwards considers Christ as the "grand medium" of the *visio Dei*, portraying Him as the ultimate theophanic manifestation of God. Furthermore, he points out that Edwards emphasizes the continual and infinite progression of the vision of God, starting in this life, extending into the intermediate state, and persisting into the eternity of the resurrection.[74]

72. "In comparison with Dante and Aquinas, Edwards gives a remarkably different account of the knowledge of God and joy in him opened to creatures in heaven. For Edwards, Jesus Christ, the incarnate God-man, continues to play an active and the central role in heaven's conversation even after that conversation has ceased to be about the great earthly events in the work of redemption, or about the heavenly events promised in Scripture to the church triumphant" (Ramsey, "Heaven," 723).

73. McClymond and McDermott, *Theology of Jonathan Edwards*, 300–301.

74. Boersma, "Grand Medium," 187–212. For more studies of Edwards's understanding on *visio beatifica*, see McDermott, *Seeing God*; Caldwell, "Brief History," 48–71; Filson, "Beatifical Vision," 61–63; Boersma, *Seeing God*, 354–84.

Jonathan Edwards's Biblical Interpretations on the Beauty of Heaven

For Edwards, Heaven is a beautiful place filled with holy love. Edwards illustrates heaven as a paradise of pleasures, where everything is conducive to the promotion and enjoyment of divine love. There will be no adversaries to sow discord, but rather, everything in heaven will reflect and augment the beauty and loveliness of God and Christ. Edwards elaborates on the heavenly light, which is a manifestation of divine love, emanating from the glory of the Lamb of God, symbolizing Christ's meekness and love (Rev 22:5). The portrayal of the heavenly environment, including the radiant glory and rainbow, symbolizes God's covenant of love and grace with humanity (Gen 9:12–15; Rev 4:3; 21:11). The New Jerusalem's light, likened to a jasper stone, represents the precious and beautiful nature of God's glory.[75]

The Christocentric Beauty of Heaven

As a continuation of the redemptive perspective, Edwards emphasizes the relationship between the beauty of heaven and the excellence of Christ. In his sermon "That the Son of God by Appearing in Our Nature Laid a Glorious Foundation for Peace to the Inhabitants of This World," Edwards states how the coming of Christ into the world has brought forth a peace that permeates the relationship between God and mankind, within individuals, and amongst one another. This divine peace is heralded by angels singing "Peace on earth," signifying its celestial origin and purpose.[76] He underscores the consummate peace that will be relished by the saints in heaven, where the manifold benefits of Christ's incarnation and sacrifice will be fully realized. In contrast to the earthly realm, where the spirit of Christ is given in part and remnants of bitterness and enmity persist, heaven is portrayed as a place of absolute righteousness, devoid of ill will, anger, and reproach. There, eternal peace reigns supreme in this kingdom specifically ordained for tranquility.

Edwards also draws attention to the exemplary nature of Christ, the Son of God, who, despite being subjected to the utmost affront and abuse, epitomized meekness and calmness. His response to maltreatment,

75. *WJE* 8:382.

76. Edwards, "Appearing," 184.

likened to a lamb's demeanor, emphasizes His unparalleled excellence in character. Christ's embodiment of meekness, even in adversity, establishes Him as the eternal Lamb, a title under which He is ceaselessly adored and exalted by angels and heavenly hosts. This relationship between the excellency of Christ and the heavenly realm illuminates the profound unity and peace that characterize the divine kingdom.[77]

In his sermon, "Jesus Christ Is the Great Mediator and Head of Union in Whom All Elect Creatures in Heaven and Earth Are United to God and to One Another," Edwards explains that the glory of the church is that Christ—the head of the church—is in heaven: "Christ's exaltation and ascension to heaven is spoken of as cause of exceeding joy to his church. . . . 'Tis a glorious privilege to the church to have their Mediator in heaven, in the holy of holies, at the right hand of God."[78] Moreover, Edwards propounds the significance of the delegated authority vested in Christ as God-man and our mediator. This authority is not inherent but is graciously bestowed upon Him by the Father, allowing Christ to govern as God's "vice regent" (Matt 28:18; Luke 22:29; Ps 2:6).[79] This divinely sanctioned rule underscores the symbiotic relationship between Christ's sovereignty and the structured order of Heaven, revealing a dimension of divine beauty manifest in authority and governance. Christ's appointment is not limited merely to governance. In a divine act of trust, the Father has entrusted Christ with the profound responsibility of judgment. It is said that when Christ returns, it will be enveloped "in the glory of his Father" (Matt 16:27). This glory is not a mere spectacle but rather a testament to Christ's capability. For he stands uniquely positioned to bridge the vast expanse between humanity and divinity. As our priest, he assumes our burdens, pleading our cause before the Father. So, Edwards examines that Christ's delegated authority denotes not just an image of divine justice, but also portrays a manifestation of heavenly glory, whereby Christ's capacity to intercede and reconcile is highlighted.[80]

Drawing on Colossians 2:9–10, Edwards argues that Christ's authority and rule is not limited to humanity, but extends to the angels who dwell in heaven. Edwards emphasizes that while Christ may not serve as a mediator between God and angels, His headship signifies an essential conduit of divine communication and fullness. The angels, through

77. Edwards, "Appearing," 185–88.

78. *WJE* 18:537.

79. Edwards, "Great Mediator," 320.

80. Edwards, "Great Mediator," 320–21.

Christ, receive their fullness from God, illuminating the Heaven with divine light and glory. This harmonious celestial symphony, under the headship of Christ, radiates the beauty and glory of Heaven, exemplifying the unity and blessedness of the divine society of saints and angels.[81] Edwards underscores the communal aspect of Heaven, wherein angels and saints form a divine society under the common headship of Christ. The Lamb, as the light of the new Jerusalem, enlightens all inhabitants, both saints and angels, with divine radiance. This shared illumination and blessedness, centered around Christ, reveal the multifaceted beauty of Heaven, a beauty characterized by light, glory, and communal unity.[82]

Trinitarian Excellencies in Heaven

Undoubtedly, for Edwards, heaven is a world of love filled with beauty. However, in Jonathan Edwards's theological perspective, heaven is not just a locale of eternal peace and happiness, but also the ultimate setting where the trinitarian nature of God fully manifests in an architecture of infinite, eternal love. Understanding this trinitarian structure is crucial for comprehending Edwards's view of heaven as the ultimate realm of love. Edwards cites 1 John 4:8, "God is love" (ὁ θεὸς ἀγάπη ἐστίν), to assert that heaven is awash with divine love because God Himself, who is the embodiment and source of infinite love, resides there. Being infinite, all-sufficient, unchangeable, and eternal, God is described as a boundless and inexhaustible fountain of love. Heaven is where all streams and even drops of holy love emanate from this divine source.[83] This divine love, for Edwards, is united in the trinitarian mutual love. Edwards identifies God the Father as the "Father of mercies" and the eternal source of love. The Father's love is not a finite or ephemeral expression but one that flows from an eternal and infinite source. This love, based on John 3:16, is obviously revealed in the fact that He gave His only Son as a sacrifice for humanity, signifying an unparalleled generosity and depth of love. Edwards emphasizes that Jesus's love is the medium through which the Father's love is made manifest to the saints. Jesus is not just a channel of divine love, but is its very embodiment, willingly laying down His life to redeem the fallen world. Edwards outlines the role of the Holy Spirit as the spirit

81. Edwards, "Great Mediator," 323–24.

82. Edwards, "Great Mediator," 324.

83. *WJE* 8:369.

of divine love, echoing Paul's words that "God's love has been poured out into our hearts through the Holy Spirit, who has been given to us" (Rom 5:5). The Spirit is neither a mere conduit nor an abstract concept but the very essence of divine love flowing out or "breathed forth" from the Father and the Son. The Holy Spirit is the one who fills the hearts of believers with divine love, making the heavenly love accessible even now, fortifying the church with the love that originates from both the Father and the Son.[84]

Central to Edwards's argument is the idea that in heaven, the saints will intimately share in Christ's joy and love towards the Father. Drawing from biblical passages such as Romans 8:34, he asserts that the saints' partaking in Christ's own joy in the Father makes them conduits through which Christ's joy is completed. This mutual sharing of the Father's infinite love elucidates the profound and eternal relationship between Christ and the saints in heaven, positioning it as an unbreakable bond anchored in divine happiness. Moreover, he emphasizes that the saints will co-reign with Christ over the new heavens and earth. This co-sovereignty, where they are seated with Christ on his throne, signifies a relationship that combines love, joy, shared authority, and governance. Thus, in Edwards's vision, saints are not merely passive beneficiaries but actively partake in Christ's eternal kingship. Employing the term *προγινώσκω* from Romans 3:34 Edwards supports the relationship between Christ and saints in heaven. He interprets that this term (*προγινώσκω*) is linked to the Hebrew terms "מוֹדָע," implying a kinsman or close friend, and "מוֹדַעַת," indicating kinship, both derive from "יָדַע"; and these linguistic nuances reveal the theological understanding of God's intimate and predetermined relationship with the elect.[85]

The Divine Beauty and the Saints in Heaven

Another focus of Edwards's theological aesthetics regarding heaven concerns the saints residing in heaven. As we have seen above, for Edwards, heaven is a place filled with the divine love of the Trinity. Edwards elucidates the dynamic and boundless nature of divine love within the Trinity and extends it to the saints and angels in heaven. All of that divine love overflows into the hearts of all the saints by the Holy Spirit, and "the

84. *WJE* 8:369–70.

85. *WJE* 24:1019–20.

Head of the body is so, and so are all the members."[86] So, heaven is a place of absolute purity and beauty, inhabited solely by lovely objects and beings. He references Revelation 21:27 to underscore that nothing defiling, abominable, or deceitful has a place in heaven. God, the glorious Father, Redeemer, and Sanctifier, is infinitely loving, and so are all the members of the heavenly society.[87] Central to this love is its infinite flow between the Father and the Son, a pure and ceaseless mutual love that makes the very core of God's being a boundless act of love. This divine love is not confined within the Godhead but radiates outward, touching all of heaven's inhabitants. God's love reaches out to Christ, and through Him, it envelops all the saints, reflecting the timeless love God held for them, which became evident through Christ's sacrifice on Earth and their ultimate union in heaven. The angels and saints become vessels of this divine love, reflecting it as planets do sunlight. Their love, although derived from God, is powerfully directed back to its source. There is no discord or animosity; instead, heaven is a harmonious realm where every inhabitant loves and is loved in return. Christ's love encompasses all his saints, and they, in unison, adore their Savior. The beauty of this celestial society is its unity: angels and saints alike cherish one another, creating an environment devoid of enmity and filled with mutual admiration.[88]

Edwards argues that in heaven, the love of angels and saints is finite, but perfectly consistent with their nature, absent of sin, envy, or any form of malice. Each inhabitant's[89] love in heaven is commensurate with their capacities, ensuring a state of completeness and satisfaction. The differing degrees of glory among the heavenly residents do not incite envy or diminish happiness; rather, they enhance the collective joy as all rejoice in one another's prosperity. Edwards underscores that the greater the holiness and glory of an individual, the greater their humility and capacity for love, fostering a state of reciprocal affection and unity. The happiness and harmony in heaven are intensified by the recognition that those of higher degrees of glory exhibit greater humility and benevolence. They are beloved by all and, in turn, demonstrate increased love to those below them, reflecting Christ's spirit of boundless love. Edwards assures that envy has no place in heaven, as the superior happiness of some is

86. *WJE* 8:371.

87. *WJE* 8:371.

88. *WJE* 8:373–74.

89. The inhabitants refer to saints and angels.

recognized as stemming from their greater humility and love, elements which contribute to the overall bliss and unity of the celestial society.[90]

Edwards continues to depict the nature of love and its expression in heaven. He contrasts the earthly experience of love with its heavenly realization, highlighting the limitations and obstacles believers face on Earth and the unbounded expression of love they will enjoy in heaven. Edwards describes how, on Earth, believers' love for God is often constrained by physical and spiritual limitations. The "heavy moulded body" symbolizes the physical constraint and the "corruption of heart" represents the spiritual impediment that hinders the full expression of divine love.[91] Earthly believers aspire to a fervent, unhampered expression of love, but often find themselves restrained, capable only of inexpressible groans (Rom 8:26). However, in heaven, these limitations are non-existent. The souls of the saints, likened to flames of fire with love, will experience no restriction or hindrance. The saints' love will be able to express itself fully, unhindered by physical or spiritual constraints, and will find a harmonious reflection in the heavenly environment and in mutual love with other saints.[92]

Edwards asserts that the saints in heaven will exhibit "the most excellent and perfect behavior" towards God and one another.[93] In heaven, the saints lead lives characterized by unwavering righteousness, embodying holiness in every action and behavior, which are divine in matter, form, and end. Although Edwards does not specify the exact nature of the saints' duties in heaven, he highlights their primary role as one of praising and serving God, citing Revelation 22:3—"And there shall be no more curse; but the throne of God and of the Lamb shall be in it; and his servants shall serve him." This service to God is executed flawlessly, under the influence of the perfect divine love.

In short, Jonathan Edwards depicts heaven as a realm of divine love, where the inhabitants, free from earthly constraints, express this love in its fullest form. He illustrates how the divine love within the Trinity overflows to all in heaven, creating a harmonious environment devoid of sin and filled with mutual admiration and unity. The differing degrees of glory among the saints enhance collective joy, with each individual reflecting and embodying Christ's boundless love through excellent and perfect behavior. Thus, every saint is a vessel of God's love, reflecting it

90. *WJE* 8:375–76.

91. *WJE* 8:379.

92. *WJE* 8:379–82.

93. *WJE* 8:383.

and directing it back to its source, ultimately contributing to the harmonious and glorious celestial society.

Seeing the Beautiful God in Heaven: *Visio Beatifica*

Edwards's exegetical understanding of the relationship between God and the saints through Christ in heaven is closely linked to his understanding of *visio beatifica*. Edwards posits that saints participate in the *visio beatifica*[94] through Christ. In other words, by participating in the *visio beatifica* through Christ, saints are sanctified to perfection, made wholly holy and blameless. In essence, those who partake in the *visio beatifica* experience the nature and outcome of divine happiness. It is worth noting that this is not a result of the saints' inherent abilities, but a reward of grace. Just as saints rely on Christ for salvation on Earth, they continue to depend on Christ in Heaven.

Edwards articulates that no being, except for Jesus Christ, can directly perceive God. This assertion is grounded in the belief that no created being can fully comprehend or see another created spirit's essence without having the ability to discern their innermost thoughts and intentions. However, such a profound understanding or insight into the heart is a distinctive feature that only God possesses, as is frequently emphasized in the Scripture. Edwards cites various passages that depict the divine characteristic of God's invisibility and inaccessibility to direct perception by any creature. He is referred to as the "invisible God" (Col 1:15), the "King eternal, immortal, invisible" (1 Tim 1:17), and "he that is invisible" (Heb 11:27). Moreover, 1 John 4:12 and 1 Timothy 6:16 explicitly state that no one has seen or can see God directly. Significantly, Jesus Christ stands out as the central medium through which all other beings come to know God. Edwards emphasizes that they can understand God through the revelations and teachings presented by Christ. This mediating role of Jesus is reiterated in passages such as Matthew 11:27, which states that only the Father knows the Son and only the Son truly knows the Father, and only those to whom the Son chooses to reveal the Father can know Him.[95] This idea is further emphasized in John 1:18 and 6:46, where it is

94. For more studies of Edwards's understanding on *visio beatifica*, see Boersma, "Grand Medium," 187–212. For more studies of Edwards's understanding on *visio beatifica*, see McDermott, *Seeing God*; Caldwell, "Brief History," 48–71; Filson, "Beatifical Vision," 61–63; Boersma, *Seeing God*, 354–84.

95. In citing this passage, Edwards points out that the Greek word οὐδείς, translated "no man" in the English Bible (KJV), means "no one" (*WJE* 18:428).

made clear that no one, except Jesus, who is in close communion with the Father, has directly seen or known God.[96]

In his sermon, "The Pure in Heart Blessed" (1730), Edwards portrays the *visio beatifica* as an intellectual sight which provides an immediate and certain understanding of God's love and glory, far surpassing any bodily or speculative understanding.[97] Edwards begins by clarifying what is meant by "seeing God," rigorously distinguishing it from physical or bodily sight. He cites Hebrews 11:27; Colossians 1:15; and 1 Timothy 1:17 to support the theological premise that God is "invisible" and beyond the perception of physical senses. Edwards also addresses how angels and saints in heaven see God, drawing on Matthew 18:10 to argue that their vision is not based on any "form or visible representation."[98] He acknowledges that while God has appeared in physical forms or signs in biblical history (e.g., to Moses in Exod 33:18–23), these manifestations were a concession to humanity's spiritual immaturity at the time. In heaven, while saints may behold the "outward glory" of Christ's human nature, the true delight comes from recognizing the "spiritual greatness and majesty" of the divine nature expressed through it. Edwards cites 2 Peter 1:16–18 and John 1:14, which describe the experiences of the disciples during Christ's transfiguration, to illustrate how physical glory serves primarily to express deeper spiritual truths.[99] Seeing God is an intellectual and spiritual exercise. It is not gained through hearsay or mere rational reasoning but through an immediate and certain understanding of God's glorious excellence and love. Edwards emphasizes that the knowledge of God that grants true happiness is intuitive and direct, not mediated through abstract reasoning. In heaven, the saints will experience God's glory and love as immediate, certain, and as vivid as any earthly sight, yet vastly superior. It will be a direct apprehension of God's divine nature, transcending any earthly means or symbols. The sight of God in heaven will not just be about his majesty and power, but also an intimate understanding of His love and grace towards the individual. In essence, to see God is to have a profound and immediate understanding of His glorious excellency and enduring love, a vision that finally and completely satisfies

96. *WJE* 18:428.

97. *WJE* 17:61–67.

98. *WJE* 17:62.

99. Edwards argues that while there can be earthly moments where we get a glimpse of God's glory (as in the Transfiguration), the ultimate vision of God that brings eternal happiness will be fully realized in heaven. See *WJE* 17:63.

the soul. Therefore, Edwards posits that the *visio beatifica* is the ultimate goal for the human soul, attainable only through spiritual purity. It is a vision so overwhelming and complete that it fulfills all human desires for understanding and love, leading to eternal blessedness.[100]

Edwards suggests that the vision of God is not only the source of our deepest joy but also the point at which we reach our highest moral and intellectual perfection. He claims that true happiness is synonymous with one's excellency and perfection, and the act of seeing God fulfills this. The vision makes the individual more excellent by elevating the faculties of understanding and will. Thus, the *visio beatifica* serves a dual purpose: it is both the epitome of human joy and the pinnacle of human excellence. Moreover, Edwards emphasizes the staggering infiniteness of God's excellency as a source of eternal joy and fulfillment for humans. His metaphor of diving into a "bottomless ocean" or soaring into an "endless expanse" evocatively captures the notion that one can never fully grasp or exhaust the grandeur and magnificence of God.[101] The capacity of the human soul, particularly the faculty of understanding, can continuously extend itself to comprehend the ever-unfolding beauty and glory of God. Edwards implies that the *visio beatifica* offers an ever-renewable source of inspiration and revelation. In this unending exploration, the soul finds its fullest delight. Edwards argues that one's understanding and perception of God can continue to deepen and expand eternally. Even after one has contemplated the divine nature for ages, there will still be facets left to explore, layers of complexity to unravel, and greater heights of glory to perceive. This limitless nature of God's excellency ensures that the joy one finds in the *visio beatifica* is perpetually fresh and never stale. The human soul, therefore, finds its true satisfaction in this endless pursuit of understanding God's incomprehensible beauty and glory.

Edwards also underscores the eternal and unchanging foundation upon which the *visio beatifica* rests. Unlike worldly pleasures and material possessions that are transient and susceptible to decay, the joy emanating from the direct intellectual apprehension of God's glory is built on an eternal foundation, which Edwards describes as "an everlasting rock." He supports this point by referencing several Biblical verses like Isaiah 26:4[102]

100. *WJE* 17:66–67.

101. *WJE* 17:71–72.

102. "Trust ye in the Lord for ever: For in the Lord JEHOVAH is everlasting strength" (Isa 26:4 KJV).

and Jeremiah 31:3.[103] In particular, suggesting that the appropriate Hebrew translation of Isaiah 26:4, "בְּיָהּ יְהוָה צוּר עוֹלָמִים," rendered "in the Lord Jehovah is everlasting strength" (KJV), is "in the Lord Jehovah is the rock of ages," Edwards explains that he who has the immediate intellectual views of God's glory and love, and rejoices in that, has his happiness built upon an everlasting rock.[104] These verses confirm the timeless and unwavering nature of God's glory and love. The perpetuity of God's glory and love not only ensures that the joy derived from them is unfading but also reinforces the individual's sense of spiritual stability and existential assurance.[105] In short, Edwards presents the vision of God as both endless in its excellency and eternal in its foundation. The human soul finds its deepest desires and unlimited capacities perfectly met in the infinite and everlasting nature of God's glory and love. This makes the *visio beatifica* not just a source of ultimate joy but also an enduring promise of eternal fulfillment.

While Edwards approached the spiritual and intellectual view of the *visio beatifica* in "The Pure in Heart Blessed," his other sermon, "True Saints, When Absent from The Body, Are Present with the Lord" (1747), talks about seeing the glory and love of Christ in heaven. In this life, according to Edwards, the perception of Christ is dim and limited. He cites 1 Peter 1:8 to point out that in the present world, believers haven't seen Jesus, yet they love him; they believe in him even though they do not see him directly. Similarly, 1 Corinthians 13:12 is invoked to contrast our current 'dark' understanding and vision of Christ with the face-to-face encounter promised in heaven. Essentially, earthly experiences offer but a glimmer of the spiritual reality, a reality fully revealed only in the afterlife. Edwards elaborates that in heaven, the saints are blessed with the *visio beatifica* of God through Christ. Matthew 5:8—"The pure in heart are blessed; for they shall see God"—is cited to support this. He explains that Christ serves as the medium through which the divine glory of God is seen. By being in the presence of Christ in heaven, the saints are given an immediate, unhindered view of God's full glory. In this state, they come to truly understand the depth of God's wisdom, love, and grace, as well as the marvel of Christ's redemptive work, in a way that is impossible while still living in their mortal bodies on Earth. Furthermore, Edwards posits that the saints in heaven not only behold the glory of Christ in a general sense but also

103. "The Lord hath appeared of old unto me, saying, Yea, I have loved thee with an everlasting love: Therefore, with lovingkindness have I drawn thee" (Jer 31:3 KJV).

104. *WJE* 17:73.

105. *WJE* 17:73.

come to understand Christ's eternal and "unmeasurable dying love" for them individually. It is a perception that is free of "darkness or delusion," unobstructed by the physical and moral limitations of earthly existence. Furthermore, Edwards argues that the saints in heaven not only behold the glory of Christ in a general sense but also come to understand Christ's eternal and "unmeasurable dying love" for them individually. It is a perception that is free of "darkness or delusion," unobstructed by the physical and moral limitations of earthly existence.[106]

Conclusion

While Edwards's ecclesiological aesthetics provide a philosophical framework that perceives the church as a community united in primary beauty and true virtue, his biblical interpretations add substantive layers to our understanding, ones that philosophy alone cannot fully capture. The theological interpretations deepen our grasp of the church as an institution grounded in divine edicts and as a participant in God's overarching plan of redemption. Edwards elaborates on the church's enduring excellency and progressive beauty through trials and tribulations, a perspective intimately tied to divine deliverance and the workings of the Holy Spirit. This supplements what might be perceived as an abstract aesthetic in his philosophical examinations by providing it with tangible historical and scriptural contexts.

Moreover, his philosophy and biblical exegesis converge remarkably well in understanding the beauty of heaven. His philosophical reflections on heavenly aesthetics accentuate how heaven serves as the ultimate realization of the church's beauty, a beauty enriched and informed by biblical teachings on the afterlife and the *visio beatifica*. The unity achieved in love and glory in heaven parallels his vision of the church on Earth, embodying the same primary beauty and true virtue. This reinforces that the church is not just a concept but a divine reality, undergoing a journey that culminates in eternal communion with God.

The synergy between Edwards's philosophical examinations and biblical interpretations elucidates facets of the church that are often neglected or overlooked in purely philosophical discourse. They show that the church is not only an embodiment of true virtue and primary beauty but is also an evolving, resilient entity shaped by divine love and celestial purpose. His

106. *WJE* 25:229–30.

biblical interpretations fill the gaps that philosophical discourse leaves—gaps concerning divine intervention, historical challenges, and the role of the Holy Spirit. In conclusion, Jonathan Edwards's multi-dimensional approach to understanding the church captures the essence of a divine institution enshrined in spiritual, aesthetic, and moral beauty.

Chapter 8

Conclusion

THIS BOOK DEMONSTRATES THE ways in which Edwards's exegesis articulates and contributes to his conceptualization of theological aesthetics. The pivotal role that aesthetics plays in the theological and intellectual framework of Jonathan Edwards is a matter of widespread scholarly agreement. Predominantly, researchers have approached Edwards's aesthetics through philosophical and systematic theological lenses, aiming to situate his work within broader conceptual paradigms. However, this focus overlooks a critical dimension of Edwards's self-identification and practice—namely, that he primarily saw himself as a pastor, preacher, and biblical interpreter. This perspective is substantiated by the fact that a considerable portion of his existing oeuvre comprises sermons and biblical exegeses.

Scholars such as Douglas Sweeney have emphasized this pastoral and interpretative facet of Edwards's identity as central to his scholarship. Despite such claims, there has been a noticeable lack of integrated research focusing on Edwards's biblical interpretations in relation to the concept of beauty, a core tenet of his theology. Such a focus is not only pertinent but essential when taking into account the existing body of theological research on Edwards.

Given this lacuna, this book contends that examining Edwards's aesthetics through the prism of his biblical interpretations is a research avenue with tremendous scholarly potential. It responds to this academic necessity by aiming to elucidate how Edwards's theological and exegetical writings articulate and contribute to his understanding of beauty.

Through this approach, this book seeks to offer a more nuanced and complete picture of Jonathan Edwards's multifaceted intellectual legacy.

Edwards has been studied extensively for his philosophical contributions; however, in focusing largely on his philosophy and theology, scholars sometimes overlook the fact that his primary vocation was as a pastor and an exegete of the Bible. Chapter two sought to shed light on how Edwards's biblical scholarship had a profound impact on his life, theology, and pastoral role. For Jonathan Edwards, the pursuit of theological understanding was a deeply religious quest rooted in the Bible. At the core of this quest lay what Edwards saw as the Christian's duty towards God, which involved a comprehensive understanding of religious truths. According to Edwards, this duty extended far beyond mere acknowledgement of God's existence; it required an intricate understanding of God's nature, His relationship with humanity, and His revealed will. In this vein, Edwards posited that true knowledge of God could only be obtained through divine revelation, particularly as found in the Scriptures. He personally attested that his most spiritually vibrant moments coincided with his deep engagements with the Bible. As a theological thinker, Edwards was heir to a Puritan tradition that prioritized the Bible as the ultimate source of truth. While he did not entirely shun the intellectual currents of his time, particularly those stemming from the Enlightenment, Edwards distinguished himself by placing the revelation of God above human reason. In other words, his biblical scholarship thus serves as a foundational layer, allowing scholars to reconstruct the intellectual and spiritual universe he inhabited. Thus, we confirmed that any serious examination of Edwards's contributions to theology and aesthetics must begin with an understanding of how he interpreted the Bible.

Chapter three explored the background and characteristics of Edwards's aesthetics. The idea of aesthetics may have been formalized in the modern era, but the quest to understand beauty had been a perennial concern for theologians and philosophers alike. Jonathan Edwards stood as a pivotal figure in this intellectual tradition, bridging the gap between classical Christian thought and the Enlightenment, all the while developing a theology deeply imbued with aesthetic considerations.

Edwards's theological aesthetics cannot be understood apart from the rich tradition that preceded him. He inherited the Western church's views on beauty, particularly through intellectual giants like St. Augustine, Thomas Aquinas, and Reformation figures such as John Calvin and John Owen. Augustine's thoughts on the excellence and beauty of the trinitarian hypostases and their loving union profoundly influenced Edwards. These theological forebears helped Edwards formulate his own understanding of beauty, emphasizing themes of harmony, excellence, and trinitarian relationships. However, Edwards was not a mere disciple of traditional theology; he was a man of his time. He engaged with Enlightenment methodologies and even its language, to make his ideas accessible and intellectually robust. While Edwards did borrow terminology from British aesthetic theories, such as "a divine taste" and "new sense of heart," he did not abide by the secular rationalism prevalent among many Enlightenment thinkers. Instead, he used these contemporary concepts as tools to build his theological framework, one that placed God's revealed truth above human reason.

In contesting the Deist worldview, which saw God as a distant Creator, Edwards employed his understanding of beauty as a compelling argument for a God who was intimately involved with His creation. He argued that the secondary beauty of the created world was a mere reflection of God's primary beauty, revealing the characteristics of a God who was both transcendent and immanent. Against the Deists, Edwards posited a God who not only created the world but continued to communicate with it through the revelation of His beauty. Edwards's varied use of terms such as excellency, symmetry, proportion, harmony, agreement, consent, union, glory, holy, and love were not rhetorical flourishes but intricate components of his theological aesthetics. These terms linked back to his trinitarian framework, reinforcing the notion that understanding God's beauty was paramount for understanding the Trinity, which Edwards saw as the archetype of beauty.

Chapters two and three explored the background research of this book, such as the importance of Edwards's biblical interpretation in the study of Edwards and the historical and philosophical backdrop of Edwards's aesthetic concepts. Chapters four through seven, each addressed important themes in Jonathan Edwards's theological aesthetics. In addressing these themes, Edwards's philosophical works were first addressed before considering his biblical interpretation of the matter. Chapter four examined Edwards's theological aesthetic understanding of the beauty of God. Edwards's theological aesthetics was not a mere extension of the theological tradition he had inherited, although figures like Augustine certainly had a significant impact. Instead, Edwards's understanding of God's beauty had been profoundly shaped by his own engagement with biblical texts. He carefully interpreted passages from both the Old and

New Testaments that discussed the beauty inherent in the trinitarian nature of God. Through the interpretation of original biblical words like אֱלֹהִים (Elohim), יהוה (Yahweh), פָּנֶה (Paneh), Λογος (Logos), and Αγαπε (Agape), Edwards formulated a trinitarian and comprehensive theology of divine beauty. A notable aspect of Edwards's theological aesthetics, was his linkage between God's beauty and His other attributes, particularly His holiness and moral perfection. To Edwards, the beauty of God was not a superficial quality but was deeply intertwined with His ethical and moral nature. The different hypostases of the Trinity each possessed their unique beauty, informed by their holiness and moral integrity.

Chapter five covered the understanding of Edwards's conception of beauty as not just a static attribute of God, but as a dynamic quality communicated to and through His creation, particularly humanity. In Edwards's theological universe, God's primary aim in creation had been the manifestation of His glory, a multifaceted glory that incorporated holiness, intelligence, and beauty. Humans, created in the *Imago Dei*, served as mirrors of this divine glory. They embodied the beauty of God in their intellectual, moral, and spiritual faculties. According to Edwards, this was not a mere abstract theological proposition but a reality rooted in biblical scholarship. He saw human intelligence and wisdom, reflecting the divine image, as excellent attributes that enabled humans to appreciate, express, and communicate the beauty of God. For Edwards, the highest honor for humans lay in embodying the holiness and righteousness that constituted the essence of divine beauty. This chapter continued to explore Edwards's aesthetics, which extended into a profound engagement with the state of the world and humanity after the Fall. After the Fall, the beauty that characterized the original creation had been marred by human sin. Despite the tarnishing of this primordial beauty, Edwards saw vestiges of beauty in the postlapsarian world. He found this residual beauty not through a philosophical framework but through a robust theological understanding grounded in biblical exegesis and typology. Edwards insisted that the dim light illuminating the fallen world was the redemptive work of Christ, and it was in this light that glimpses of God's beauty could still be found. This chapter confirmed that it was crucial to recognize the interconnected nature of Edwards's intellectual framework: from the transmission of divine beauty within the Trinity itself to its diffusion into the created world (both *ad intra* and *ad extra*), to the unique position of humans as the apex of creation designed to absorb and echo this divine beauty, down to the remnants of this divine beauty that persisted even in a world tainted by sin. Rather than considering these elements as discrete entities, Edwards had fused them into a unified, harmonious system with each component mutually enhancing the others and all anchored in his hermeneutical engagement with the Bible.

Chapter six established Edwards's understanding of the excellency of Christ. Confronting deistic critiques directly, Edwards orchestrated a multifaceted defense, fusing theological astuteness with biblical exegesis. A cornerstone of Edwards's theology was his articulation of Christ as a harmonious amalgam of diverse excellencies, transcending the dichotomies and contradictions that confounded human understanding. Edwards did not merely catalog these excellencies; rather, he elucidated their intimate integration in Christ's character and actions. From Christ's divine majesty and human humility to his perfect righteousness and boundless grace, Edwards demonstrated how these seemingly incongruent attributes found their synthesis in the person of Jesus Christ. Through extensive biblical interpretation, Edwards established that Christ was a unique entity, beyond human categorization, embodying a union of attributes and roles that would seem contradictory to finite understanding. Furthermore, this chapter covered that Edwards navigated the complex dimensions of Christ's earthly and heavenly life, offering keen observations on the manifestations of these diverse excellencies. Whether it was the incarnation that juxtaposed divine dignity with human humility or the crucifixion that melded lamb-like meekness with lion-like majesty, Edwards depicted these acts as revelations of God's glory, accessible yet awe-inspiring. Edwards's theological aesthetics extended beyond the majesty of God to its transformative impact on believers. According to Edwards, redemption was not merely an abstract doctrine but an operative principle that led to sanctification. This sanctification was not just about moral refinement; it was about embodying the holiness and beauty of Christ, becoming a reflection of the divine excellencies that Edwards so meticulously detailed.

Therefore, as we had anticipated examining Edwards's contributions to ecclesiological and eschatological themes in the subsequent chapter, it was evident that his theology served as an intellectually coherent and aesthetically rich framework. This framework was not only consistent with orthodox Christian beliefs but also served as a polemic against the deistic thought of his time, fortifying the edifice of Christian doctrine against intellectual and spiritual corrosion. Edwards, through his keen interpretations, not only defended but elevated the Christian understanding of redemption, providing a compelling vision that celebrated the beauty and glory of God as manifested in Jesus Christ.

The final chapter examined Jonathan Edwards's work on ecclesiological aesthetics and biblical interpretation which offered an enriching composite of theological insight and philosophical nuance. Whereas his philosophical framework posited the church as a community marked by primary beauty and true virtue, his biblical exegesis added tangible depth and substance to this abstract conceptualization. In doing so, Edwards constructed a holistic understanding of the church that was both grounded in divine edicts and actively involved in the unfolding God's redemptive plan. This chapter also established that one of Edwards's seminal contributions lay in his treatment of the church's resilience and progressive beauty, even amidst trials and tribulations. This viewpoint was not a mere philosophical observation but was deeply rooted in the biblical narrative, especially as it related to divine deliverance and the transformative influence of the Holy Spirit. By harmonizing philosophy and scriptural interpretation, Edwards bridged the gap between abstract aesthetics and lived ecclesiastical experience, situating the church within specific historical and spiritual contexts. Equally significant was Edwards's exploration of heavenly aesthetics, where his philosophical musings found remarkable consonance with biblical teachings. According to Edwards, heaven represented the ultimate realization of the church's beauty—a transcendent form of beauty corroborated and enriched by biblical insights of the afterlife and the *visio beatifica*. The harmonious relationship between love and glory in heaven served as a celestial mirror to his vision of the church on Earth. It confirmed that the church was not a mere conceptual framework but a divine reality, journeying towards eternal communion with God. This chapter discovered that Jonathan Edwards's multi-pronged approach brought to light aspects of the church that might otherwise have gone unnoticed in a purely philosophical dialogue. His work illuminated the church as not just a static embodiment of virtue and beauty but as a dynamic, evolving institution shaped by divine imperatives and celestial objectives. The fusion of Edwards's philosophical and biblical perspectives closed gaps inherent in isolated philosophical or theological treatments, notably in areas concerning divine intervention, historical evolution, and the role of the Holy Spirit. Therefore, Edwards's ecclesiology provided a comprehensive lens through which to appreciate the church as a divine institution steeped in aesthetic, moral, and spiritual beauty.

This book, then, has endeavored to elucidate the intricate relationship between Jonathan Edwards's theological aesthetics and his biblical interpretation. As has been demonstrated, Edwards's biblical exegesis is not a peripheral element but rather a central, integrative force that shapes and enriches nearly all facets of his theological discourse. The core tenets of his theology are not disparate ideas; rather, they are harmoniously woven around the pivotal concept of beauty. It is also evident that an isolated examination of Edwards's philosophy risks misrepresenting or oversimplifying his theological aesthetics. This research has shown that such potential pitfalls are mitigated when Edwards's philosophy is considered in concert with his biblical exegesis. By bringing these two dimensions into dialogue, a fuller, more nuanced understanding of Edwards's theological aesthetics emerges—one that is richly supported by scriptural interpretation. In sum, this book contends that a well-rounded comprehension of Jonathan Edwards's theological aesthetics is incomplete without considering the substantial role played by his biblical interpretation. As this study has demonstrated, Edwards's theological perspectives are not merely theoretical constructs but are deeply embedded in his scriptural analysis, forming an integrated framework that centers around the thematic richness of beauty.

Finally, building on the insights of this book, which highlights the profound connection between Jonathan Edwards's theological aesthetics and his biblical exegesis, I suggest that future research should concentrate on the theme of beauty within Edwards's extensive biblical commentaries, examined in canonical order. Such studies would be instrumental in deepening our understanding of how Edwards integrates the concept of beauty into his interpretation of various biblical texts. Investigating this theme throughout his commentaries will not only enrich our grasp of his theological and philosophical views on beauty but also illuminate the wider implications of his aesthetic principles within the scriptural narrative. This proposed research direction holds the promise of offering a more comprehensive and nuanced understanding of Edwards's contributions to theology and aesthetics.

Bibliography

Aquinas, Thomas. *The Summa Theologica*. Translated by the Fathers of the English Dominican Province. Complete ed. New York: Catholic Way, 2014.

Arendt, Hannah. *Love and Saint Augustine*. Edited by Joanna Vecchiarelli Scott and Judith Chelius Stark. Chicago: University of Chicago Press, 1996.

Aristotle. *Aristotelis De Caelo*. Edited and Translated by Donald James Allan. Scriptorum Classicorum Bibliotheca Oxoniensis. Oxford: Oxford University Press, 2005.

Augustine. *Against the Academicians*. Translated by Mary Patricia Garvey. Mediaeval Philosophical Texts in Translation 2. Milwaukee, WI: Marquette University Press, 1993.

———. *Confessions*. Translated by Henry Chadwick. Oxford World's Classics. Oxford: Oxford University Press, 2008.

———. *De natura boni of Saint Augustine: A Translation with an Introduction and Commentary*. Translated by Anthony A. Moon. Washington, DC: Catholic University of America Press, 1955.

———. *Of True Religion*. Translated by John H. S. Burleigh. Edited by Louis O. Mink. Chicago: H. Regnery, 1959.

———. *On Christian Doctrine*. Pickerington, OH: Beloved, 2014.

———. *On Order*. Translated by Silvano Borruso. South Bend, IN: St. Augustine's, 2007.

———. *The Trinity*. Edited by John E. Rotelle. Translated by Edmund Hill. Hyde Park, NY: New City, 2007.

Balthasar, Hans Urs von. *Word and Revelation*. New York: Herder and Herder, 1964.

Barshinger, David P. *Jonathan Edwards and the Psalms: A Redemptive-Historical Vision of Scripture*. New York: Oxford University Press, 2014.

Barshinger, David P., and Douglas A. Sweeney, eds. *Jonathan Edwards and Scripture: Biblical Exegesis in British North America*. New York: Oxford University Press, 2018.

Batschelet, Margaret Susan. "Jonathan Edwards' Use of Typology: A Historical and Theological Approach." PhD diss., University of Washington, 1977.

Baumgarten, Alexander G. *Reflections on Poetry: Alexander Gottlieb Baumgarten's Meditationes Philosophicae de Nonnullis Ad Poema Pertinentibus*. Translated by Karl Aschenbrenner and William B. Holther. Berkeley: University of California Press, 1954.

Beeke, Joel R., and Randall J. Pederson. *Meet the Puritans: With a Guide to Modern Reprints*. Grand Rapids: Reformation Heritage, 2007.

Beutler, Keith. "Reason." In *The Jonathan Edwards Encyclopedia*, edited by Harry S. Stout et al., 486–88. Grand Rapids: Eerdmans, 2017.

Bezzant, Rhys S. *Jonathan Edwards and the Church*. New York: Oxford University Press, 2014.

Bibber, James Joe van. "The Concepts of Church Membership and Ministry in the Covenantal Theology of Jonathan Edwards." PhD diss., Southwestern Baptist Theological Seminary, 1984.

Boersma, Hans. "The 'Grand Medium': An Edwardsean Modification of Thomas Aquinas on the Beatific Vision." *Modern Theology* 33.2 (2017) 187–212.

———. *Seeing God: the Beatific Vision in Christian Tradition*. Grand Rapids: Eerdmans, 2018.

Brissett, Wilson N. "Beauty among the Puritans: Aesthetics and Subjectivity in Early New England." PhD diss., University of Virginia, 2007.

Bychkov, Oleg V. "What Does Beauty Have to Do with the Trinity? From Augustine to Duns Scotus." *Franciscan Studies* 66 (2008) 197–212.

Caldwell, Robert W. "A Brief History of Heaven in the Writings of Jonathan Edwards." *Calvin Theological Journal* 46.1 (2011) 48.

Calvin, John. *Institutes of the Christian Religion*. Translated by Ford Lewis Battles. Edited by John T McNeill. Louisville, KY: Westminster John Knox, 2006.

Campagnac, E. T., ed. *The Cambridge Platonists: Being Selections from the Writings of Benjamin Whichcote, John Smith and Nathanael Culverwel*. Oxford: Clarendon, 1901.

Chapman, Emmanuel. *Saint Augustine's Philosophy of Beauty*. Saint Michael's Mediaeval Studies Monograph Series. New York: Sheed & Ward, 1939. Reprint, Sacramento, CA: Creative Media Partners, 2018.

———. "Some Aspects of St. Augustine's Philosophy of Beauty." *The Journal of Aesthetics and Art Criticism* 1.1 (1941) 46–51.

Cherry, Conrad. *The Theology of Jonathan Edwards: A Reappraisal*. Gloucester, MA: Peter Smith, 1974.

Cho, Hyun-Jin. *Jonathan Edwards on Justification: Reformed Development of the Doctrine in Eighteenth-Century New England*. Lanham, MD: University Press of America, 2012.

Chubb, Thomas. *A Discourse Concerning Reason, with regard to Religion and Divine Revelation*. London: T. Cox, 1731.

Colacurcio, Robert Eugene. "The Perception of Excellency as the Glory of God in Jonathan Edwards: An Essay Towards the Epistemology of Discernment." New York: Fordham University, 1972.

Cooper, Anthony Ashley. *Characteristics of Men, Manners, Opinions, Times*. Edited by Lawrence E. Klein. New York: Cambridge University Press, 2003.

Copleston, Frederick Charles. *British Philosophy: Hobbes to Hume*. Vol. 5 of *A History of Philosophy*. Reprint, London: Continuum, 2011.

Crisp, Oliver. *Jonathan Edwards on God and Creation*. New York: Oxford University Press, 2012.

———. "Jonathan Edwards's Ontology: A Critique of Sang Hyun Lee's Dispositional Account of Edwardsian Metaphysics." *Religious Studies* 46.1 (2010) 1–20.

Crisp, Oliver D., and Kyle J. Strobel. *Jonathan Edwards: An Introduction to His Thought*. Grand Rapids: Eerdmans, 2018.

Danaher, William J., Jr. *The Trinitarian Ethics of Jonathan Edwards*. Louisville, KY: Westminster John Knox, 2009.

Daugaard, Curtis Lee. "God, Glory, and the Good: A Study in the Theological Aesthetics of Jonathan Edwards." PhD diss., Boston University, 1993.

Delattre, Roland André. "Beauty and Sensibility in the Thought of Jonathan Edwards." PhD diss., Yale University, 1966.

———. *Beauty and Sensibility in the Thought of Jonathan Edwards: An Essay in Aesthetics and Theological Ethics*. New Haven, CT: Yale University Press, 1968.

Dicker, Georges. *Locke on Knowledge and Reality: A Commentary on An Essay Concerning Human Understanding*. New York: Oxford University Press, 2019.

Dyrness, William A. *Reformed Theology and Visual Culture: The Protestant Imagination from Calvin to Edwards*. New York: Cambridge University Press, 2004.

Eco, Umberto. *Art and Beauty in the Middle Ages*. Translated by Hugh Bredin. New Haven, CT: Yale University Press, 2002.

Edwards, Jonathan. *The Blessing of God: Previously Unpublished Sermons of Jonathan Edwards*. Edited by Michael D. McMullen. Nashville, TN: Broadman & Holman, 2003.

———. *Charity and Its Fruits: Christian Love as Manifested in the Heart and Life*. Edited by Tryon Edwards. New York: Robert Carter & Brothers, 1852.

———. *The Glory and Honor of God: Previously Unpublished Sermons of Jonathan Edwards*. Edited by Michael D. McMullen. Nashville, TN: Broadman & Holman, 2004.

———. *The Sermons of Jonathan Edwards: A Reader*. Edited by Wilson H. Kimnach et al. New Haven, CT: Yale University Press, 1999.

———. *An Unpublished Essay of Edwards on the Trinity: With Remarks on Edwards and His Theology*. Edited by George P. Fisher. New York: Scribner's Sons, 1903.

———. *Works of Jonathan Edwards*. Edited by Edward Hickman. Vol. 2. Carlisle, PA: Banner of Truth Trust, 1974.

———. *The Works of Jonathan Edwards*. Vol. 2, *Religious Affections*. Edited by John E. Smith. New Haven, CT: Yale University Press, 2009.

———. *The Works of Jonathan Edwards*. Vol. 3, *Original Sin*. Edited by Clyde A. Holbrook. New Haven, CT: Yale University Press, 1970.

———. *The Works of Jonathan Edwards*. Vol. 6, *Scientific and Philosophical Writings*. Edited by Wallace E. Anderson. New Haven, CT: Yale University Press, 1980.

———. *The Works of Jonathan Edwards*. Vol. 8, *Ethical Writings*. Edited by Paul Ramsey. New Haven, CT: Yale University Press, 1989.

———. *The Works of Jonathan Edwards*. Vol. 9, *A History of the Work of Redemption*. Edited by John Fredrick Wilson. New Haven, CT: Yale University Press, 1989.

———. *The Works of Jonathan Edwards*. Vol. 10, *Sermons and Discourses, 1720–1723*. Edited by Wilson H. Kimnach. New Haven, CT: Yale University Press, 1992.

———. *The Works of Jonathan Edwards*. Vol. 11, *Typological Writings*. Edited by Wallace E. Anderson et al. New Haven, CT: Yale University Press, 1993.

———. *The Works of Jonathan Edwards*. Vol. 13, *The "Miscellanies": (Entry Nos. a–z, aa–zz, 1–500)*. Edited by Thomas A. Schafer. New Haven, CT: Yale University Press, 1996.

———. *The Works of Jonathan Edwards*. Vol. 14, *Sermons and Discourses, 1723–1729*. Edited by Kenneth P. Minkema. New Haven, CT: Yale University Press, 1997.

———. *The Works of Jonathan Edwards*. Vol. 15, *Notes on Scripture*. Edited by Stephen J. Stein. New Haven, CT: Yale University Press, 1998.

———. *The Works of Jonathan Edwards*. Vol. 16, *Letters and Personal Writings*. Edited by George S. Claghorn. New Haven, CT: Yale University Press, 1998.

———. *The Works of Jonathan Edwards*. Vol. 17, *Sermons and Discourses, 1730–1733*. Edited by Mark Valeri. New Haven, CT: Yale University Press, 1999.

———. *The Works of Jonathan Edwards*. Vol. 18, *The "Miscellanies": (Entry Nos. 501–832)*. Edited by Ava Chamberlain. New Haven, CT: Yale University Press, 2000.

———. *The Works of Jonathan Edwards*. Vol. 19, *Sermons and discourses, 1734–1738*. Edited by M. X. Lesser, New Haven, CT: Yale University Press, 2001.

———. *The Works of Jonathan Edwards*. Vol. 20, *The "Miscellanies": (Entry Nos. 833–1152)*. Edited by Amy Plantinga Pauw. New Haven, CT: Yale University Press, 2002.

———. *The Works of Jonathan Edwards*. Vol. 21, *Writing on the Trinity, Grace, and Faith*. Edited by Sang Hyun Lee. New Haven, CT: Yale University Press, 2003.

———. *The Works of Jonathan Edwards*. Vol. 22, *Sermons and Discourses, 1739–1742*. Edited by Kyle P. Farley et al. New Haven, CT: Yale University Press, 2003.

———. *The Works of Jonathan Edwards*. Vol. 23, *The "Miscellanies": (Entry Nos. 1153–1360)*. Edited by Douglas A. Sweeney. New Haven, CT: Yale University Press, 2004.

———. *The Works of Jonathan Edwards*. Vol. 24, *The Blank Bible*. Edited by Stephen J. Stein. New Haven, CT: Yale University Press, 2006.

———. *The Works of Jonathan Edwards*. Vol. 25, *Sermons and Discourses, 1734–1738*. Edited by M. X. Lesser. New Haven, CT: Yale University Press, 2001.

———. *The Works of Jonathan Edwards*. Vol. 26, *Catalogues of Books*. Edited by Peter J. Thuesen. New Haven, CT: Yale University Press, 2008.

———. *The Works of Jonathan Edwards Online*. Vol. 46, *Sermons, Series II, 1731–1732*. Edited by the Jonathan Edwards Center at Yale University. New Haven, CT: Jonathan Edwards Center at Yale University, 2008. http://edwards.yale.edu/archive?path=aHRocDovL2Vkd2FyZHMueWFsZS5lZHUvY2dpLWJpbi9uZXdwaGlsby9zZWxlY3QucGw/d2plby40NA.

Emerson, Everett H. *Puritanism in America, 1620–750*. Twayne's World Leaders Series 71. Boston: Twayne, 1977.

Erdt, Terrence. "The Calvinist Psychology of the Heart and the 'Sense' of Jonathan Edwards." *Early American Literature* 13.2 (1978) 165–80.

Fiering, Norman. *Jonathan Edwards's Moral Thought and Its British Context*. Chapel Hill, NC: Wipf and Stock, 1981.

Filson, David Owen. "Beatifical Vision". In *The Jonathan Edwards Encyclopedia*, edited by Harry S. Stout et al., 61–63. Grand Rapids: Eerdmans, 2017.

Floyd D. Anderson. "'De Doctrina Christiana' 2. 18. 28: The Convergence of Athens and Jerusalem." *Rhetoric Society Quarterly* 15.3/4 (1985) 102–4.

Frame, John M. *A History of Western Philosophy and Theology*. Phillipsburg, NJ: P&R, 2015.

Frei, Hans W. *The Eclipse of Biblical Narrative: A Study in Eighteenth and Nineteenth Century Hermeneutics*. New Haven, CT: Yale University Press, 1974.

Geisler, Norman L. *The Big Book of Christian Apologetics: An A to Z Guide*. Kindle ed. Grand Rapids: Baker, 2012.

Glacken, Clarence J. *Traces on the Rhodian Shore: Nature and Culture in Western Thought from Ancient Times to the End of the Eighteenth Century.* Berkeley: University of California Press, 1973.

Glauser, Richard, and Anthony Savile. "Aesthetic Experience in Shaftesbury." *Proceeding of Aristotelian Society* 76 (2002) 25–74.

Gleason, Randall C., and Kelly M. Kapic. "Who Were the Puritans?" In *The Devoted Life: An Invitation to the Puritan Classics*, edited by Kelly M. Kapic and Randall C. Gleason, 15–37. Downers Grove, IL: InterVarsity, 2004.

Guyer, Paul. "Monism and Pluralism in the History of Aesthetics." *The Journal of Aesthetics and Art Criticism* 71.2 (2013) 133–43.

Hedley, Douglas. "Reason and Beauty in Cambridge Platonism." Lecture delivered online for the Lumen Christi Institute, August 4, 2020. https://www.lumenchristi.org/event/2020/08/reason-beauty-in-cambridge-platonism-douglas-hedley.

Helm, Paul. "John Locke and Jonathan Edwards: A Reconsideration." *Journal of the History of Philosophy* 7.1 (1969) 51–61.

———. "Jonathan Edwards: Reformed Apologist." In *The Rationality of Theism*, edited by Paul Copan and Paul K. Moser, 43–56. Leiden: Brill, 2009.

Holmes, Stephen R. "Does Jonathan Edwards Use a Dispositional Ontology? A Response to Sang Hyun Lee." In *Jonathan Edwards: Philosophical Theologian*, edited by Kelly M. Kapic and Randall C. Gleason, 99–114. Burlington, VT: Ashgate, 2003.

Hopkins, Samuel. *The Life and Character of the Late Reverend, Learned, and Pious Mr. Jonathan Edwards: President of the College of New Jersey*. North Hampton, MA: Andrew Wright, 1804.

Hume, David. *Dialogues Concerning Natural Religion and Other Writings*. Edited by Dorothy Coleman. Cambridge Texts in the History of Philosophy. New York: Cambridge University Press, 2007.

Hutcheson, Francis. *An Inquiry into the Original of Our Ideas of Beauty and Virtue: In Two Treatises*. Edited by Wolfgang Leidhold. Natural Law and Enlightenment Classics. Indianapolis, IN: Liberty Fund, 2008.

Jackson, F. J. Foakes, and Kirsopp Lake. *The Beginnings of Christianity: The Acts of the Apostles*. Vol. 2. Eugene, OR: Wipf and Stock, 2002.

Jolly, Nicholas. "Locke on Faith and Reason." In *The Cambridge Companion to Locke's Essay Concerning Human Understanding*, edited by Lex Newman, 436–55. New York: Cambridge University Press, 2007.

Kang, Kevin Woongsan. "Justified by Faith in Christ: Jonathan Edwards' Doctrine of Justification in Light of Union with Christ." PhD diss., Westminster Theological Seminary, 2003.

Kloosterman, Nelson D. "The Use of Typology in Post-Canonical Salvation History: An Orientation to Jonathan Edwards' *A History of the Work of Redemption*." *Mid-America Journal of Theology* 14 (2003) 59–96.

Knight, Janice. "Typology." In *The Princeton Companion to Jonathan Edwards*, edited by Sang Hyun Lee, 190–209. Princeton, NJ: Princeton University Press, 2005.

Koerner, Joseph Leo. *The Reformation of the Image*. Chicago: University of Chicago Press, 2008.

Landrum, Doug. *Jonathan Edwards' Exegesis of Genesis: A Puritan Hermeneutic?* Mustang, OK: Tate, 2015.

Lane, Belden C. *Ravished by Beauty: The Surprising Legacy of Reformed Spirituality*. New York: Oxford University Press, 2011.

LaShell, John K. "Jonathan Edwards and the New Sense." *Reformation & Revival* 4.3 (1995) 87–97.

Layton, John K. "The One and the Many: The Influence of Neoplatonism on the Theology of Jonathan Edwards." PhD diss., Southern Baptist Theological Seminary, 2012.

Lee, Sang Hyun. "God's Relation to the World." In *The Princeton Companion to Jonathan Edwards*, edited by Sang Hyun Lee, 59–71. Princeton, NJ: Princeton University Press, 2005.

———. *The Philosophical Theology of Jonathan Edwards*. Expanded ed. Princeton, NJ: Princeton University Press, 2000.

Lesser, M. X. *Reading Jonathan Edwards: An Annotated Bibliography in Three Parts, 1729–2005*. Grand Rapids: Eerdmans, 2008.

Locke, John. *The Correspondence of John Locke*. Vol. 8, *Letters Nos. 3287–3648*. Edited by E. S. de Beer. Clarendon Edition of the Works of John Locke. Oxford: Clarendon, 1989.

———. *A Paraphrase and Notes on the Epistles of St. Paul*. Edited by John W. Yolton. Vol. 2. New York: Oxford University Press, 1987.

———. *The Reasonableness of Christianity: As Delivered in the Scriptures*. Edited by John C. Higgins-Biddle. Clarendon Edition of the Works of John Locke. New York: Oxford University Press, 1999.

Louie, Kin Yip. "The Theological Aesthetics of Jonathan Edwards." PhD diss., University of Edinburgh, 2007.

Lovi, David S. *The Power of God: A Jonathan Edwards Commentary on the Book of Romans*. Eugene, OR: Pickwick, 2013.

Manuel, Frank Edward. *The Broken Staff: Judaism Through Christian eyes*. Cambridge, MA: Harvard University Press, 1992.

Marsden, George M. *Jonathan Edwards: A Life*. New Haven, CT: Yale University Press, 2004.

McClymond, Michael James, and Gerald R. McDermott. *The Theology of Jonathan Edwards*. New York: Oxford University Press, 2012.

McDermott, Gerald R. *Jonathan Edwards Confronts the Gods: Christian Theology, Enlightenment Religion, and Non-Christian Faiths*. New York: Oxford University Press, 2000.

———. "Types in Nature: Jonathan Edwards on Typology." *Bibliotheca Sacra* 175.699 (2018) 271–83.

McMahon, C. Matthew, et al. *The Writings of A Puritan's Mind*. Vol. 1. Coconut Creek, FL: Puritan, 2001.

McNeill, John T. *The History and Character of Calvinism*. New York: Oxford University Press, 1967.

Miller, Perry. *Jonathan Edwards*. New England Writers Series. Amherst: University of Massachusetts Press, 1981.

Minkema, Kenneth P. "A 'Dordtian Philosophe': Jonathan Edwards, Calvin, and Reformed Orthodoxy." *Church History & Religious Culture* 91.1/2 (2011) 241–53.

———. "Jonathan Edwards: A Theological Life." In *The Princeton Companion to Jonathan Edwards*, edited by Sang Hyun Lee, 1–15. Princeton, NJ: Princeton University Press, 2005.

Mitchell, Louis J. "The Experience of Beauty in the Thought of Jonathan Edwards." ThD diss., Harvard Divinity School, 1995.

———. "The Theological Aesthetics of Jonathan Edwards." *Theology Today* 64 (2007) 36–46.

Morimoto, Anri. *Jonathan Edwards and the Catholic Vision of Salvation*. University Park: Penn State University Press, 1995.

Murray, Iain H. *Jonathan Edwards: A New Biography*. Edinburgh: Banner of Truth Trust, 1987.

Nichols, Stephen J. *Jonathan Edwards: A Guided Tour of His Life and Thought*. Phillipsburg, NJ: P&R, 2001.

Nichols, Stephen R. C. "Typology." In *The Jonathan Edwards Encyclopedia*, edited by Harry S. Stout et al., 575–77. Grand Rapids: Eerdmans, 2017.

Nygren, Anders. *Agape and Eros*. Translated by Philip S. Watson. Philadelphia: Westminster, 1953.

Owen, John. *The Works of John Owen*. Edited by William H. Goold. Vols. 6–7. Logos. Edinburgh: T&T Clark, 1862.

Pauw, Amy Plantinga. "The Church as Mother and Bride in the Reformed Tradition: Challenge and Promise." In *Many Voices, One God: Being Faithful in a Pluralistic World*, edited by Walter Brueggemann and George W. Stroup, 122–36. Louisville, KY: Westminster John Knox, 1998.

———. "Jonathan Edwards' Ecclesiology." In *Jonathan Edwards as Contemporary: Essays in Honor of Sang Hyun Lee*, edited by Don Schweitzer, 175–86. New York: Peter Lang, 2010.

———. *The Supreme Harmony of All: The Trinitarian Theology of Jonathan Edwards*. Grand Rapids: Eerdmans, 2002.

———. "The Trinity." In *The Princeton Companion to Jonathan Edwards*, edited by Sang Hyun Lee, 44–59. Princeton, NJ: Princeton University Press, 2005.

Piper, John, and Jonathan Edwards. *God's Passion for His Glory: Living the Vision of Jonathan Edwards, with the Complete Text of the End for Which God Created the World*. Wheaton, IL: Crossway, 1998.

Polinska, Wioleta. "John Locke, Christian Doctrine and Latitudinarianism." *Zeitschrift Für Neuere Theologiegeschichte* 6.2 (1999) 173–94.

A Puritan's Mind (APM). "The Being of God: Miscellanies by Jonathan Edwards (1703–1758)." *APM*, n.d. https://www.apuritansmind.com/puritan-favorites/jonathan-edwards/miscellaneous-writings/god-the-being-of-god.

Robertson, Archibald, ed. *St. Athanasius: Select Works and Letters*. Vol. 4 of *A Select Library of Nicene and Post-Nicene Fathers of the Christian Church, Second Series*. Edited byPhilip Schaff and Henry Wace. Buffalo, NY: Christian Literature, 1892.

Schafer, Thomas A. "Jonathan Edwards." *Encyclopedia Britannica*, January 16, 2019. Revised June 9, 2025. https://www.britannica.com/biography/Jonathan-Edwards.

Schultz, Walter J. "Is Jonathan Edwards a Neoplatonist? The Concept of Emanation in End of Creation." *Jonathan Edwards Studies* 8.1 (2018) 17–36.

Sevier, Christopher Scott. *Aquinas on Beauty*. Lanham, MD: Lexington, 2015.

Sherry, Patrick. *Spirit and Beauty: An Introduction to Theological Aesthetics*. New York: Clarendon; Oxford University Press, 1992.

Smith, John E. *Jonathan Edwards: Puritan, Preacher, Philosopher*. Notre Dame: University of Notre Dame Press, 1993.

———. "Jonathan Edwards as Philosophical Theologian." *The Review of Metaphysics* 30.2 (1976) 306–24.

Stang, Charles M. *Our Divine Double*. Cambridge, MA: Harvard University Press, 2016.

Stein, Stephen J. "Edwards as Biblical Exegete." In *The Cambridge Companion to Jonathan Edwards*, edited by Stephen J. Stein, 181–95. New York: Cambridge University Press, 2007.

———. "The Spirit and the Word: Jonathan Edwards and Scriptural Exegesis." In *Jonathan Edwards and the American Experience*, edited by Nathan O. Hatch and Harry S. Stout, 118–30. New York: Oxford University Press, 1988.

Strachan, Owen, and Douglas A. Sweeney. *Jonathan Edwards on Beauty*. New ed. Chicago: Moody, 2010.

Strader, Ronald Edwin. "The Chronological Development of the Spiritual-Aesthetic in the Philosophical-Theology of Jonathan Edwards and Its Relationship to Seventeenth and Eighteenth Century British Philosophy." PhD diss., Claremont Graduate School, 1981.

Stuart, Matthew. *Locke's Metaphysics*. New York: Oxford University Press, 2013.

Sweeney, Douglas A. *The American Evangelical Story: A History of the Movement*. Grand Rapids: Baker Academic, 2005.

———. "The Church". In *The Princeton Companion to Jonathan Edwards*, edited by Sang Hyun Lee, 167–89. Princeton, NJ: Princeton University Press, 2005.

———. *Edwards the Exegete: Biblical Interpretation and Anglo-Protestant Culture on the Edge of the Enlightenment*. New York: Oxford University Press, 2016.

———. "Edwards, Jonathan (1703–1758)." In *Historical Handbook of Major Biblical Interpreters*, edited by Donald K. McKim, 309–12. Downers Grove, IL: InterVarsity, 1998.

———. *Jonathan Edwards and the Ministry of the Word: A Model of Faith and Thought*. Downers Grove, IL: IVP Academic, 2009.

Tatarkiewicz, Władysław. *History of Aesthetics*. Translated by Adam Czerniawski et al. Edited by J. Harrell and Cyril Barrett. Vols. 1–2. Warsaw: PWN-Polish Scientific, 1970.

———. *A History of Six Ideas: An Essay in Aesthetics*. Boston, MA: Polish Scientific, 1980.

Thilly, Frank. *A History of Philosophy*. Edited by Ledger Wood. New York: Holt, Rinehart and Winston, 1962.

Thuesen, Peter J. "Editor's Introduction." In *Catalogues of Books*, by Jonathan Edwards, 1–113. Vol. 26 of *The Works of Jonathan Edwards*. New Haven, CT: Yale University Press, 2008.

———. "Edwards's Intellectual Background." In *The Princeton Companion to Jonathan Edwards*, edited by Sang Hyun Lee, 16–33. Princeton, NJ: Princeton University Press, 2005.

Tindal, Matthew. *Christianity as Old as the Creation: Or the Gospel a Republication of the Religion of Nature*. Vol 1. London: 1730.

Tracy, Patricia J. *Jonathan Edwards, Pastor: Religion and Society in Eighteenth Century Northampton*. American Century Series. New York: Hill and Wang, 1980.

Uzgalis, William. "John Locke." *Stanford Encyclopedia of Philosophy*, September 2, 2001. Revised November 8, 2024. https://plato.stanford.edu/entries/locke.

Walton, Brad. "'Formerly Approved and Applauded': The Continuity of Edwards's *Treatise Concerning Religious Affections* with Seventeenth-Century Puritan Analyses of True Piety, Spiritual Sensation and Heart-Religion." ThD diss., Wycliffe College, 1999.

Wolterstorff, Nicholas. "Locke's Philosophy of Religion." In *The Cambridge Companion to Locke*, edited by V. C. Chappell, 172–98. New York: Cambridge University Press, 1994.

Wooddell, Joseph D. "Aesthetic Christian Apologetics." PhD diss., Southwestern Baptist Theological Seminary, 2005.

Zachman, Randall C. *Image and Word in the Theology of John Calvin*. Notre Dame, IN: University of Notre Dame Press, 2009.

Zakai, Avihu. *Jonathan Edwards's Philosophy of Nature: The Re-Enchantment of the World in the Age of Scientific Reasoning*. T&T Clark Theology. London: T&T Clark, 2010.

www.ingramcontent.com/pod-product-compliance
Lightning Source LLC
LaVergne TN
LVHW050629100826
845148LV00011B/1797